TRIBUTES FROM TH~~~~~~~~~TS

"This is the finest travel guide ~~~~~~~~~~~~~~~~~~~ngly beautiful, solidly biblical, and ~~~~~~~~~~~~~~~~ this outstanding resource. It will i~~~~~~~~~~, ~~~ your heart and bless your soul. It is a keepsake treasure for life."

DR. ED HINDSON, *Founding Dean & Distinguished Professor of Religion at Liberty University, host of the nationally-syndicated television broadcast The King is Coming, and author of more than twenty books*

"*Israel for the Christian Traveler* helps make Israel come alive. It is a beautiful quality publication with magnificent pictures that couldn't help but delight every Christian."

RAY COMFORT, *co-host of the award-winning television program The Way of the Master, CEO of Living Waters, best-selling author, pastor, and evangelist*

"*Israel for the Christian Traveler* is an essential guide to receiving the best from your visit to the Holy Land. The details and graphics about Israel are fabulous! It's a genuine work of art and excellent in design, with all the necessary information to make every moment of one's pilgrimage significant. It's a complete journal to follow the Way of the Lord and bring one home to the roots of our faith."

REV. ROSEMARY SCHINDLER GARLOW, *great niece of Oskar Schindler, president of Schindler's Ark International, accredited Israeli Tourism Ambassador and partner with Israeli government leaders, host of nearly 60 trips to Israel*

"*Israel for the Christian Traveler* is YOUR 'bible' for a life-changing trip to the Land of THE Bible! A perfect companion for believers in Yeshua (Jesus). Everyone should make this pilgrimage at least once in their lifetime, but the thought of it can be overwhelming. Now, you can go with 'Peace,' with this complete and exhaustive book by Joan Peace as your guide! Shalom and enjoy the journey!!"

MARTY GOETZ, *Emmy-nominated, modern-day Messianic psalmist*

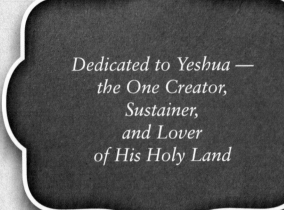

Dedicated to Yeshua —
the One Creator,
Sustainer,
and Lover
of His Holy Land

ISRAEL

for the

CHRISTIAN

TRAVELER

JOAN PEACE

REVISED *&* UPDATED

Inspiration Israel
USA

*Israel for the
Christian Traveler*
Copyright © 2019
by Inspiration Israel
(a subsidiary of
Walk About Zion)

All Scripture quotations,
unless otherwise indicated,
are taken from the New
International Version, NIV.

Editor: Linda Stubblefield

Cover and interior design
by TLC Book Design,
TLCBookDesign.com

Printed in Canada

ISBN 978-0-9914745-7-8

ACKNOWLEDGMENTS

THIS BOOK WOULD HAVE NOT BEEN POSSIBLE
without 1) the Lord who restored my health and gave
me an enormous love and passion for His Holy Land
and 2) my friend, Bruce Gregg, who accompanied me
to Israel in 2012, and who tenaciously encouraged me
to pursue this project to benefit other Israeli pilgrims.

Thank you to Cheri Walker, my longtime friend,
who provided hundreds of beautiful photographs as
well as unwavering support throughout the entire
process. I could never have done this without her!

A huge thank you to Yosef Rachamim, better known
as "Rami," of Tour Your Roots. Rami was a significant
contributor to the first edition of this travel guide, investing countless hours reviewing every detail of the content.
This perspective from a native-born Israeli and a Messianic Jewish tour guide was invaluable.

Thank you to Rev. Rosemary Schindler-Garlow
who helped me understand the vital importance of
directing the media's "West Bank" label to its proper,
God-given name, the biblical heartland of "Judea and
Samaria"—the literal piece of land with specific
boundaries where God made His everlasting covenants
with Abraham, Isaac, and Jacob.

Thank you to my family for their enthusiastic support and encouragement! Special thanks to Michelle
and Mike for their vital assistance in the original
editing process. And special thanks to my daughter,
Rebekah Peace (bekahpeacephotography.com), who
donated her professional, artistic eye to the selection
and placement of photos. I am blessed to have an
amazing family!

Thank you to my incredibly patient and thorough
book editor, Linda Stubblefield.

And most importantly, thank you to my incredibly
gifted and gracious book designer, Tamara Dever of
TLC Book Design. Her relentless, phenomenal work
is the reason this book won several national awards! I
highly recommend Tamara to any author or publisher
desiring exceptional design and Christian integrity.
Visit TLCBookDesign.com.

Incredibly Blessed, Joan Peace

TABLE OF CONTENTS

CHAPTER 7:
GOLAN HEIGHTS & UPPER GALILEE

CHAPTER 8:
FROM GALILEE TO JERUSALEM

CHAPTER 9: GREATER JERUSALEM

CHAPTER 10: THE OLD CITY

CHAPTER 11:
OUTSIDE THE CITY WALLS

MAPS

INTRODUCTION

BEFORE THE BOOK

Please allow me to briefly share some of my background and the "God Story" of how this book came into existence.

My professional training was in education, with a master's degree in Curriculum and Instruction. I have worked over twenty years in education—homeschooling, teaching most grades, writing curriculum and founding several charter schools, including Escondido's "The Classical Academy," which currently has seven campuses in several cities and over 4,500 TK–12 students.

Fast forward to 2001. This year marked the beginning of an exceedingly long, tough journey. I became very sick with multiple, debilitating health conditions; at the end of 2009, I was diagnosed with advanced uterine cancer. My prognosis: six months of the most aggressive chemotherapy followed by six weeks of radiation would be essential for survival. I would have followed this regimen; however, eight years of debilitating illnesses had seriously weakened my body. I made the difficult decision to forego the treatments and simply trust God—no matter what the outcome. I had already invested over $150,000 on at least 200 different modes of healing—to no avail. After exhausting all financial resources and human means of healing, for the first time I totally surrendered my health to the Lord. I gave Him permission to do whatever He wanted to do—heal me, give me a prayer ministry in bed for the rest of my life, or take me home to heaven. What I wanted no longer mattered. Over the next year and a half, through prayer, worship, Bible reading, and repentance, our amazing Lord graciously healed me of every one of my health conditions and the cancer.

At the end of 2011, as my strength returned, I developed an intense passion to visit Israel. In March of 2012, I set out for Israel—the beginning of an amazing journey! I fell in love with the Israeli people, the land, and the Lord even more; I've been back many times since. This book, along with the journal, study guide, and map are the results of my life-changing journeys.

The writing of the book catapulted me into doing what I truly love: bringing groups to Israel, helping travelers with their itineraries, and founding a non-profit for Israel, the "Israel Now Project," with a major focus on Holocaust Survivors. (www.IsraelNowProject.com)

The "other part" of what I truly love at this season in my life is residing near the greatest blessings of my life and the source of tremendous joy—my three wonderful children, their amazing spouses, and nine super-wonderful grandchildren pictured with their parents from left to right: Seth, Levi, Caleb, Juliet, Natasha, Sabrina, Ashton, Wynter, and Sienna. God is good!

ABOUT THE BOOK

IT NEEDS TO BE STATED THAT THIS BOOK IS BIASED. WITH ALL DUE RESPECT TO other beliefs, this author has chosen to remain as pure to literal scripture as possible. As such, many of the views expressed in these pages reflect this author's understanding of what is taught in the Bible and how it relates to present-day issues in Israel and their implications. The use of the three identifying terms below, the last two being quite controversial, stem from this bias.

EXPLANATION OF TERMS

Yeshua: The word Yeshua is used interchangeably with "Jesus," a derivation of *Yesous*, its Greek translation literally meaning "salvation."

West Bank: The "West Bank" is often referred to as "the occupied territories" with Israel being the "occupying power." The term is used within quotation marks in this book because the region's proper biblical name is "Judea and Samaria." Historically, it is the biblical heartland of Israel.

Palestine: "Palestine" is also in quotation marks because biblically, the term never existed. In AD 135, Roman Emperor Hadrian maliciously renamed Israel *Syria-Palestinia* (a Latinized version of *Philistine*, the arch enemy of the Jewish people). Hence, Palestine has long been a despised name to the Jews. The name "Israel" first appears in the Bible in Genesis 32:28. Other biblical names for the land include Canaan and "from Dan to Beersheba," but never Palestine. The word "Palestinian" also came from the Philistines. However, the Philistines were not indigenous to Canaan. There may be traces of Philistine blood in those who identify as "Palestinian" today; they are nevertheless a distinctly different people with a distinctly different culture.

ISRAEL FOR THE CHRISTIAN TRAVELER POWER PACK

The revised travel guide has many updates, additional sites, and extras. However, please understand this travel guide is not meant to be exhaustive in content; it is an overview of the most important highlights of Israel and the Jewish people, as well as information relevant to the sites included in the bulk of Christian tours to Israel. You will find bottom-line answers for "Who?," "What?," "When?," and "I wonder...." The internet contains a plethora of information for those who wish to dig deeper.

ADDITIONAL ONLINE SITE INFORMATION: Information regarding sites that are generally not included in basic Israel tours is provided at www.walkaboutzion.com. Click "Inspiration Israel." See included sites in this guide at the beginning of chapters 4, 6, 7, 9, 12, and 15 on the map pages.

JOURNAL/STUDY GUIDE: This journal is also a place to keep track of your itinerary, your expenses, and more—as well as a comprehensive study guide with maps—allowing you to become an "Israel Pro" before your trip! It is written to go hand-in-hand with this travel guide. The reader will be directed back to the travel guide for answers to Study Guide questions. (These books are also sold independently on Amazon).

TWO LAP MAPS: The accompanying "Lap Maps" provides the most important information for group tours to Israel and, due to their size, they can be easily read on your lap. If you would like additional LAP MAPS, simply go online to Amazon and type in "LAP MAP."

GROUP DISCOUNTS are available for ten or more resources shipped to the same address. Email Joan@WalkAboutZion.com.

Enjoy and be blessed
with the trip of a lifetime!

ORIENTATION TO ISRAEL

I will insist the Hebrews have [contributed] more to civilize men than any other nation. If I was an atheist and believed in blind eternal fate, I should still believe that fate had ordained the Jews to be the most essential instrument for civilizing the nations ... They are the most glorious nation that ever inhabited this Earth. The Romans and their empire were but a bubble in comparison to the Jews. They...have influenced the affairs of mankind more...than any other nation, ancient or modern. – PRESIDENT JOHN ADAMS

1

ONLY JEWISH COUNTRY IN WORLD: Number of countries worldwide with religion practiced by 50% or more of their population: Roman Catholic (45), Protestant (27), Eastern Orthodox (15), Muslim (52), Hindu (3), Buddhist (6), Jewish (1)

MINISCULE SIZE: Israel spans approximately 8,000 square miles (12,875 sq. km) in total area, 263 miles in length (423 km), and ranges from 9 miles (14 km) to 71 miles (114 km) in width. She is smaller than New Jersey and could fit into the state of California 19 times. 22 predominantly Arab Middle Eastern countries surround Israel, dwarfing her in size by 4,500 to 1. In regard to population, there are 6 million+ Jews in the Middle East compared to 423 million Arabs. Israel's total population currently exceeds 9 million.

CONTINUOUS JEWISH PRESENCE IN THE LAND FOR 3,000 YEARS: Jews are indigenous to Israel with a continuous presence for over 3,000 years according to archaeological, historical, and biblical evidence. "Who can challenge the rights of the Jews in Palestine? Good Lord, historically it is really your country." Yusef Diya al-Khalidi, Arabic Mayor of Jerusalem, 1899

OLDEST LANGUAGE IN WORLD REVIVED: Hebrew was virtually dead for almost 2,000 years (throughout the *diaspora*—the scattering of the Jews throughout the world); it was not used for daily conversation, business, or education. However, Hebrew was amazingly resurrected at the end of the 19th century when the Jews started returning to Israel. This phenomenon was prophesied over 2,500 years prior: "For then will I turn to the people a pure language, that they may all call upon the name of Hashem, to serve him with one consent." (Zephaniah 3:9)

FIRST RESPONDERS IN EMERGENCY: With 60 years of expertise in emergency response, Israel is typically among the first on the scene at international disaster sites.

RISKS LIVES FOR ISLAMIC MILITANTS: Elite Israeli troops rescue wounded Syrians almost every night. They have saved the lives of more than 2,000 Syrians (many even from terrorist groups) since 2013—at a cost of more than $13 million.

EXCELS IN UNIVERSITY DEGREES: Israelis rank second in number of university degrees per capita in the world.

LEADER IN VENTURE CAPITAL: Israel attracts more venture capital investments per capita than any other country in the world.

FORERUNNER IN HIGH-TECH STARTUPS: Israel has the most high-tech start-up companies per capita in the world.

ENERGY AND WATER EFFICIENCY EXPERTS: Over 90% of Israel's water heaters are solar-powered. Drip irrigation was invented in Israel. One of the driest countries on earth, Israel now has more than enough water for all her needs and leads the world in water recycling. Desalination plants were invented in Israel and account for 55% of their domestic water supply.

WORLD-CLASS TECHNOLOGY: Jews founded Google, Amazon, and Facebook. Israelis created WAZE, instant messaging, firewall security software, Intel wireless computer chips, Windows NT operating systems, voicemail technology, and the USB drive. A sampling of Israel's countless medical inventions include PillCam, Biowelds1, MicronJet, VitalGo Systems' Total Lift Bed, Robotic exoskeleton ReWalk, and ApiFix to correct scoliosis.

*All Bible prophecies below concerning Israel were prophesied over 2,500 years ago;
all have seen their continuing fulfillment over the last seventy years!*

1. **JEWS WILL RETURN TO ISRAEL FROM THE ENDS OF THE EARTH.** "Do not be afraid, for I am with you; I will bring your children from the east and gather you from the west. I will say to the north, `Give them up!' and to the south, `Do not hold them back.' Bring my sons from afar and my daughters from the ends of the earth..." Isaiah 43:5–6

2. **ISRAEL WILL BE FRUITFUL AND PROSPER.** "I will increase the number of men and animals upon you, and they will be fruitful and become numerous. I will settle people on you as in the past and will make you prosper more than before. Then you will know that I am the Lord." Ezekiel 36:11

3. **THE RUINS OF ISRAEL WILL BE REPAIRED, RESTORED, AND REBUILT.** "In that day I will restore David's fallen tent. I will repair its broken places, restore its ruins, and build it as it used to be..." Amos 9:11

4. **ISRAEL'S DESERTS AND WASTELANDS WILL BECOME LIKE THE GARDEN OF THE LORD.** "The Lord will surely comfort Zion and will look with compassion on all her ruins; he will make her deserts like Eden, her wastelands like the garden of the Lord. Joy and gladness will be found in her, thanksgiving and the sound of singing." Isaiah 51:3

5. **TREES AGAIN WILL GROW IN ISRAEL.** I will put in the desert the cedar and the acacia, the myrtle and the olive. I will set pines in the wasteland, the fir and the cypress together, so that people may see and know, may consider and understand, that the hand of the Lord has done this, that the Holy One of Israel has created it. " Isaiah 41:19–20

6. **THE GROUND WILL BECOME FRUITFUL.** The seed will grow well, the vine will yield its fruit, the ground will produce its crops, and the heavens will drop their dew. I will give all these things as an inheritance to the remnant of this people. " Zechariah 8:12

7. **THE JEWS WILL RETURN TO JERUSALEM.** "I will save my people from the countries of the east and the west. I will bring them back to live in Jerusalem; they will be my people, and I will be faithful and righteous to them as their God." Zechariah 8:7–8

8. **ISRAEL WILL PREVAIL OVER HER ENEMIES THROUGH THE LORD'S HELP.** "Though you search for your enemies, you will not find them. Those who wage war against you will be as nothing at all. For I am the LORD, your God, who takes hold of your right hand and says to you, Do not fear; I will help you. Do not be afraid, you worm Jacob, little Israel, for I myself will help you," declares the Lord, your Redeemer, the Holy One of Israel." Isaiah 41:12–14

9. **ISRAEL'S FRUIT WILL BE SHIPPED THROUGHOUT THE WORLD.** "In days to come Jacob will take root, Israel will bud and blossom and fill all the world with fruit." Isaiah 27:6

10. **JERUSALEM WILL BECOME THE MOST IMPORTANT RELIGIOUS SITE IN THE WORLD.** "In the last days, the mountain of the Lord's temple will be established as chief among the mountains; it will be raised above the hills, and peoples will stream to it." Micah 4:1 (Note: From 2018–2019, tourism increased 50% to 4.5 million.)

1. **THE WORD OF GOD ENCOURAGES US TO VISIT.**

   "Walk about Zion, go around her, count her towers, consider well her ramparts,
   and view her citadels that you may tell of them to the next generation. For this is
   our God forever and ever; he will be our guide even to the end." Psalms 48:12–14

   "I rejoiced with those who said to me, 'Let us go to the house of the Lord.'
   Our feet are standing in your gates, Jerusalem. Jerusalem is built like a city that is closely
   compacted together. That is where the tribes go up—the tribes of the Lord—to praise the
   name of the Lord according to the statute given to Israel." Psalms 122:1–4 (song of ascents)

2. **WHEN WE ARRIVE IN ISRAEL, WE FEEL WE HAVE COME HOME.** Jerusalem is the
   only city in the world on which God chose to place His name. "But I have chosen
   Jerusalem, that my name might be there…" 2 Chronicles 6:6a. An anonymous visitor to
   Israel stated this sentiment beautifully:

   "The unplanned tears that come down your face as you experience the pain of
   what was lost, alongside the hope of what will come—promised through the
   prophets long ago… It is awesome beyond words. When you depart, you cannot
   say goodbye, only that you will be back. There is an unseen force that draws you in
   and assures you that you will be back again. It's where you belong; it is home."

3. **SEEING AND EXPERIENCING THE ROOTS OF OUR FAITH, FIRST-HAND, INSPIRES
   US.** The Holy Land is the very cradle of our faith. Every believer must visit Israel at least
   once in his or her lifetime to *truly* understand the Jewish roots of of Christianity. It is only
   here, in this small country chosen by God, that we can smell the same air and feel the same
   dirt as our biblical ancestors. Their voices and their stories live on as our hearts and souls
   become entrenched in our rich spiritual history. When we remember where the Jews have
   been as a people and see where Israel is now, we can only stand in awe—of what this small,
   seemingly insignificant group of people have miraculously overcome and of the immense
   blessings God has placed on this Land and His people.

4. **WE ARE RENEWED SPIRITUALLY.** A trip to Israel is life-changing! It will transform our
   souls, make our prayers come alive, and build our faith in God in a way no other experience
   can. The Bible, sermons, Jewish feast days, and Christmas and Easter are never the same
   again. Each one comes to life upon recalling the biblical sites we touched with our own
   hands and saw with our own eyes! Dancing in the streets of Jerusalem, praying at the Western Wall, viewing miracles at every turn—many of us are never the same again! We return
   home with a greater love and understanding of the Bible, a renewed passion for Christ, and
   a deepened prayer life.

"To visit this land is like a pilgrimage into the past, and walking in the shadow of greatness.
But, it is more. Here, today, one rubs elbows with the descendants of Abraham,
Isaac and Jacob. With Bible in hand, one can see the fulfillment of biblical prophecy,
and can sense God's promise for the future."
– Billy Graham

5. **MANY ARE INSPIRED IN MINISTRY.** Church leaders are strengthened in their own spiritual walk, while new leaders emerge. Those who may have been hesitant to teach or serve in church often return home with an entirely new motivation and passion. Some even feel called to ministry or missions.

6. **DEEP, LASTING INTERPERSONAL BONDS ARE GENERATED.** Extended time together, close fellowship, and shared spiritual experiences result in lasting ties with new friends within the body of believers. New bonds are created while existing bonds are strengthened.

7. **WE FALL IN LOVE WITH THE ISRAELI PEOPLE—AND THEIR FOOD!** Israelis are known for being *very* real and *very* caring. Where else do people open their homes to total strangers? In Israel, we savor a "sense of community" that we may never have before experienced. And with the amazing Israeli people comes their delectable food. We just can't get seem to get enough shawarma, falafel, Israeli salad, and decadent halvah!

8. **WE ARE CAPTIVATED BY THE LAND AND EVERYTHING IT REPRESENTS.** The diversity and beauty of the landscape of Israel, within such a small piece of real estate, is unparalleled. Towering mountains, fertile plains, thriving farmland, lush valleys, and arid deserts all thrive within its mere 8,000+ square miles (12,875 sq. km) of landmass. We can stand at the Dead Sea, the lowest place on earth (1,388 ft or 423 m below sea level), while just 20 miles (32 km) away, we can ascend "up to Jerusalem" to an altitude of 3,800 ft (1,158 m) above sea level. Israel abounds in beauty; her oceans, seas, rivers, and waterfalls, are breathtaking! The flora of Israel can be described as "one large botanical garden" born out of the ashes of the Holocaust. This botanical harvest was conceived from resolute Jewish immigrants who relentlessly tilled the soil of a desert, a land that had never been naturally conducive to agriculture. The resilience of these Jewish immigrants, their strength of character, and sweat of their brow resulted in an innovation in agricultural technology unsurpassed by any other people group. The desert has truly become alive!

9. **WE "EXPERIENCE" WORLD NEWS.** Travel to Israel is an opportunity to better understand the Middle East conflict and to gain new insights into the political, social, and economical state across the different regions of Israel. Before visiting, the Palestine/Israel conflict was just a CNN news byte heard in the comfort of our home. Once in Israel, we better understand the joys and the pain, the tension and the discouragement, and *especially* the comradery among neighbors never mentioned in the news. We better understand the realities of the Jewish heart and the Palestinian challenges; we better understand the hopes and dreams of the Israeli people.

10. **OUR HEARTS AND OUR SPIRITS YEARN TO SUPPORT ISRAEL.** The people of Israel (Jews and Arabs, Christians and non-Christians) are positively affected by our visits. All of the people groups of Israel want and need the support of Christians around the world, and visiting is an important statement of that support. As hostility against Israel continues to escalate globally and the media continues to portray Israel in a negative, destructive light, Israel desperately needs our encouragement—no matter what our personal opinions. Through our visits, the spirits of *all* Israelis are elevated, their economy is strengthened, and they feel they are not alone.

Visit Israel!
You'll never be the same.

IS ISRAEL SAFE TO VISIT? DEFINITIVELY "YES!!!"

IN 2019, 4.5 MILLION TOURISTS VISITED ISRAEL. THE ISRAEL MINISTRY OF Tourism reports that all visitors have returned home safely with glowing stories of warmth, welcome, and a new perspective on the roots of their faith. The Israeli government would not encourage tourists to come if they felt they would be in the slightist danger.

WHAT ARE THE REALITIES CONCERNING SAFETY IN ISRAEL?

As of the printing of this book, there has not been even a single report of any person on a group tour that has been negatively affected or injured by political activity in Israel.

AIRPORT SECURITY FOR FLIGHTS TO AND FROM ISRAEL IS INCREDIBLY THOROUGH. Ben Gurion Airport in Tel Aviv is known for having the tightest security in the world.

TOUR GUIDES ARE TRAINED TO BE PROACTIVE IN PROTECTING THEIR GROUPS. Tour guides maintain ongoing contact with their ground tour operators, as well as other guides and drivers. They are trained to take every measure necessary to protect their groups and insure they have a safe visit. Tour guides do NOT place their groups in dangerous situations or potentially troubled areas or sites (which typically are far from traditional tour sites). They will reroute if necessary.

THE ISRAELI GOVERNMENT PRIORITIZES TOURISTS. If, in the unlikely event, a war or skirmish did break out while on tour, tourists are the government's priority and would be taken care of immediately. Israeli officials, together with foreign embassy and consulate officials have clear and efficient procedures in place to quickly remove at-risk visitors from a potentially dangerous place or situation, and if necessary, transport them safely back home.

TERRORISTS DO NOT TYPICALLY TARGET TOUR BUSES AND TOURIST SITES. Terrorists, as much as peace-loving Israelis, need the tourist business for survival.

WARS ARE GENERALLY SHORT AND IT'S "BUSINESS AS USUAL." Those living in Israel know that when a terrorist attack occurs, it is predictably *not* as described by the media. The media (both international and domestic) continually broadcast the same, horrible scenes throughout the day—while giving the impression that what occurred in one location is happening throughout Israel. The standard reality is that one or two hours after the grievous incident, Israelis fully return to "normal life" (i.e., the area is cleaned up, shops reopen, residents continue with their same daily tasks; and public transportation continues as usual).

PERSONAL SAFETY IN ISRAEL IS INCREDIBLY HIGH AND CRIME VERY LOW. Travel to Israel is generally safer than staying home in the US—especially if you live in a large city like Los Angeles, or New York. Unlike the US, most Israelis do not lock their homes. In fact, with increasing global terrorism, Israel is now becoming one of the safest places in the world to visit!

STILL CONCERNED? Could some harm come to a tourist? Of course; that could happen anywhere in the world. As believers, the safest place to be is in God's will! If you're still concerned, online safety updates for traveling to Israel are available. Check either the Bureau of Consumer Affairs or the US Department of State website online.

Bottom Line: Don't let others' fears rob you of a trip of a lifetime!

Much of the content below is extracts from the highly recommended book, *IDENTITY THEFT: How Jesus was Robbed of His Jewishness* by Ron Cantor.

JESUS—RABBI YESHUA: Jesus' Hebrew name is *Yeshua*, which means "salvation." Yeshua's disciples called Him "Rabbi." He went to synagogue on the Sabbath, dressed as a biblical Jew with tzitzit (fringes on his garments), and lived His days on earth as a totally observant Jew. Yeshua never intended to break with Jewish tradition or to be the founder of a new religion; He differed with the traditions of men, not with the teaching of the Torah.

JOHN THE BAPTIST—RABBI YOHANAN: John the Baptist was not a "Baptist," as Baptists are known today. He was the cousin of Yeshua, as well as the last and greatest of the Hebrew prophets in the likes of Jeremiah, Isaiah, and Ezekiel. *Rabbi Yohanan* is the one who prophesied the coming of Yeshua, the Jewish Messiah.

ALL OF THE ORIGINAL FOLLOWERS OF JESUS WERE JEWISH. Mary's Hebrew name was *Miriam*; she was an Israeli Jew. James, the author of the book of James, was *Jacob*, or *Ya'akov* in Hebrew. In the time of Yeshua, His followers were simply recognized as another Jewish sect (akin to Pharisees or Sadducees). Almost thirty years subsequent to Yeshua's death and resurrection, His followers in Jerusalem were still zealous for the Torah and totally devoted to the Jewish way of life (Acts 21:17-25). Never did it enter the mind of His Jewish followers that they were no longer Jewish. In fact, once Gentiles began to believe in Yeshua, many felt they had to convert to Judaism first (which, of course, they did not).

ALL SEVEN JEWISH FEASTS POINT TOWARDS YESHUA. Christ died on Passover, rose from the dead on the Feast of Firstfruits, and the Holy Spirit was poured out on Jerusalem during the Feast of Weeks (Shavuot). These are three of the most significant days in history, and God caused each one of them to occur on the three Jewish feast days during the spring of AD 30. (A concise overview of the seven feasts of Israel and their fulfillment in Christ can be found online. Type "Hebrew4 Christians Feasts of Israel" into your search bar).

THE ENTIRE NEW TESTAMENT WAS WRITTEN BY JEWS. Some controversy exists as to whether Luke was Jewish (however, he was a doctor…); every other writer was undoubtedly Jewish.

COMMUNION WAS INSTITUTED IN THE UPPER ROOM AT A PASSOVER SEDER. Yeshua picked up the *Afikomen*, a special piece of matzah (unleavened bread) used during the Passover Seder. He then lifted the third of four cups that are blessed during the Passover meal, the Cup of Redemption, and asked that His Jewish disciples continue this Jewish tradition; this was the first communion.

JEWISH RITUAL BATHS WERE A PREDECESSOR TO CHRISTIAN BAPTISM. In Bible times, centuries before John began to baptize his Jewish followers, Jewish *mikvahs* (ritual baths) were used for cleansing and purification. Jews would walk down the steps on one side of the mikvah, fully immerse themselves in the water at the bottom, then walk up the steps on the other side, exiting the pool totally cleansed. This cultural water immersion was one of the reasons Jewish believers did not resist baptism.

OUR FAITH BEGINS AND ENDS WITH THE JEWS. Our Christian faith not only began in Israel, focusing on the Jewish people, but it will also end in Israel—still focused on the Jewish people. The final blow to anti-Semitism will be when a "glorified Jew" plants His feet on the Mount of Olives (Zechariah 14:4)!

What is the time difference between Israel and the U.S. & Canada? Israel's time is ahead of the U.S. and Canada. The following are the time differences between Israel and the U.S./Canada time zones: **PST:** 10 hours behind; **MST:** 9 hours behind; **CST:** 8 hours behind; **EST:** 7 hours behind; **AST** (Canada only): 6 hours behind; **NST** (Canada only): 5 hours behind. For instance, if it is 8:00 AM in New York (EST), it will be 3:00 PM in Israel.

What languages are spoken in Israel? Hebrew and Arabic are the official Israeli languages. English is widely spoken and understood in all hotels and most restaurants and stores. In prominent cities and roads, most signs are posted in Hebrew, Arabic, and English.

What is appropriate dress in Israel? Israel is a casual country; comfort dress is the norm. Some dress up for church; some don't. However, it is important that your dress is respectful to other belief systems. Dress modestly and be prepared for religious sites which require your shoulders, legs, and head to be covered.

What if I need healthcare in Israel? Israel's healthcare facilities, including emergency rooms, are state-of-the-art. Most health care professionals understand and speak very good English. Well-stocked pharmacies are throughout Israel; some are open 24 hours. Contact your healthcare provider to check your coverage when traveling abroad; many medical plans are not recognized in Israel. **A good travel insurance will cover all your medical needs and emergencies.**

Do I need any immunizations? No immunizations are required in Israel, though you'll want to make sure your tetanus shot is current.

What about medications and supplements? Consult your physician if you have any medical condition(s) that may impact your ability to fully participate in your tour. In case of emergency, it would be prudent to bring your written prescriptions with you to Israel. Many doctors will write a prescription for an antibiotic—just in case it is needed abroad. Bring all potentially important medications: sleep aids, decongestants, motion sickness medication such as Dramamine, digestive meds like Pepto-Bismol or Tums, cold/flu/allergy medications, cough lozenges, medication for diarrhea or constipation, and any others you may need. Don't forget your regular daily supplements, as well as supplements to boost your immune system such as Emergen-C, Wellness Formula, or Airborne. **Keep your medications and supplements in your carry-on luggage.**

Special dietary needs? Hotel breakfasts and dinners are generally all-you-can eat buffets that feature a wide variety of breads, salads, vegetables, and meat. Nearly every hotel caters to gluten-free or special dietary needs—just ask. Most lunch stops will be roadside vendors or restaurants serving traditional Israeli fare. If this fare potentially presents a problem, bring your own food from home for lunches; protein bars or healthy snacks suffice for many.

Is everything closed on the Shabbat (Sabbath)? Shabbat, the Jewish holy day of the week, is observed from sunset Friday through sunset Saturday. All public offices, banks, as well as most stores, kosher restaurants, public transportation, and private businesses are closed during the Shabbat—most by 1:00 PM Friday. Many hotels have "Shabbat elevators" which stop at every floor (to avoid working, i.e., pressing a button on the Sabbath). Radio stations, television channels, Christian sites, and many non-kosher restaurants operate as normal. If you are not on an organized group tour, it would be wise to check the operating hours of all applicable sites and businesses prior to your visit.

EMERGENCY NUMBERS: Police: 100 / Emergency Medical Services: 101

Is Israel's water safe to drink? Tap water across Israel is both safe and delicious, and bottled water is sold in abundance. Cold water is generally available in the tour buses for $1 a bottle. It is critical to stay hydrated in Israel's dry, desert climate; keep water with you at all times.

What about mobility challenges? If you need a cane or wheelchair, use one! **Yad Sarah,** Israel's largest organization for the disabled, provides a spectrum of free and nominal cost services designed to make life easier for the sick, disabled, and elderly, as well as their families. Their website is www.yadsarah.org.il; click on the U.S. flag for English. Yad Sarah has more than 100 branches throughout Israel with thousands of items—from crutches and wheelchairs to oxygen concentrators and electronic monitors. They will even arrange for airport and intercity transport and assist in ensuring that your hotel rooms are suitable for your special needs. Although most services are free, deposits are required for equipment. Yad Sarah is always happy to offer advice for special-needs travelers to Israel. Contact them prior to your trip departure so your needs can be efficiently coordinated. Email info@yad-sarah.org.il or call 972-2-644-4633.

Avis Rental Cars currently offers **Avis Access,** which provides a wide array of services and car features for customers with special travel needs. To ensure availability, reserve at least one day in advance via phone reservation. Call 1-888-879-4273.

If you are participating in a regular tour and you have physical challenges, use wisdom. Keeping up with the group may be difficult. Plan ahead for possible difficult situations and be prepared with back-up plans. The following are some proactive suggestions:

- The best-case scenario is to bring a travel partner who is willing and happy to take responsibility for you and help as needed. If this is not possible, you may want to ask others for assistance. However, don't assume they will help and don't take it personally if they decline; they did not sign up to be a caregiver. You are ultimately the one responsible to meet your needs. Use sensitivity and wisdom to ensure that you are not detracting from or limiting another traveler's experience.

- Prior to departure, you can contact your travel agent or tour operator to inquire about the sites of your specific itinerary. Which sites do you need to avoid or limit your participation? Inquire about steep or uneven surfaces. It might be wise to avoid all tunnels and trails without handicap access. *Ask your guide about easy access through Old City Jerusalem. Let your tour group leader and tour guide know about your special circumstances and needs ahead of time, and don't hesitate to ask them or your driver questions.

- You may even want to sit out at one or more sites. It's not all that bad. Make these sites your special, pampered time to do whatever you feel like doing—rest on the bus, sip on a cup of coffee, enjoy the site's gift shop. Just relax and enjoy!

- Only want to tour for half a day? Ask about options to return to your hotel before the touring day is over. How about a taxi? Make an informed decision not to participate at a particular site or even not to tour the entire day. This is far better than possibly injuring yourself, depleting your immune system, or ultimately reaching a point of exhaustion that would hinder you from enjoying the next day or unnecessarily slowing down the rest of the group. A day off to relax at your hotel can be refreshing and revitalizing. Our loving, gracious Lord knows each of your needs intimately and He's got you covered!

- Try to remember that it's all about attitude. You still will experience the great majority of your planned tour. Understand that there is never enough time for any traveler to see everything he or she would like. Make up your mind beforehand that you will enjoy "to the max" every site or activity that you *are* able to see or experience.

CALLING U.S. AND ISRAEL

Calling instructions from the U.S. to Israel:

- Step 1: Dial "011" (USA exit code).
- Step 2: Dial "972" (Israel country code).
- Step 3: Dial the Israel phone number, minus the initial "0." For instance, if the Israel number is 03-520-2552, the caller would dial: 011-972-3-520-2552.

Calling instructions from Israel to the U.S.:

- Step 1: Dial "00" (Israel exit code).
- Step 2: Dial "1" (USA country code).
- Step 3: Dial the USA phone number: the 3-digit area code followed by the 7-digit local phone number. For instance, calling 760-379-8812, you would dial: 001-760-379-8812.

WI-FI

Israel is a leader in technology; Wi-Fi is provided free throughout the country at most hotels, tourist sites, restaurants, tour buses, and on public transportation. You can ask your tour guide or bus driver about Wi-Fi access on the bus or at a specific site.

Israeli SIM cards provide unlimited Wi-Fi use. If you are using an international plan with your cell provider, you may want to restrict your phone usage to complimentary Wi-Fi hotspots, especially for web browsing and app use. The real culprit behind overseas bill shock is the cost of data usage. The average cost of overseas, pay-as-you-go data charges is between $.50 and $3.00 per megabyte. In practical terms, this means you could be charged this amount simply for viewing a single web page, uploading one photo to Facebook, or even utilizing your "free" GPS which is high in data usage. Do your homework and check with your provider beforehand.

COMPUTERS

Many tourists like to bring small computers like a Samsung Galaxy Tab or an iPad. The iPad mini is currently quite popular. These small computers allow you not only to have Internet access, but to journal, take photos, and Skype your loved ones back home. An important additional benefit is Bible access. You will want access to some sort of Bible in Israel and the weight of most Bibles is burdensome while touring. Small, easy-to-carry Bibles are also an option for those who can read small print.

If the glare of the sun is an issue with your tablet or pad, you can purchase a film guard with a matte finish to cover the screen. Film guards are easily found on Amazon and most stores that carry electronics.

ELECTRICITY

Power in Israel is 220V—the same as in Europe. Israeli outlets have three round holes. If you need to plug in a laptop, cell phone charger, iPad charger, or similar device, you should only need a **Type H** travel plug adapter (found on Amazon and stores that carry electronics) that will adapt the shape of your plug to fit the Israeli plug. Although Israeli sockets are three-pronged, they will generally accept European two-pronged **Type C** travel plug adapters as well. A three-outlet plug, used with an adapter, is a good investment for multiple cords.

Make sure your hair dryers, curling irons, flat irons, etc. are 220 volts or dual voltage. *Most, but not all, hotels provide hairdryers, but they frequently lack power; Conair and BaByliss offer some great dual voltage travel hair dryers.*

Warning: NEVER plug a 110-volt device into Israel's 220-volt outlets without a converter. Your item will crash and burn—sometimes even with a converter!

PHONE AND INTERNET

You may not wish to have phone or Internet capability at all. If so, you can skip this section. For simple calls and texts, consider **WhatsApp**, **Skype** or **FaceTime**. However, these do require internet.

From this author's experience, most travelers to Israel have, or more often *wish* they had, an effective and affordable cell phone plan in which they could utilize their own phone for calls and texts to and from home, as well as enjoy unlimited Internet use. You can utilize your phone and Internet service in Israel in two main ways.

The most stress-free and inexpensive option is to rent an Israeli SIM card that inserts into your own smartphone. If you choose to use a SIM card, make sure you have an unlocked SIM card in your smartphone. Call your cell phone provider to ask if your phone is unlocked. If not, ask if they will unlock it for you. Israeli phone providers will ship the SIM card prior to the trip. *Be sure to order at least ten days prior to departure to allow adequate time for shipping.*

Currently, one very affordable plan with excellent coverage and comprehensive services for SIM card use is **Group Sims**. This company also provides group discounts for three or more travelers purchasing their plans together. Go to www.GroupSims.com. *Israel for the Christian Traveler* readers are offered an additional discount on both SIM card and Israel phones if you type in this code: **ICT10OFF**. Group Sims' daily rates, which include the use of an Israeli phone number, feature:

- Unlimited calling within Israel
- Unlimited calling to USA and Canada
- 30 GB of data allotment
- 10 GB of texting, both within Israel and abroad
- Affordable upgrade to a U.S. number

For phone use only, you can rent an Israeli flip phone; also available through Group Sims, as well as various companies online and at the airport.

The second option is to use your cell phone provider's international plan. This option can be great; however, use caution. There are often "hidden" fees and disclaimers that you find when you arrive in Israel, and/or after you return home. Although pricier than a SIM card, the good news is that you're only charged for the days that you actually use your device abroad. Additionally, you can typically use your minutes, messages, and data allowances from your domestic plan.

You should be aware that if you make or accept a phone call, listen to a voicemail, send a text, use data, or simply have apps running in the background that use data, you'll be charged the daily fee—even if you don't use the phone. On these days, you need to remember to turn off all of your apps and data roaming to avoid the daily charge. If you don't know how to disable apps, get help before you leave home or do a Google search to find out how to completely disable your data usage. You may also want to turn off all your location services, automatic updates, and push notifications that are enabled for apps.

IMPORTANT QUESTIONS TO ASK YOUR CELL PHONE PROVIDER:

- What are the coverage areas in Israel? Sometimes locations, such as Tiberias (Sea of Galilee region) are not included.

- Are there any roaming or data charges? If so, how can you prevent these charges?

- Does the plan include both outgoing and incoming calls and texts? If not, what are the additional costs?

- What is the data speed per day and are there limits in data use? Some plans start with 4G of data and are soon reduced to 2G. With these reduced speeds, you will most likely experience significantly slow connectivity, potentially waiting a long time just to open an email.

- Are additional taxes included in the cost? If so, how much? Some plans charge taxes that are up to 30% more than the basic cost of your plan.

ISRAELI CURRENCY

ISRAEL'S CURRENCY IS THE **NEW ISRAEL SHEKEL (NIS)** OR "SHEKEL" FOR SHORT. An "average conversion rate of 3.5 NIS to $1 USD is used below for examples. *Search online to find out the **current exchange rate** for your country's currency.* For instance, if you are a U.S. citizen, type in: "How many NIS in one-dollar USD?"

ISRAELI BANK NOTES

Bank notes are available in the following denominations:
20 NIS, 50 NIS, 100 NIS, & 200 NIS.

How much are Israeli bank notes worth?

Based upon an average conversion value of
3.5 NIS (shekels) to $1, here are the
approximate USD values:

20 NIS = $5.70	50 NIS = $14.30
100 NIS = $28.50	200 NIS = $57.00

ISRAELI COINS

Israeli coins are available in silver **shekels (NIS)** and gold **Agorot**. 100 *agorot* is equal to one shekel. Be aware that even 10 agorot is worth less than 3 cents! You'll save time if you pull out just your silver coins (and ½ NIS when appropriate) for purchases.

SILVER shekel coins come in denominations of **1 NIS, 2 NIS, 5 NIS, 10 NIS** (gold with silver border), and the gold **½ NIS** is equivalent to **50 agorot**.

GOLD agorot coins are available in denominations of **1, 5, 10,** and **50** (**½ NIS**).

How much are Israeli coins worth?

Based upon an average conversion value of 3.5 NIS (shekels) to $1,
here are the approximate USD values:

1 agorot = $.003
5 agorot = $.015
10 agorot = $.03

½ NIS = $.14
(½ NIS = 50 agorot)

1 NIS = $.29

2 NIS = $.57

5 NIS = $1.42

10 NIS = $2.85

CHANGING MONEY
TO ISRAELI CURRENCY

If you want to avoid the hassle of exchanging money, U.S. currency is accepted throughout most of Israel. Local currency, however, does yield better prices. You will receive the best exchange value, with no fees, by bringing $100 bills to a reputable exchange vendor in Tiberias or Old City Jerusalem. Be aware that storeowners and service providers are not required to accept foreign currency and will often provide change in Israeli shekels—even if the payment was made in foreign currency. The average spender will want to exchange about $200 or more for NIS (New Israeli Shekels). Be sure to keep your exchange receipts for accurate expense accounting.

Major credit cards such as **Visa, Master-Card, Discover,** and **American Express** are widely accepted. **Travelers' checks** are not recommended as they are usually not accepted. Some businesses will accept **U.S. checks,** so you may want to bring a checkbook with you. Foreign currency of all kinds may be exchanged at the airport, banks, post offices, most hotels, and licensed exchange agencies in major cities. Rates vary at different locations, and banks charge a commission. Credit cards usually provide the best exchange rate.

You can withdraw local or foreign currency at banks which accept credit cards, and you will generally find ATM machines just outside the bank entrance. BANKING HOURS: Banks are generally open from 8:30AM–12:00 PM Sundays through Fridays and Jewish holiday eves; they are also open from 4:00 PM–6:00 PM on Sundays, Tuesdays, and Thursdays. All banks are closed on Shabbat and Jewish holidays. Try to avoid banking on Sundays; exchange fees are considerably higher.

Utilizing a DEBIT/ATM CARD from your home bank will enable you to extract cash at most ATM machines in Israel. ATM machines are the fastest, easiest way to change money at the best rates. If you access an ATM, be prepared to pay a modest ATM fee. Look for ATMs with posted international flag decals and images of foreign debit cards. Note: ATMs are not restocked during Shabbat or on Jewish holidays.

IMPORTANT: Before you leave home, find out the exchange rate and any additional usage fees determined by your credit card provider and know your debit and credit card PIN codes; chances are you will need them. Additionally, confirm that your bank will allow your debit card to be used in Israel (as not all do) and notify your credit card provider of the use of the card within Israel to avoid a potential temporary suspension due to suspicious fraudulent activity. Leave all unnecessary credit cards at home for protection in the unlikely event your wallet is stolen.

CASH ON HAND

Establish your spending budget to determine how much cash should you bring from home. Expenses over and above a "typical" all-inclusive tour may include:

- Souvenirs and gifts
- Lunches at $10–$15 a day per person (Note: protein bars or other snacks from home may suffice for some, due to the substantial breakfast and dinner buffets at the hotels.)
- $5 a day for snacks or beverages like coffee, tea, water, or cold drinks
- Tips for restaurants and baggage handling at the airport
- A few shekels for the use of bathrooms at some of the touring sites

CASH is mainly used for tipping, small item purchases, and emergencies. A minimum suggested amount to bring is $100–$200 USD in cash. This amount is adequate for tips, small item purchases like water, bottles, and postcards, and for times you run out of shekels, etc. Small bills ($1 and $5) are best, allowing you to keep a minimal amount of cash on your person. About twenty $1 bills will be quite useful.

CUSTOMARY TIPPING (2019)

If you are on a group tour, you have most likely paid for the bulk of your tips up front. These include tips to your tour guide, bus driver, and hotels. Be sure to consult with your travel arranger regarding which tips have already been paid and which you need to add. Consider tipping generously for great service as making a living in Israel is difficult.

Baggage Handlers at airport: For basic baggage handling, the standard tip is $1 per bag. If you need special service or assistance (such as expedited handling at curbside check in at the airport), an extra $1 per bag or a flat $5–$10 (if you have several bags) is reasonable and acceptable.

Tour Guide: If your tips were not included in your tour package, prepare to tip your guide between $6–$8 per day. A guide whom you hire directly has no expectation of a tip. A *private* guide hired through a company or service does NOT receive the full amount you paid and should be tipped; the going rate is $8–$10 per person per day.

Vehicle or Bus Driver: If tips were *not* included on your prepaid tour, tip your bus driver $3–$5 per person per day. On a *private* tour, you would want to tip your driver $4–$6 per person per day.

Hotels: Tip $1–$2 per day for the hotel staff; pay at reception desk. This tip is generally included in the package price of group tours.

Restaurants: Tipping at Israeli restaurants is similar to the U.S. Based on the level of service received, 10–15% is standard. Make sure to check your receipt; sometimes, it will say, "10% service fee included." In this case, a tip is unnecessary.

Taxi Drivers: Do not tip taxi drivers in Israel. Pay only what the meter shows unless the cab driver is handling baggage for you.

MONEY MATTERS WHEN DEPARTING ISRAEL

A maximum of $500 USD can be converted back from shekels at banks in the Ben Gurion Airport. Anything exceeding this amount, up to $5,000 USD, (acquired during a single visit to Israel) can be reconverted with bank receipts substantiating the original conversion of the foreign currency. So keep those bank receipts!

Israeli tourists can qualify for a V.A.T. ("Value Added Tax") refund. This tax is added on to most purchased merchandise. The current V.A.T. in Israel is a whopping 17 percent! Thankfully, tourists can apply for a refund of that extra tax money upon departure at the airport. The following are the requirements for a V.A.T. refund:

- The purchase amount in **one** tax invoice, including V.A.T., must **exceed** 400 NIS.

- Food, drink, and tobacco products do not qualify for V.A.T. refunds.

- You cannot be an Israeli citizen.

- Goods must have been purchased in stores that participate in the V.A.T. refund program. If in doubt, ask.

- Goods must be recognized for export from the State of Israel.

- Purchases must be for personal use only and in a non-commercial quantity.

When you arrived in Israel, you received a paper inserted in your passport. Have this paper available for inspection at the V.A.T. refund counter.

Pack your goods in a Ziploc bag together with the applicable invoices. Present the package to the official at the "MILGAM" counter at the airport.

SHOPPING TIPS

Predetermine your spending budget; this will help to resist the temptation to buy something at almost every gift shop. Unless you see something you cannot live without, hold off. You'll probably find something better and less expensive down the road. *Tip: Some of your best deals are in the smaller national park bookstores in the north, like Megiddo and Caesarea Philippi.*

Souvenirs can be found for as low as a couple of dollars; high-end jewelry and artwork can run into thousands of dollars. The most popular souvenirs in Israel are Dead Sea cosmetics and skin care products, religious articles, reproductions of museum items, olive-wood products, biblical spices, cashmere scarves, clothing, and jewelry. Popular jewelry includes items made from silver and/or Roman glass, gemstones, and authentic ancient coins or coin replicas. A favorite jewelry choice is the Eilat stone, Israel's national stone. It is a beautiful green-blue mixture of malachite, azurite, turquoise, and other minerals. Generally, upscale gift shops provide the best quality and selection of jewelry.

Do not use a debit card for major souvenir purchases such as jewelry. A possible scenario is purchasing a $200 silver bracelet, returning home, and finding it's fake. You call the bank, and much to your dismay, you're told your cash has already been transferred because you used a debit card. By using a regular CREDIT CARD, the payment by the bank can be postponed until an investigation is completed.

Conventional stores, restaurants, and public transportation have fixed prices and are not open to bargaining. However, in the open-air marketplace (as in Old City Jerusalem), bargaining is expected—and that's half the fun! The price quoted is never the final price; it is often two to three times higher. Typically, the further into the market you venture, the better the deals. Tip: don't look too excited about a find and don't show them too much of your money...or your final price may be higher!

It is important to keep an updated, written record of your purchases. You will need to provide a list of items bought, along with their value, in your U.S. airport customs form on your return flight home.

PUBLIC TRANSPORTATION

ISRAEL'S PUBLIC TRANSPORTATION IS convenient and reasonably priced. Tourists arriving at the Ben Gurion Airport are approximately 16 miles (22 km) from the center of Tel Aviv and 34 miles (55 km) from Jerusalem. Traffic is generally quite congested in the morning and late afternoon/early evening Sunday through Thursday, especially between and within Tel Aviv and Jerusalem.

To access public transportation at the airport, take the elevator to the lowest level. Destinations include Jerusalem, Tel Aviv, and Haifa.

BUS: The most popular form of public transportation in Israel is the bus. The very affordable **Egged** operates the bulk of the bus transportation. Call 03-694-8888.

TRAIN: Israel Railways is a convenient and inexpensive train service. Part of the long-awaited Tel Aviv-Jerusalem high-speed train is currently open—between Jerusalem and the airport. Check to see if the Tel Aviv section is open yet. The **Jerusalem Light Rail** opened in late 2011. The line is 8.6 miles (13.9 km) long with 23 stops at popular destinations in Jerusalem, including the Old City. Call 072-256-4333. During heavy traffic times, the train is by far the fastest mode of transportation.

Note: Israel Railways and most bus lines are closed on Jewish holidays. On Shabbat, they stop operating early Friday afternoon and resume Saturday evening.

FLIGHTS WITHIN ISRAEL: Arkia Airline offers affordable commuter flights between Eilat & Tel Aviv and Eilat & Haifa.

TAXI: Although more expensive, taxis are popular. By law, fares are fixed by the Ministry of Transportation and charged according to the meter reading. Avoid unnecessary haggling and stress; request the driver turn on his meter. Drivers may attempt collecting a fixed, higher price. If you prefer a fixed price, confirm the rate prior to service and refuse to pay more! Taxis can be ordered in advance by telephone or flagged down on main streets.

SHARE TAXI: A "share taxi," known as a *sherut*, is an economical alternative to a conventional taxi. Sheruts take their passengers on regular bus routes, offer flexible scheduling, and depart when their ten seats are filled. Some operate on Saturdays. The **Nesher Airport Shuttle** is a great bargain, operating between Ben Gurion Airport and Jerusalem. They will deliver you straight to your Jerusalem destination. Call 02-625-7227 for more information. Most Jerusalem hotels will book a Nesher for you to return to the airport. For preferred departure time, arrange service at least two days prior to departure.

CAR RENTALS

If you are not part of a tour, you may want to rent your own car to have the flexibility to visit the sites of your choice at your own pace. You must be 21 years of age or older with an international driver's license. Rental car companies are in all of Israel's major cities, as well as the airport. Reserve your car before your trip; the longer you wait, the higher the price. **Typically, you will get the best price about three months prior to your departure.**

A good **GPS** is vital to make your way through Israel. Most car rental companies offer GPS systems. **Google Maps** and **WAZE** (developed by Israelis) are available for free on most smartphones and tablets.

Driving caution: Be aware that Israelis are typically quite aggressive drivers; many are even reckless. Defensive driving is imperative; vigilantly be on the alert for swerving cars and mopeds. Allow impatient drivers to pass and use your horn as needed. It really works!

*Note: Aroma Espresso Bar and coffee shop,
the "Starbucks" of Israel, has 125 branches across the country.*

FALAFEL
Traditional Middle Eastern food; deep-fried balls or patties made from ground chickpeas, fava beans, or both; usually served in a pita

SCHNITZEL
Thin slices of boneless meat (generally veal or chicken) dipped in flour, egg, and bread crumbs; then fried in butter or oil

SHAWARMA
Arabic dish of lamb or other meat that is "shaved" and placed on a spit to grill for many hours; often enjoyed in pita or laffa bread

ISRAELI SALAD
Chopped salad made of finely diced tomatoes and cucumbers (described as the "most well-known national dish of Israel")

POTATO LATKES
Grated or ground potato, flour, and egg "pancakes" fried in oil and often seasoned with onion and garlic; typically served during Hanukah

BAMBA
Israel's exclusive all-natural peanut butter-flavored snack, made of peanuts, corn, palm oil and salt (Bamba is Israel's best-selling snack food)

TAHINI
A delicious spread made from ground sesame seeds; PITA, the "national bread" of Israel is often served with tahini or hummus

JERUSALEM BAGELS
Long and oblong-shaped, soft and chewy — Jerusalem bagels are made from bread dough, covered in sesame seeds, and served with the spice hyssop

HUMMUS
A popular Arabic food dip (made from garbanzo beans, or chickpeas)

BABA GANOUSH
Tangy Levantine dish; an eggplant spread mixed with olive oil and various seasonings

HALVAH
Flaky, dense, tahini-based delicacy sweetened with honey or sugar

BUREKAS
Baked or fried pastries filled with cheese, minced meat, potatoes, or vegetables

The dates on the Gregorian Calendar change each year;
check online for current dates.

ENGLISH NAME	HEBREW NAME	JEWISH CALENDAR	GREGORIAN CALENDAR
Esther's Triumph	Purim	Adar 14–15	late Feb. thru March
Feast of Passover	Erev Pesach	Nisan 14	late Mar. thru late Apr.
Feast of Unleavened Bread	Pesach	Nisan 15–21	late Mar. thru late Apr.
Feast of First Fruits	Omer	Nisan 15	late Mar. thru late Apr.
Holocaust Remembrance Day	Yom Hashoah	Nisan 28	mid-Apr. to early May
Memorial Day	Yom Hazikaron	Iyar 5	mid-Apr. to mid-May
Independence Day	Yom Ha-Atzmaut	Iyar 6	mid-Apr. to mid-May
Jerusalem Day	Yom Yerushalayim	Iyar 28	late May
Feast of Weeks (Harvest)	Shavuot (Pentecost)	Sivan 6	late May
Feast of Trumpets (New Year)	Rosh Hashanah	Tishrei 1–2	mid-Sept. to early Oct.
Day of Atonement	Yom Kippur	Tishrei 10	mid-Sept. to mid-Oct.
Feast of Tabernacles	Sukkot	Tishrei 15–23	late Sept. to late Oct.
Assembly of the 8th Day	Simchat Torah	Tishrei 23	beg. to mid-October
Feast of Rededication	Hanukkah	Kislev 25–Tevet 2	December

On Mt. Sinai, God gave Moses instruction for the dates and observances of the seven feasts:
four in the spring (past fulfillment) and three in the fall (future fulfillment).
Note: the Day of Atonement will be fulfilled in the second coming of Jesus when
"all Israel will be saved," and the Jewish people finally experience true atonement.

SPRING FEASTS	NEW TESTAMENT FULFILLMENT	FALL FEASTS	NEW TESTAMENT FULFILLMENT
Feast of Passover	Crucifixion of Jesus	Feast of Trumpets	Gathering of Church (rapture)
Feast of Unleavened Bread	Burial of Jesus	Day of Atonement	Second Coming of Jesus
Feast of First Fruits	Resurrection of Jesus	Feast of Tabernacles	Beginning: Millennium
Feast of Weeks	Descent of Holy Spirit (Pentecost)		

C: Centigrade/F: Fahrenheit	JAN	FEB	MAR	APR	MAY	JUNE	JULY	AUG	SEPT	OCT	NOV	DEC
TEL AVIV High °C/°F	18/64	18/64	19/67	23/73	25/77	28/82	29/85	30/86	29/85	27/81	23/74	19/67
TEL AVIV Low °C/°F	10/49	10/50	12/53	14/58	17/63	21/69	23/73	24/75	23/73	19/66	15/58	11/52
TEL AVIV # of Rainy Days	12.8	10.0	8.5	3.1	0.8	0.0	0.0	0.0	0.3	3.2	7.5	10.9
TIBERIAS High °C/°F	17/63	19/65	22/71	27/81	32/89	35/94	36/97	36/97	35/94	30/87	24/75	20/66
TIBERIAS Low °C/°F	8/47	8/47	10/50	13/56	17/62	20/68	22/72	23/73	21/70	18/65	19/56	10/50
TIBERIAS # of Rainy Days	13.7	11.8	9.7	5.1	1.9	0.1	0.0	0.0	0.3	3.7	6.7	12.2
JERUSALEM High °C/°F	12/53	13/55	15/60	22/71	25/78	28/82	29/84	29/85	30/83	28/77	25/66	19/57
JERUSALEM Low °C/°F	6/44	6/44	8/47	13/55	16/60	18/64	19/67	20/67	20/66	19/62	17/54	12/47
JERUSALEM # of Rainy Days	12.9	11.7	9.6	4.4	1.3	0.0	0.0	0.0	0.3	3.6	7.3	10.9
MASADA/EILAT High °C/°F	21/69	22/72	26/78	31/88	35/96	39/102	40/104	40/104	37/99	33/91	27/81	22/72
MASADA/EILAT Low °C/°F	10/49	11/51	14/57	18/64	22/71	24/76	26/79	26/79	25/76	21/70	16/60	11/52
MASADA/EILAT # of Rainy Days	2.1	1.8	1.6	0.9	0.7	0.0	0.0	0.0	0.1	0.7	0.8	1.9
DAYLIGHT HRS. (15th of month)	10	11	12	13	13.5	14	14	13	12.5	11.5	10.5	10
SUNRISE AM SUNSET PM (15th of month)	6:40 4:54	6:21 5:22	5:46 5:46	6:07 7:08	5:38 7:30	5:29 7:47	5:41 7:46	6:01 7:22	6:21 6:43	6:42 6:04	6:08 4:36	6:33 4:33

ENGLISH	HEBREW	ENGLISH	HEBREW
Hello! Goodbye! Peace be with you.	Shalom!	What's your name?	Ma shimkha?
Good morning!	Boker tov!	My name is ….	Shmi …..
Good evening!	Erev tov!	Nice to meet you!	Naim meod!
Good night!	Lila tov!	Welcome!	Baruch haba!
Peace upon you	Shabbat Shalom!	I don't understand.	Lo hevanti.
How are you?	Ma shelomkha?	Today/Now	Hayom/Akhsh
Good	Tov	Tomorrow/Yesterday	Mahar/Etmol
Thank you very much.	Toda raba!	Here you go! (giving something)	Hine!
Please You're welcome!	Bevakasha!	Sorry! (for a mistake)	Ani mitstaer meod!
Yes/No	Ken/Lo	I feel sick.	Ani chole.
Way to go! Great!	Yoffi!	I need a doctor.	Ani zakuk lerofe.
Come on! Hurry up!	Yalla!	one, two, three	echad, shtaim, shalosh
Excuse me! (to pass by or interrupt)	Slicha!	four, five, six	arba, chamesh, shesh
Fine! or All right!	Beseder!	seven, eight, nine, ten	sheva, shmone, tesha, eser
Cool! or No problem!	Sababa!	How much is this?	Kama ze ole?

HEBREW	ENGLISH	HEBREW	ENGLISH
Mazel Tov!	Congratulations!	mishegas meshugener	insanity, craziness "crazy man"
L'Chaim	To life! (toast before drinking alcoholic beverages)	mensch	good, honorable person
Gesundheit!	Health! (response to a sneeze)	nosh	to nibble or eat a light snack
Nu?	So? Huh? Well? What's up?	chutzpah	"He's got chutzpah!" nerve, arrogance (not a compliment)
Le´hit!	See you! I gotta go now!	kvetsh	complain, whine, or fret
Mitzvah	Good deed done for God	goy goyim (plural)	non-Jew or gentile
Oy vey!	Exclamation of dismay, grief, or exasperation	kibbitz	verbal joking around

"Ch" is guttural "h." (akin to the beginning sound of spitting!)

COMMON ISRAELI TERMS

PREFIX	MEANING	USAGE/EXAMPLES
"beit" "bet" "beth"	These three terms all mean "house of..." Many synagogues use these terms as part of their name, such as *Beth Israel*.	Beit She'an: "House of 'Security' or 'Rest'" Bethesda: "House of 'Mercy' or 'Grace'" Bethlehem: "House of Bread" Beit Shemesh: "House of the Sun"
"ein"	"Ein" refers to a **spring of water**.	Ein Harod: "Spring of Harod" Ein Karem: "Spring of the Vineyard" Ein Gedi: "Kid Spring"
"gan"	"Gan" means "**garden**."	Gan Hashlosha: "Garden of the Three" Ganei Chaim: "Gardens of Life"
"tel" "tell"	A once-occupied archaeological **mound or hill**, generally with a flat top and sloping sides. Most are biblical ruins of fortified cities;	Tel Megiddo, Tel Hazor, Tel Dan, Tel Beit She'an, Tel Jericho, Tel Beit Shemesh Tel Be'ersheva, Tel Gezer, Tel Lachish, Tel Arad
"via"	"Via" means "**way of**."	Via Maris: "Way of the Sea" Via Dolorosa: "Way of the 'Cross' or 'Sorrows'"
"wadi"	"Wadi" is an Arabic term referring to a **valley or dry riverbed**.	Wadi David: "Valley of David" in Ein Gedi Wadi Qelt: beautiful valley in Jericho Wadi Elah: Valley of Elah (David & Goliath)

Described as a wasteland for thousands of years, God has made His promised land prosper once again, as prophesied over 2,500 years ago in Zechariah 8:12:

"The seed will grow well, the vine will yield its fruit, the ground will produce its crops, and the heavens will drop their dew..."

ISRAELI AGRICULTURE

From drip irrigation to natural pesticides, Israeli innovations are helping to feed the world, especially in developing countries. Israel remains a world leader in agricultural technology, even though water scarcity has created unfavorable farming conditions. Greater than 40% of Israel is desert and only 20% of the land is naturally arable. These grim realities make it even more remarkable that Israel has increased her agricultural productivity sevenfold over a twenty-five-year period with no corresponding increase in water usage. An astonishing 95% of Israel's food is produced locally and over $1.3 billion worth of agricultural products are exported each year.

Drip irrigation originated in Israel. Soon after Israel became a state in 1948, Simcha Blass, Director of Government Water Institutions, came up with the idea of drip irrigation. His ideas were developed over the years, and in 1965, a new drip irrigation system came into fruition on a kibbutz in the Negev desert. The rest is history. Drip irrigation is now used in over 75% of Israeli farming. Israeli irrigation systems have been sold to more than 100 countries throughout the world.

Israel has become one of the world's chief exporters of fresh produce. Her attractive,

succulent fruit commands a high price in today's world market—also a fulfillment of prophecy: *"...Israel will bud and blossom and fill all the world with fruit"* (Isaiah 27:6).

WINE PRODUCTION

Wine has been produced in the Holy Land since biblical times, as evidenced in the miracle at Cana. However, the wine industry was virtually non-existent for well over one thousand years, with only two wineries operating in the late eighties. In the past twenty years, Israel's wine production has grown exponentially—generating over 250 wineries of various sizes, some producing millions of bottles of wine annually. About one-third of these wineries produce kosher wine (wine handled by observant Jews from the moment the grapes are crushed). Israelis drink an average of 4.6 liters of wine per capita, less than half of the U.S.—to where most of their wine is exported.

Israel's climate, especially in the mountains of the North, has proven conducive to productive vineyards—as prophesied in the book of Amos almost 3,000 years ago: *"New wine will drip from the mountains and flow from all the hills..."* (Amos 9:13)

WILDLIFE OF ISRAEL

The desert-dwelling **Nubian ibex** is a large wild goat found in mountainous regions of the Middle East. Its population in the wild is estimated at approximately 1,200. Ibex are secure ascending steep and challenging cliffs because of their strong, supple legs and grooved hooves. *"The high hills are a refuge for the wild goats; and the rocks for the conies"* (Psalm 104:18).

The **coney**, or rock hyrax, is a rodent-like animal that makes its home in the rocks, a reminder to God's people that they must trust in the Rock to dwell safely—*"hyraxes are creatures of little power, yet they make their home in the crags"* (Proverbs 30:26, KJV). The coney can be seen in abundance in the rocks and cliffs of Ein Gedi National Park.

Camels were created to thrive in the hot desert regions, such as the Negev. They have a thick covering of hair that protects them from the high temperatures and lengthy eyelashes to shade them from the hot desert sun. Also, camels have the ability to close off their nostrils during sandstorms and their upper lip is divided, enabling consumption of prickly vegetation. Of chief importance is their ability to go without water for prolonged periods of time, up to a week or more.

The **donkey** is known for its strength, gentleness, and loyalty to its master (Genesis 49:14; Numbers 22:30). The donkey was ridden by diverse classes of people in the Bible, including Abraham, Balaam of Mesopotamia, King David's household, and women and children (Genesis 22:3; Numbers 22:21; 2 Samuel 16:2; Exodus 4:20). Israel's future king, or Messiah, is depicted by the prophet Zechariah as arriving *"humble and mounted on a donkey"* (Zechariah 9:9, ESV). This prophecy was fulfilled in Matthew 21:1–5.

Sheep are the most frequently-referenced animal in Scripture, since they were a key part of Israel's sacrificial offerings to the Lord. Their dependent and helpless nature is frequently compared to that of man. Sheep continue to hold great significance in Israel through their provision of wool, milk, and meat.

ISRAEL DEFENSE FORCES (IDF)

Military service is compulsory for both males and females—Israel is the only country in the world to require women to serve in the military. Males serve in the IDF three years and females almost two years. Israel is a world leader in her exemplary military recruitment, generating approximately 80% compliance of all who receive summons. Legal exemptions include Muslims, Christians, Ultra-Orthodox Jews (currently disputed), and delinquent youth. Bedouin often volunteer assistance in tracking and scouting. Every recruit participates in a basic training program of military discipline, physical conditioning, first aid essentials, and riflery.

Due to her small population, Israel has never had the luxury of a substantial permanent army—which is a necessity with her immense, ongoing security and terrorist threats. Israel deals with this challenge by utilizing discharged soldiers as reservists into their early 50s. These reservists are expected to donate a minimum of thirty or more days of army service each year, inclusive of training as well as active service. It is commonplace for two, or even three, generations to be serving concurrently in the army—the son or daughter in compulsory service and the father, and even some grandfathers, serving in the reserves.

THE KNESSET

THE KNESSET, ISRAEL'S LEGISLATURE, first assembled on February 14, 1949. The term *Knesset* originated from the "Great Assembly" or "Great Synagogue"—which functioned over 500 years, from the end of the Old Testament prophet era (roughly 450 BC) through to the destruction of Jerusalem in AD 70. Traditionally, Jews have believed this assembly encompassed 120 scribes, sages, and prophets.

The Knesset is responsible for electing both the President and Prime Minister, approving the cabinet, passing all legislative laws, as well as supervising all government projects. The 120 members of the Knesset generally serve four-year terms and are divided into permanent and special interest committees for amending specified bills.

Israelis are typically quite outspoken about their values and beliefs. Civil rights and freedom of the press are foundational to Israel's democratic system.

It's both important and difficult to grasp the complexities of the Israeli-Palestinian relations. However, we do know the Lord created both Jews and Arabs, and Yeshua died for both. Blessing Israel includes also blessing Israeli Arabs. Any persuasion or discussion on this volatile issue wishing to stay true to Scripture must keep in mind our Lord's personal, authoritative direction in His Word:

"The foreigner residing among you must be treated as your native-born. Love them as yourself, for you were foreigners in Egypt. I am the Lord your God."
Leviticus 19:34

"You shall allot it as an inheritance for yourselves and for the sojourners who reside among you and have had children among you. They shall be to you as native-born children of Israel. With you they shall be allotted an inheritance among the tribes of Israel."
Ezekiel 47:22

This biblical understanding is relevant to our understanding of the people living in the region often referred to as the "Occupied Territories." Historically, the term "**Occupied Palestinian Territories**" was conferred by the United Nations (UN) and other international organizations between the years 1998 and 2013; the purpose was to refer to areas under the jurisdiction of the Palestinian National Authority, which the UN continues to believe are "occupied" by Israel. These areas encompass the "West Bank," East Jerusalem, and the Gaza Strip. The East Jerusalem disputed territory includes the Old City as well as neighborhoods to its north, east, and south. Borders are defined by the **Green Line**, a demarcation line determined by the 1949 Armistice Agreements—a line that marked the de facto borders of the State of Israel and those of her four bordering neighbors (Egypt, Jordan, Lebanon and Syria) spanning 1949–1967.

WEST BANK

Historyically, the "West Bank" is an area that borders Israel and Jordan, covering an area of 3,641 sq. miles, or 5,860 sq. km. The name "West Bank" is an Arabic term given to all of the land on the west side of the Jordan River. The purpose was to differentiate the west bank of the Jordan River (East Jerusalem, Judea and Samaria) from its east bank.

Please note: this sensitive issue is the author's perspective and others are free to respectfully disagree. "West Bank" is used by the modern news media to reference what they consider the "occupied territories," with Israel as the "occupying power." This is a hotly debated subject focusing on historical interpretation and the nature and recipients of the biblical covenants. The Palestinians currently have great global support for their cause, including the United Nations. They demand Israel withdraw from these contested regions. However, most Bible-believing Christians believe Israel is justified both historically and biblically to settle this area.

In this book, the term "West Bank" is used loosely in quotations marks because the Bible provides a different name to this region. In the Bible, it is actually the biblical heartland of Israel, known as Judea (which includes Jerusalem) and Samaria. These names were reiterated by Yeshua Himself in Acts 1:8. Every part of this territory is included in the land that God granted to Israel under the Abrahamic Covenant (Genesis 15:18–21). *You can read more about the four primary biblical covenants regarding the "Land" of Israel on pp. 44–45.*

However, even outside of clear Bible teaching, the Jewish people have maintained a well-documented, continuous presence in this region for well over 3,000 years; the only time they were prohibited from living here was during Jordan's rule from 1948 to 1967.

"West Bank" barrier: In response to numerous suicide bombings and "Palestinian" terrorist threats, the Israeli government has authorized and directed the ongoing construction of the Israeli "West Bank" barrier, or security fence (photo above). The construction of this network of fences, which loosely followed the armistice Green Line in this region, began in 2003. In 2006, approval was granted for the barrier's final length of 437 miles (703 km). As of 2013, almost 60% of the fence was complete, with concrete walls up to 26 ft (8 m) high and barrier trenches ranging from 98 ft (30 m) to 492 ft (150 m) in width.

According to Wikipedia, *"The number of fatalities due to terror attacks (in this region) have continued to exhibit a steady decline since 2002, from four-hundred fifty-two in 2002 to nine in 2010."* However, the erection of the security barrier has sparked great controversy and heated emotions among many groups of people.

Demographics: As of 2017, the population of the contested area of Judea and Samaria (the "West Bank") encompassed an estimated 500,000 Israeli Jews and close to three million "Palestinian" Arabs. Another roughly 200,000 Jewish settlers populate East Jerusalem.

According to the official U.S. Department of State Country Report of the UN Refugee Agency, 95–98% of the Palestinian population live on 40% of the land, while 60% of the land remains unpopulated. Israeli settlements encompass less than 2% of this contested land and close to 80% of these settlements are located close to, or adjacent to, the Green Line. This "occupation" continues to spark controversy throughout the world.

Administrative Divisions of "West Bank" Territory: The Oslo II Accords, signed by the U.S. in 1993, divided the entire region into three administrative divisions: areas A, B, and C—as described in the chart below.

	AREA A	AREA B	AREA C
Governing Authority	Palestinian Authority	Palestinian Authority; Israel	Israel
Inhabitants	Palestinians	Palestinians; Israeli Jews	Palestinians; Israeli Jews
Percentage of "West Bank" Land (2013)	18%	22%	60%
Land Utilization and Composition	Cities/Towns: Nablus (Shechem), Jenin, Tulkarem, Qalgilya, Ramallah, Bethlehem, Jericho, 80% of Hebron	20% of Hebron; 440 Palestinian villages and surrounding lands; Jewish Settlements	Jewish Settlements (Ariel, Gush Etzion, Karnei Shomron, Ma'ale Adumim, etc.); outposts; 21% closed military zones

Ma'ale Adumim is Israel's third largest settlement with a population close to 40,000. It is one of Israel's more controversial settlements due to the fact that many Palestinians view Ma'ale Adumim as a threat to a future Palestinian state because of its strategic location between the northern and southern parts of the "West Bank" (Samaria and Judea).

GAZA STRIP

The Gaza Strip (known as "Gaza") is a self-governing Palestinian territory that borders the most southwestern part of Israel and the Mediterranean Sea for 32 miles (51 km); its southwest borders Egypt for 7 miles (11 km). The width of the entire region ranges from 3–7 miles wide (5–11 km) and is roughly 146 sq. miles (235 sq. km) in total area. More than 99% of Gaza's 1.5 million Palestinian Arab residents are Sunni Muslims—mostly refugees; there is also a small Christian contingent of 2,000–3,000. 80% of Gaza's citizens live below the poverty line.

Gaza has a long history of occupation—beginning with the ancient Egyptians, followed by the Philistines, the Arabs, the Christian Crusaders, and continuing with the Ottomans through the end of World War 1. The occupation continues through today:

- Post-World War I (beginning in 1918), the region was officially part of the British Mandate of Palestine.

- In the aftermath of the first Arab-Israeli war of 1948, Gaza came under the occupation of Egypt.

- In the 1967 Six-Day War, Israel took control of Gaza, along with the "West Bank," eastern Jerusalem, the Golan Heights, and the Sinai Peninsula.

- In 1994, Israel withdrew from portions of the Gaza Strip. The Palestinian National Authority and Israel held joint power over Gaza for the next ten years.

- In 2005, Israeli Prime Minister Ariel Sharon unilaterally ended military rule in Gaza, removing all Israeli settlements. Almost the entire Gaza Strip was now under Palestinian administration.

- In 2007, Hamas seized control of Gaza, resulting in an economic and political boycott from both Israel and the U.S. The Hamas "rule of terror" continues to this day.

- Since 2012, the two "Palestinian" territories of Gaza and the "West Bank" constitute what is referred to as the "State of Palestine," both falling under the jurisdiction of the Palestinian Authority.

Since Hamas' rise to power, Gaza has lived in extreme contention with Israel, engaging in numerous conflicts and battles. Some of the major historical clashes include: the 2007 Fatah-Hamas conflict, the Israeli blockade of 2007, Operation "Hot Winter" of 2008, the 2008 Israel-Hamas ceasefire, the 2008–2009 Gaza War, the 2011 cross-border attack, Operation "Returning Echo" of March-2012, Operation "Pillar of Defense" of October-2012, and the 2014 Gaza War (widely publicized for Gaza's "terror tunnels"). The relationship between Israel and the Gaza Strip has sparked public sentiment and worldwide controversy.

RELIGION IN ISRAEL PLAYS A KEY ROLE in shaping Israeli culture and lifestyle. According to the Israel Central Bureau of Statistics, Jews, Muslims, and Christians account for roughly 96% of Israel's population. The remaining 4% include minority faiths and belief systems such as Baha´i, Samaritanism, Hinduism, and diverse secular beliefs.

JUDAISM

Dad teaching his son from
the Hebrew holy books in Jerusalem.

Woman lighting Shabbat candles

Judaism is made up of three primary movements: Reform, Conservative and Orthodox. **Reform** Judaism, the most liberal, rejects the belief that the Torah was written by God and does not emphasize keeping the commandments. However, they do integrate some Judaïc values, practices, and culture into their lifestyle and worship. **Conservative** Judaism falls into a broad spectrum between Orthodoxy and Reform. While they adhere to Judaic values, they believe the Law should conform more to the prevailing culture. **Orthodox** Judaism spans a wide range of sects. However, they all strictly observe the Jewish law and share various similarities in observances and beliefs.

In Israel, practicing Jews generally identify themselves as "observant" rather than belonging to one of the three primary movements. Some of the more prominent communities of Jews in Israel include the following:

Ultra-Orthodox Jews consist of two main sects: *Haredi* and *Hasidic*; both are strongly opposed to Zionism.

Haredi is Hebrew for "those who tremble [before God]." Haredi Jews *(Haredim)* commit themselves to full-time Torah study, *accounting for the nearly 60% living in poverty.* Haredim tend to segregate themselves from the rest of society.

Hasidic Judaism (Hebrew for "piety") is slightly different from Haredi Judaism. Hasidics are *Ashkenazi* Jews which constitute the majority of American Jewry, originally from France, Germany, and Eastern Europe. The minority, primarily from Spain, Africa, and the Middle East, are known as *Sephardic* Jews. Hasidics emphasize joy in their mitzvah (good deed) observances and their mystical Jewish prayers, while their community revolves around their *Rebbe* (Grand Rabbi). The predominant language of Hasidim is *Yiddish* (a German dialect of Ashkenazi origin). Many Hasidics practice Jewish mysticism, known as *Kabblism. See following page.*

The **Dati Leumi** community is actively Zionistic (maintain a strong belief in a Jewish homeland) and Orthodox, but not as strict as the ultra-Orthodox sects.

The **Masorti** "Conservative" branch of Judaism integrates both traditional and secular observances and beliefs. Masorti are both Zionists and egalitarians encompassing a broad range of ideologies and practices. Masorti Jews can be Orthodox (Dati Leumi), traditional and religious, or just traditional.

Hilonis are secular Jews who may observe some traditional practices such as bar mitzvahs, Jewish weddings and funerals, lighting of the Shabbat candles, limiting activity on the Shabbat, and/or keeping partly kosher. The principal values of Israel's secular Jews are freedom of expression, democracy, and minority rights.

OBSERVANCE STATISTICS

According to a 2010 report released by the Israel Central Bureau of Statistics, the following are the approximate percentages of Israel's Jewish population:

8% ultra-Orthodox (Haredim, Hasidic)

12% Orthodox (Dati Leumi)

13% traditional-religious

25% traditional

42% secular, non-religious (Hiloni)

KABBALISM

Mysticism is an integral part of Hasidic practice. The primary stream of mystical Judaism is known as **Kabbalism,** parts of which Hasidim frequently include in their traditional prayer books. Kabbalah is a philosophical framework for interpreting Jewish texts and practices. The word *Kabbalah* means "to receive." In Kabbalism, secret "heavenly revelation" is received by Jews and orally passed on to subsequent generations. They believe this "secret" revelation explains the true meaning of the Hebrew Scriptures, as well as the nature of the universe, the nature of man, and the purpose of existence. They also believe these secrets are only revealed to those who are "spiritually ready to receive them." Kabbalah teaches that God, or "En Sof" (the "Endless One") is infinite, transcendent, incomprehensible, and cannot make direct contact with finite beings—except through divine revelation.

Kabbalism began among Babylonian Jews somewhere between AD 600–1300. For some time, it was practiced in mainstream Judaism, but as it became more esoteric, only certain sects continued their observance. There is quite a diversity in practice; observance may include prayer, revelation, visions, asceticism, numerology, talismans, amulets, incarnation of divine names and words, and even predictions of the coming Messiah. In reality, the principles of Kabbalah have more in common with the belief system of Deepak Chopra than with authentic Jewish sources.

The most important text in Kabbalah is the **Zohar**. The Zohar encompasses mystical and subjective commentaries on the Torah, seeking to both explain and construct a visual picture of the relationship between God and man. Furthermore, the Zohar is believed to have special powers which its adherents can experience simply by running their finger over the text as if reading Braille.

Today, as many seek to experience "contemporary spirituality," Kabbalah followers have crossed over not only into various sects of Judaism, but into other religions and faiths as well. Many "spirituality" seekers, Hollywood personalities, and even professing Christians are being drawn into Kabbalism. However, it is critical to understand that Kabbalah is completely incompatible with historic Judeo-Christianity. Its core philosophy is *pantheism*, the belief that God is everything and everyone, and everyone and everything is God. It teaches that man can attain a level in which he can become one with God, and that reincarnation and soul migration occur after death. Kabbalah will take its devoted followers on a dangerous path of "awakening the consciousness" through "self-realization" and "secret revelation," which is essentially an *occultic* revelation of God and existence—in direct opposition to the biblical gospel.

Since 1492, the Upper Galilee city of Tzfat (or Safed), has been the center of Kabbalistic practice and the home to countless Talmud and Zohar sages, Jewish mystics, and Kabbalists. Many claim the city generates a supernatural ambience, energy, and inspiration. Tzfat draws many tourists today who are seeking to experience this dangerous Jewish "spirituality" and "self-realization."

TRADITIONAL JEWISH DRESS

Ultra-Orthodox Jews strictly adhere to both traditional and scriptural teachings; some of their modern-day apparel originated in the Torah. For example, the Torah prohibits cross dressing: *"A woman shall not wear anything that pertains to a man, nor shall a man put on a woman's garment, for all who do so are an abomination to the Lord your God."* (Deuteronomy 22:5, NKJ). They contend that traditional clothing must differ between the genders; i.e., women cannot wear pants.

TRADITIONAL DRESS OF MEN

Ultra-Orthodox men can be identified by their black suits or long black coats (*kapotas* in Hebrew), white shirts, traditional black hats, beards, and sidecurls or sidelocks, known as **peot**. *Peot* originated from an interpretation of the biblical instruction laid forth in Leviticus 19:27, "Do not cut the hair at the sides of your head or clip off the edges of your beard."

To demonstrate piety and respect, observant Jewish men wear head coverings. The most common is a **kippah**—a thin, slightly rounded skull cap (above). In Yiddish, a kippah is known as a **yarmulke**. *Yarmulke*, in Aramaic, denotes "fear of the King." Some men wear them only inside a synagogue; others wear them at all times. A wide variety of kippahs are available, signifying various ideologies. Married Ultra-Orthodox men generally wear large kippahs (signifying greater piety). These larger hats can substitute for the conventional kippahs and range from traditional black top hats, or **fedoras** (below left) to **shtreimels** (below right). A *shtreimel* is a large kippah encircled by pieces of fur (typically gray fox, Russian sable, or stone marten). Fedoras and shtreimels are typically worn by the Ultra-Orthodox men during Shabbat, Jewish festivals, and other special celebrations.

A **tallit** is a prayer shawl, or robe, wrapped around Orthodox Jewish men during prayer services and other special occasions. Tied to the four corners of the tallit (and other four-cornered garments) are **tzitzit**, special twined and knotted wool fringes, or tassels. Religious Jews wear these in obedience to Deuteronomy 22:12, *"Make tassels on the four corners of the cloak you wear."* Tzitzit also serve as a precious reminder of God's laws while going about daily life. As such, they are kissed at specified times during the Jewish prayer service.

Tichels come
in a variety of styles.

Andrea Grinberg,
creator of Wrapunzel,
wearing a tichel

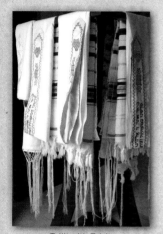

Tallit with Tzizit

Tefillin

Tzniyut

Tefillin, also called phylacteries, are small, cube-shaped black leather boxes which contain parchment scrolls of four Torah verses (Exodus 13:9,16 and Deuteronomy 6:8 and 11:18). Tefillin are attached to the head and the left arm of observant Jewish men, thirteen years and older. They are worn during weekday morning prayers to encourage spirituality, while discouraging worldliness.

TRADITIONAL DRESS OF WOMEN

Ultra-Orthodox women are required to dress modestly, known as **tzniyut** in Hebrew. They must wear long skirts which extend past the knee, long sleeves which extend past the elbow, high necklines which cover the collar bone, and thick stockings. High heels are not allowed. The purpose of this dress is to discourage improper thoughts in men, while increasing spirituality and decreasing materialism.

Married women cover their hair with wigs, scarves, or hats. A woman's hair is regarded sacred and intended only for her husband's pleasure. Consequently, married Orthodox Jewish women are required to cover their natural hair. They have two options: a headscarf or a wig. A headscarf, or **tichel** (Yiddish for "kerchief"), is available in a wide range of styles and fabrics. A wig is known as a **sheitel.**

SACRED JEWISH LITERATURE, SIGNS, AND SYMBOLS

The **Law, Pentateuch,** or **Written Torah** are the Books of Moses, the first five books of the Hebrew Bible (Old Testament)—Genesis through Deuteronomy.

The **Talmud,** or **Oral Torah,** explains and interprets the Written Torah. Jews believe that when Moses was on Mt. Sinai writing down the words of the Torah, God also provided him with additional explanations.

The **Whole Torah** includes both the Written Torah and Oral Torah.

The **Mishnah,** completed in AD 200, was the first written, authoritative compendium of Rabbinic Judaism's Oral Torah, or Talmud.

The **Tanach,** or **Hebrew Bible,** is the entire body of Jewish law and teachings *(known to Christians as the Old Testament).*

The **Midrash** is a body of stories told by Jewish rabbinic sages to explain passages of the Tanach.

The **Siddur** is a contemporary Jewish prayer book with ordered daily prayers.

The **Magen David,** better known as the **Star of David,** is the symbol most commonly asso-

ciated with Jewish culture today. Even though many believe the symbol represented the shape of King David's shield, early rabbinic literature provides no substantiation for this belief. Today, the Magen David, imprinted on the Israeli flag, is the universally-recognized symbol of the Jewish people.

The word G_d is often written without the "o" because it is believed that to avoid writing out the name of the Holy God is a sign of respect.

The symbol, **Chai,** is commonly seen on necklaces and other jewelry and ornaments. *Chai,* Hebrew for "living," comes from the two Hebrew letters *Cheit* and *Yod* attached to each other. Some say it refers to the Living G_d; others say it simply reflects Judaism's focus on the importance of life. Whatever the meaning, the concept of *chai* is very important in Jewish culture. The typical Jewish toast is *L'chaim!,* "To life!"

The ornamental **mezuzah** (Hebrew for "doorpost") adorns the right side of the doorframe of a Jewish home, typically affixed at an angle. The mezuzah contains a rolled-up parchment scroll with an inscription of Deuteronomy 11:13-21, known as the "Shema." The Shema is the oldest traditional Jewish prayer, which the people are instructed to recite morning and evening—in obedience to its command to "... *write them upon the doorposts of thy house.*" Jews commonly believe the mezuzah protects their home.

MESSIANIC JUDAISM

In 1948, when Israel became a nation, there were 23 Messianic Jews in Israel. Today, there are over 30,000! Physical Jews who believe that Yeshua (Jesus) is the long-awaited Jewish Messiah and Savior are today known as Messianic Jews. Christians are non-Jews, or Gentiles, who believe Jesus is their Savior. Though the term *Messianic Jew* is relatively new, Jews began following Yeshua nearly two thousand years ago. For many years, this faith in Yeshua was exclusively Jewish. Many scholars believe there were literally hundreds of thousands of Messianic Jews in the first century AD. *Learn more about the Jewish Roots of the Christian faith on page 7.* There were also Gentiles, *not Jewish converts,* known as *"God-fearers,"* who followed Yeshua. In this period, a Jew or Gentile who identified as a *Christian* was connecting himself to both the Jewish faith and to Yeshua, the promised/prophesied Messiah. The **"grafted-in"** image (to the right) is believed to be the symbol used in the early church to identify and acknowledge other believers in Yeshua.

Through the years, the numbers of Gentile believers increased dramatically. By the third century AD, under the leadership of the Christian Council of Nicaea, the word *Christian* completely lost its original Jewish understanding or context. This is when the church's position changed to the belief that a Jewish person who believed in Yeshua no longer remained Jewish. Today, this belief continues in mainstream Judaism, as well as parts of Christendom.

However, this conclusion contradicts even *Jewish* history. In AD 132, Rabbi Akiva and his numerous followers proclaimed that Simon Bar-Kochba was the Jewish messiah. More recently, many members of the contemporary Jewish Chabad movement believe that their late Rabbi Schneersohn, who passed away in 1994, was the Jewish messiah. These followers would still be considered Jewish by the traditional Jewish community. Even Jews who have become Hindu, Buddhist, or Baha'i are still considered Jewish. Only one belief precludes a Jew from remaining Jewish in the eyes of mainstream Judaism—belief in the Jewish Messiah, Yeshua.

Romans 11:17, 18 : all believers, Jew and Gentile, are grafted into the Jewish Root through faith in Yeshua.

The Bible teaches that both "Jew" and "gentile" are ethnic, not religious, terms. *All* descendants of Abraham, Isaac, and Jacob are Jewish. **Biblically, one who is born a Jew will die a Jew; it is as involuntary as being Irish or Polish.** One who is born a gentile will die a gentile. The gentile may at some point become a Christian by faith, or even convert to Judaism, but he will still remain a gentile.

The modern Messianic Jewish movement began in the early 1970s as new Jewish believers multiplied. Its mission has been to return to the faith of the first-century Messianic Jews and return the Jewish Messiah to His original biblical and Jewish context. Messianic Judaism encompasses both the Tanakh (Old Testament) and the B'rit Chadashah (New Testament). Many Messianic believers (not all) embrace their Jewish heritage and maintain their Jewish identity through regular, systematic Torah reading, abstaining from pork and shellfish, observing the Shabbat, and observing most of the Jewish feast days and holidays. Many Messianic Jews are ardent Zionists. (p. 50)

BIBLICAL PROPHECY OF ISRAEL'S RESTORATION

... as I was prophesying, there was a noise, a rattling sound, and the bones came together, bone to bone. I looked, and tendons and flesh appeared on them and skin covered them, but there was no breath in them... 'This is what the Sovereign Lord says: Come, breath, from the four winds and breathe into these slain, that they may live.' So I prophesied as he commanded me, and breath entered them; they came to life and stood up on their feet—a vast army.

EZEKIEL 37:7-10

In Ezekiel's vision, the physical restoration of Israel precedes the nation's spiritual restoration. The physical restoration of the Jews to their biblical homeland is one of the most frequently prophesied events in the Bible. *One for Israel*, an Israeli-based ministry at the forefront of proclaiming the gospel to Jews worldwide, provides a concise summary of the historic timeline of Israel's physical and spiritual restoration. This summary includes the results of an in-depth survey of Israeli Messianic believers they conducted in 2017. *The numbers are approximate.*

- *Stages of physical restoration up to Israel's becoming a state in 1948*: Balfour Declaration, 1917; San Remo's Mandate, 1920; League of Nations, 1922; UN Partition Resolution #181, 1947; Declaration of Independence, 1948.

- *1948*: Approximately ten million Jews globally survived the Holocaust, 600,000 of whom were living in Israel. Only 23 out of this 600,000 believed in Yeshua as their Messiah and there were no Messianic congregations.

- *1989*: 3.5 million Jews in Israel, 1,200 Messianic believers, 30 Messianic congregations

- *1999*: 4.8 million Jews in Israel, 5,000 Messianic believers, 81 Messianic congregations

- *2017*: 6.5 million Jews in Israel (for the first time in history rivaling the number of Jews in the United States), 30,000 Messianic believers, 300 Messianic congregations

The center of gravity for the Messianic world is shifting. The exponential growth of Messianic believers in Israel is no longer only by immigration, but now more than ever, homegrown Israelis are accepting Yeshua as the Messiah in unprecedented numbers. God is reviving the people of Israel! A November 2017 Barna Group survey of 599 Israeli-Jewish millennials concluded that 21% believed Jesus was "God in human form who lived among people in the first century." Today, the knowledge of Messianic Jews in Israel is commonplace. As soon as someone starts searching for the Messiah, testimonies of Jewish believers and answers to common objections to faith can all be easily be found at www.oneforisrael.org. Even though there are only 6.5 million Jews in Israel, these videos in *Hebrew* have been viewed, as of this writing, more than 25 million times!

The gospel has come from all four corners of the earth, back to its place of origin. Many nations have had a part to play in restoring Israel both physically and spiritually, and as God promises, the nations will also be greatly blessed by Israel's eventual restoration which is to come. As Paul writes in Romans 11:11, *"Now if their trespass means riches for the world, and if their failure means riches for the Gentiles, how much more will their full inclusion mean!"* More and more Jews are coming to believe in Yeshua as prophesied in Romans 11. The foretold re-establishment of the Jewish state has risen out of the ashes of the Holocaust, and the promised spiritual revival is building momentum. There is a fresh harvest of "Jews born anew" every month. What exciting days we live in!

CURRENTLY, THE ARAB POPULATION in Israel is estimated at nearly 1.8 million, or 21% of the country's population (excluding the nearly four million Palestinians of the "West Bank" and Gaza Strip). Over 80% of Israeli Arabs are Muslim (mostly Sunni Muslims) and the remaining are primarily Bedouin, Druze, and Christian. The Bedouin and Druze generally identify more as Israeli than other Arab citizens of Israel. Most Israeli Arabs speak Arabic and self-designate as "Israeli Palestinians." Many have family ties to "West Bank" and Gaza Strip Palestinians, as well as Jordanian, Syrian, and Lebanese refugees. For the most part, Israeli Arabs attend separate schools from Israeli Jews. Most Arabs living in East Jerusalem and the Golan Heights have been offered Israeli citizenship. However, the majority refused, not wishing to recognize Israel's sovereignty. They became permanent residents instead, with the option to apply for citizenship if desired, along with the rights to utilize Israeli community services and participate in voting.

MUSLIMS

Muslims are the second largest religious group in Israel. 2017 data from Israel's Central Bureau of Statistics indicates 1.54 million Muslims reside in Israel, making up 17.7% of the population. Their growth rate of 2.4% per year over the past three years is the highest birth rate among Israeli minorities.

Jerusalem is Islam's third holiest city, following Mecca and Medina in Saudi Arabia. According to Wikipedia, while Muslims living in Israel are typically more religious than Israeli Jews, they are less religious than Muslims living in most other countries in the Middle East. Recent surveys of Israeli Muslims revealed the following: 83% fast during Ramadan (the lowest rate among Muslims in all Middle-Eastern countries), 97% believe in Allah and his Prophet Muhammad, 61% pray daily, and roughly 50% visit a mosque at least once a week. Muslim women tend to value religion more than their male counterparts and younger Muslims are generally less observant than their elders.

A 2016 report of the Israel Ministry of Foreign Affairs states, *"There are over 400 mosques in Israel, of which some 73 are located in Jerusalem. The number of mosques in Israel has increased about fivefold since 1988, when there were 80 mosques... The Muslim community regulates its own unique court system and handles marriage and divorce under Islamic law. Eight regional Islamic law courts and one national appeals court operate in Israel, under the supervision of Israel's Ministry of Justice."*

Five times a day, throughout Israel, outdoor loudspeakers atop tall minarets (towers) project *Adhan*, the Muslim call to prayer. The call to prayer can be heard up to three miles (five km) away. When hearing the call, Muslims stop and pray wherever they are. The first Adhan of the day is about 4:50 AM; the last around 6:00 PM.

Israeli Muslims are very slowly opening up to the prospect of volunteering for military service, with several dozen serving today. Israel's two prevalent Muslim subcultures, the Bedouin and the Druze, are much more open to volunteering. Approximately 200 Bedouin and 80% of the Druze community serve in the IDF today.

BEDOUIN

The Bedouin of Israel are nomadic desert-dwellers of Arabic origin and the majority are Sunni Muslims. However, they hold an additional belief in *jinnis*—spirits that confer supernatural influence over people while assuming human or animal forms. The Bedouin are a minority within the Arab population, comprising less than three percent of the entire population of Israel. They reside in three primary localities across Israel: roughly 50,000 Bedouin live in the Galilee, close to 10,000 Bedouin inhabit central Israel, and approximately 100,000 Bedouin live across southern Israel's Negev within seven Bedouin towns.

Bedouin communities are structured around clans of extended family who practice polygamy—accounting for their birth rate ranking as one of the highest in the world. Bedouin predominantly support their families through raising livestock and dry farming. Their primary crops are barley, wheat, and vegetables such as cucumbers and tomatoes. Many supplement their income through selling their unique Bedouin-style products such as exquisitely embroidered pillows, handbags, coin purses, wall hangings, table runners, jewelry, and clothing. Bedouin wealth is established by the tent size: the longer the tent, the more affluence. Most live in short rectangular tents, either woven from the hair of goats or camels or constructed from prefabricated metal.

The Bedouin community has traditionally been fraught with significant challenges due to the widespread poverty and prevalent crime rate in the nomadic lifestyle. Many of the Bedouin in the Negev region still do not have running water or electricity. Even so, the Bedouin in Israel, compared to their counterparts in other Arab countries, fare much better regarding standard of living and land ownership. Over the last few years, the Israeli government has provided their communities with a much-needed increase of financial allocations.

DRUZE

The Druze are believed to originate from Lebanon, most identifying with the wider Lebanese and Syrian communities. There are approximately one million Druze worldwide with over 125,000 living in Israel today. The Druze constitute over eight percent of the Israeli-Arab population and about two percent of Israel's overall population.

They primarily inhabit twenty-two villages within the Galilee and Golan Heights regions. In 1981, Israel annexed the Syrian Druze community in the Golan Heights, creating a complex quandary for them. The majority in this community refuse Israeli citizenship, choosing instead to remain primarily affiliated with Syria.

The Druze are a "minority within a minority," functioning as a distinct religious and legal entity in Israel. Though the Druze culture and language are Arabic, they have purposefully separated themselves from mainstream Arabic life and government since Israel became a state in 1948. Although loyal to the State of Israel, the Druze are a proud people who have not assimilated into Jewish society. While maintaining some form of Arab nationalism, a relatively small number identify as Palestinian. The Druze tend to marry within their own community and live somewhat isolated in remote mountain ranges.

In the eleventh century AD, the Druze broke away from mainstream Islam and created their own spiritual leadership and belief system, which included a strong belief in reincarnation. They refer to themselves as "People of Monotheism" or "Unitarians," and they regard Moses, Jesus, and Mohammed as prophets, and the first prophet Jethro, father-in-law of Moses.

The minority of Druze, which includes those who live in the Golan Heights, refuse to serve in Israel's army—*some even choosing prison sentences instead*. However, most willingly serve in both the IDF and the Border Police; many have been decorated for bravery. The Druze military participation service rate is even higher than that of Israeli Jews, though their women are exempt.

Druze are renowned throughout Israel for their tremendous hospitality and amazing food! Their villages in the Mt. Carmel and Golan regions offer wonderful opportunities for tourists to share meals in their homes while learning about the Druze culture. *Find out more on p. 92.*

ARAB CHRISTIANS

Roughly 117,000 Arab Christians live in Israel today, comprising about nine percent of Israel's Arab population and a little over two percent of Israel's total population. Almost three-quarters of the Arab Christian population resides in northern Israel, primarily in Nazareth and Haifa. Nazareth is home to Israel's largest Arab Christian population and almost all of Haifa's Arabs are Christians. Most of these Christians identify as Greek Catholic or Greek Orthodox. Evangelical Arab Christians represent the minority. *More than 35,000 Christians living in Israel are not Arab.*

Not all Arab Christians are comfortable identifying as Arabs. The Aramean Christian Foundation in Israel is a non-profit organization for Arab Christians who prefer to assimilate into an Israeli lifestyle. Since 2014, Christian families or clans who can speak the Aramaic language have been eligible to register as Arameans in Israel. In July 2016, an article in the Israeli *Ha'aretz* newspaper stated that 13,000 Arab Christians were eligible.

Israeli Arab Christians excel in education! The Israel Central Bureau of Statistics concluded that Arab Christians fared better in education in comparison to any other group receiving an education in Israel. More Arab Christians, including the women, have attained a higher education degree than the median Israeli population. As of 2010, 63% of Israeli Christian Arabs had received a college or postgraduate education. In 2014, this Israeli minority of just over two percent accounted for almost seventeen percent of the country's university and college students.

It is noteworthy that 34% of these graduates had received a Christian education growing up. Christian schools in Israel, receiving both public and private funding, rank among the best in the country. Many Arab Christians have achieved a high degree of success in the medical and the high-tech industries.

Arab Christians are viewed as upper middle class, hard-working, and educated. Their socio-economic status is closer to that of Israeli Jews than to the Muslims. Arab Christians have both the lowest incidence of poverty and the lowest percentage of unemployment in all of Israel, while maintaining the highest median household income among Israeli Arabs.

The following data has been extracted from a March 2016 Pew Research Center article:

POLITICS: Many Arab Christians have been prominent in Arab political parties in Israel; they are vocal and resolute in their political views which tend to be fairly similar to those of their Muslim counterparts. Some believe even more staunchly than Muslims on some fundamental issues. 72% believe Israel cannot be a democracy and a Jewish state simultaneously and 79% denounce the continued building of Jewish settlements in the "West Bank" as a serious hindrance to Israel's security.

COMMUNITY: Arab Christians in Israel tend to be their own community, engaging in only limited interaction with either Israeli Jews or non-Christian Arabs.

- 86% assert that either all or most of their close friends are Christian.
- Almost all marry within the Arab Christian community.
- 90% are uncomfortable with their children marrying either Muslims or Jews.

RELIGION: Israeli Arab Christians tend to be less religious than Israeli Muslims, and surprisingly more religious than Israeli Jews on key elements of their religious practice.

- 34% pray daily.
- 38% attend weekly religious services.
- 39% tithe a percentage of their income to the church.
- 60% fast during Lent.
- 81% possess icons of saints, or other holy figures, in their homes.
- 94% have been baptized.
- 83% have been anointed with holy oil.

HISTORY HIGHLIGHTS

The view of Jerusalem is the history of the world;
it is more, it is the history of earth and of heaven.

BENJAMIN DISRAELI

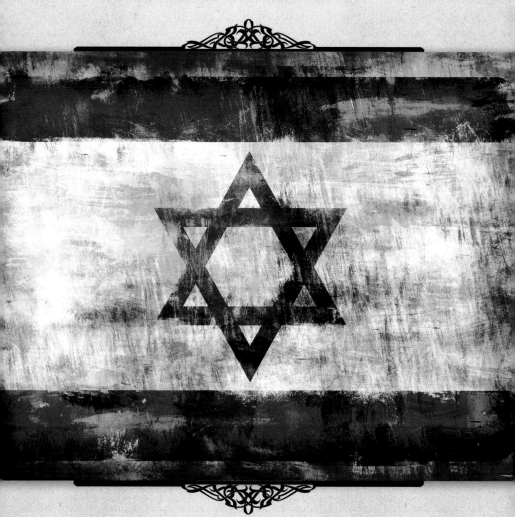

ABRAHAM: Around 2000 BC, God called Abram (later named Abraham) out of Ur of the Chaldeans and made promises of blessings and land to his seed—this was the **Abrahamic Covenant.** God spoke to Abram and said,

"Leave your country, your people and your father's household and go to the land I will show you. I will make you into a great nation and I will bless you; I will make your name great, and you will be a blessing. I will bless those who bless you, and whoever curses you I will curse; and all peoples on earth will be blessed through you." (Genesis 12:1-3)

When Abraham was 100 years old and Sarah was 90, their promised seed, Isaac, was born. Abraham's first son, Ishmael, came through Sarah's handmaid, Hagar. Ishmael's descendants would become the Arab peoples. However, the promised Messianic line would come through Isaac, not Ishmael. Isaac married Rebekah and from them came twins, Jacob and Esau. Although Esau was firstborn, Jacob deceptively stole his birthright, so the promises to Abraham were passed on to Jacob. Abraham, Isaac, and Jacob are, therefore, the patriarchs of the Jewish people. Jacob had twelve sons from his two wives, Leah and Rachel, and their handmaids. Ten of these sons became the fathers of the twelve tribes of Israel. While returning to Canaan, Jacob persisted in wrestling all night with an angel of the Lord, and his name was changed to *Israel*. The messianic line continued through Jacob's son, Judah.

JOSEPH (1934 BC): Jacob's favorite son, Joseph, was sold into slavery and eventually became ruler over Egypt, second to Pharaoh. After a number of years had passed, his family moved to Egypt for food and shelter due to a prolonged famine of the land.

MOSES (1446 BC): Long after Joseph passed, a successive Egyptian Pharaoh (Ramses II) came into power and persecuted the Hebrews, making them his slaves. God chose Moses to lead His people out of Egypt (the **Exodus**), parting the waters of the Red Sea to let them pass through. Pharaoh's pursuing army drowned, and Israel began its 40-year journey through the Sinai desert, seeking their **Promised Land** of Genesis 12:1. During this period, God gave Moses the **Ten Commandments** on Mount Sinai. This was the period of the **Mosaic Covenant** (Exodus 19-40).

JOSHUA (1399 BC): After Moses died, God appointed Joshua to conquer the land of Canaan and lead the people into the Promised Land. He then divided the land into parcels, assigning them to the tribes of Israel (right).

JACOB'S TWELVE SONS IN BIRTH ORDER

SON	MOTHER	SON	MOTHER	SON	MOTHER
1. Reuben	Leah	5. Dan	Bilhah	9. Issachar	Leah
2. Simeon	Leah	6. Napthali	Bilhah	10. Zebulun	Leah
3. Levi	Leah	7. Gad	Zilpah	11. Joseph	Rachel
4. Judah	Leah	8. Asher	Zilpah	12. Benjamin	Rachel

THE TWELVE TRIBES OF ANCIENT ISRAEL

The Levites, as priests, had no land allotment; neither did Joseph—Jacob had adopted Joseph's two sons, Ephraim and Manasseh, essentially giving Joseph a double portion.

"The initial, unconditional land promise made through the Abrahamic Covenant has become the foundational promise upon which every other covenant has been built. The conditional Mosaic Covenant provides Israel with the conditions and regulations necessary to maintain unbroken occupancy of the land. The Davidic Covenant, built upon the Abrahamic Covenant, promised a King who would rule over Israel at the time when she inherits the land." The New Covenant, built upon the foundation of the Abrahamic and Davidic Covenants, was originally made specifically with the people of Israel, with the purpose of later grafting in the Gentiles.

From *When a Jew Rules the World* (pp.44-49)
by Joel Richardson (HIGHLY RECOMMENDED)

ABRAHAMIC OR "LAND" COVENANT:

The *unconditional* Abrahamic Covenant was made specifically to Abraham, Isaac, Jacob, and their descendants—known as "Israel" in the Scriptures (repeated 20 times in Genesis). The promises of this covenant were twofold: Abraham would have a multitude of descendants and his descendants would be heir to a *specific* and *literal* piece of land for which God pronounced specific boundaries—including all of modern-day Israel, large segments of the Sinai desert (Sinai Peninsula), modern-day Lebanon, Syria, and Jordan, as well as all of the Golan Heights, the "West Bank" (Judea and Samaria) and the Gaza Strip (Genesis 15:12–21). Scripture is clear that the Abrahamic Covenant was passed on solely to Isaac, the son of Sarah (Genesis 17:18–21; Genesis 21:8–13). This promise was not contingent on the obedience of Abraham or his descendants; it was completely unconditional, irrevocable, and eternal—based upon the faithfulness of God. Since there was no one greater to swear by, *God took an oath in His own name*. This promise was reiterated to Israel frequently throughout Scripture.

MOSAIC COVENANT:

Approximately 650 years after the Abrahamic Covenant, God gave the *conditional* Mosaic Covenant to Moses at Mount Sinai. This covenant contained the regulations and requirements for Israel to possess the land and remain in it (Deuteronomy 4:1–2; 25–27). The three components included the Ten Commandments, the ordinances, and the worship system. One of the punishments for disobedience was a *temporary* season of exile from the land. God would ultimately remember this covenant and restore the land to Israel (Deuteronomy 4:30–31). The blessings that God promised were directly related to Israel's obedience to the Mosaic Law. Its purpose was to provide direction for the physical and spiritual health of Israel, to set apart Israel as distinct from all other nations, and to reveal the holiness of God, the sinfulness of man, and the need for a Savior. Christ said that He did not come to abolish the Mosaic Law, but to fulfill it (Matthew 5:17).

DAVIDIC COVENANT:

Approximately 450 years after the Mosaic Covenant, the *unconditional* Davidic Covenant was delivered to King David through the prophet Nathan. This covenant had two parts and begins with the reiteration of the Abrahamic Covenant. The first part would be realized during King David's lifetime (2 Samuel 7:8–11) and the second part would be fulfilled after his death (2 Samuel 7:12–16). The first part promised King David a great name, a place for his people, and rest from his enemies. The second part promises that a descendent of David would inherit his royal dynasty, and that dynasty, or rule, would be everlasting. *"I will establish the throne of his kingdom forever…"* (2 Samuel 7:13). This part of the covenant will ultimately be fulfilled when the Messiah Yeshua, a descendant of the line of David, takes the throne. At this time, the land promises of the Abrahamic covenant and the promise of a Davidic king will find their fulfillment together—both based upon the faithfulness of God and His Word.

NEW COVENANT: The irrevocable and everlasting New Covenant, foretold by prophets Moses, Jeremiah, and Ezekiel, was promised to replace the Mosaic Covenant. Originally made specifically with Israel ("all the families of Israel," "the house of Israel," "the house of Judah," "My people"), the New Covenant promised a new heart and a new spirit for Israel—resulting in her final and permanent forgiveness, and the culmination of her relationship with the Lord. The old Mosaic Covenant was written in stone, but the New Covenant is written on our hearts. The Mosaic Covenant is fulfilled in the New Covenant, which is referred to as a "better covenant" (Hebrews 7:22). Though national Israel has not yet identified Yeshua as her Messiah (not until her future repentance), the New Covenant is already identified with the church—which commenced at the resurrection of Christ. Jeremiah 31:34 declares, "... *for I will forgive their iniquity, and their sin I will remember no more.*" Yeshua is the mediator of the New Covenant, and His death on the cross is the foundation of its promises (Luke 22:20). He came to fulfill the Law of Moses (Matthew 5:17) and to establish the New Covenant between God and His people. Yeshua's sacrificial death brought an end to the Law's sacrifices. **Now both regenerated Jews and Gentiles share in the unconditional inheritance of the New Covenant and have become "one new man" in an everlasting relationship with the God of Abraham, Isaac, and Jacob** (Ephesians 2:14-16). This is made possible only by faith in Christ who shed His blood to take away our sins.

COVENANT	RECIPIENTS	PROMISE	NATURE	SCRIPTURE
ABRAHAMIC COVENANT (~2100 BC)	Abraham, Isaac, Jacob, and their descendants	Innumerable descendants and a literal piece of land with specified boundaries	• Unconditional • Everlasting • Irrevocable	Genesis 17:8; 18–21 Genesis 21:8–13 Genesis 28:13 Psalm 105:6–11
MOSAIC COVENANT (~1450 BC)	Corporate nation of Israel, spoken to Moses at Mt. Sinai	Regulatory statutes for Israel to maintain permanent occupancy of the land promised in the Abrahamic Covenant	• Temporary • Conditional upon obedience • Disobedience: temporary exile from the land	Deuteronomy 4:1–2, 25–31 Exodus 19:5–8 Galatians 3:21, 25 Galatians 3:16–18
DAVIDIC COVENANT (~1010 BC)	Spoken to King David through the prophet Nathan	A great name, a place for his people, rest from his enemies; a future descendant of to sit on the throne and reign forever.	• Unconditional • Everlasting • Irrevocable • Ultimately fulfilled in Jesus	2 Samuel 7:8–16 1 Chron. 17:10–14 Isaiah 9:6–7 Jeremiah 23:5–6 Jeremiah 33:17–26 Matthew 1:1
NEW COVENANT (~4100 BC)	Prophesied by Moses, Jeremiah, and Ezekiel; made initially to Israel; Gentiles later grafted in	A new heart and spirit, permanent forgiveness of sin through God's anointed Son, Yeshua the Messiah	• Unconditional • One way • Everlasting • Ultimately fulfilled in Jesus	Isaiah 59:20–21 Jeremiah 31: 31–34 Jeremiah 32:37–42 Ezekiel 36 Matthew 5:17 Hebrews 8:10

PERIOD OF THE JUDGES (1350–1025 BC) AND PROPHETS (1025-586 BC): God gave the Israelites *judges—godly men and women to guide them during times of crisis.* Samuel was the last judge and the first prophet. *Prophets were men raised up by God to speak His word to the kings of Israel.*

PERIOD OF THE KINGS (1050–586 BC): While Samuel was serving as prophet, the people of Israel rejected God as their King and demanded a human king, like the nations around them. God reluctantly obliged, providing Saul—who ultimately rebelled and was defeated by the Philistines.

UNITED MONARCHY (1050–930 BC): Three kings ruled in the "United Monarchy"—Saul, David and Solomon. David became king of Judah upon the death of Saul. David first ruled in Hebron, then from Jerusalem—which he conquered. In 950 BC, King Solomon built the First Temple that would house the Ark of the Covenant. After Solomon's death, his son Rehoboam came to power and treated the Israelites harshly. Ten of the tribes revolted and withdrew to start their own kingdom, prompting the end of the "United Monarchy."

THE DIVIDED MONARCHY (930–712 BC): The kingdom split into two: ten tribes who revolted formed the **Kingdom of Israel** to the north. Its first king was Jeroboam and its capital was Shechem. The remaining two tribes, Judah and Benjamin (as well as some Levites, who being priests, had no land of their own), formed the **Kingdom of Judah** to the south and called themselves *"Jews"* (a shortened form of "Judah," Jacob's son). Their first king was Rehoboam, and Jerusalem was their capital.

THE FALL AND RESTORATION OF THE TWO KINGDOMS (722–538 BC): In 722 BC, the Kingdom of Israel was taken into captivity by the Assyrians, and many intermarried in distant lands, largely losing their identity. Hence the expression, the **"lost tribes of Israel."** The southern Kingdom of Judah fell to the Babylonians in 586 BC. This was the period of destruction of the First Temple. As prophesied in Jeremiah 25:11–18, God freed the Babylonian captives after 70 years of captivity and restored them to their land. This prophetic event was fulfilled through Cyrus of Persia, whom God raised up to defeat the Babylonians. About 50,000 exiles returned home. After returning to Israel, they constructed the Second Temple.

CONQUERING CIVILIZATIONS: Israel was conquered and ruled by a succession of superpower civilizations.

Intertestamental Period (420 BC—appearance of John the Baptist): Greece/Hellenism (prohibition of Jewish customs and spread of the Greek culture—to the extent of sacrificing a pig in the temple)

New Testament Era: In 63 BC, Rome invaded Israel and ruled for seven centuries.

Diaspora Era: This includes the empires of Rome and Byzantine (AD 135–638), Muslim (AD 638–1099), Christian Crusaders (AD 1099–1291), Mamluk (AD 1187–1517), and Ottoman (AD 1517–1917). During the Ottoman rule, Suleiman the Magnificent built the walls of Jerusalem. In 1546, a devastating earthquake damaged the Temple Mount area; Suleiman ordered the rubble of homes adjacent to the Western Wall (which had previously blocked access to this side) to be cleared for a Jewish prayer site—hence, the beginning of the Western Wall!

Modern Era: The British Empire (1917–1947) was called upon to facilitate the establishment of a Jewish national homeland, but that did not occur. It granted both Jewish and Arab communities the right to manage their own internal affairs. During this period, Israel's economy expanded, immigration increased, a Hebrew education network was implemented, and Jewish culture and construction thrived. All new construction within Jerusalem was mandated to be fashioned from Jerusalem stone.

On May 14, 1948, the last British forces left. The new state of Israel became its own sovereign power, never again to be conquered by another civilization.

THE KINGS OF ISRAEL

Saul	1050–1010 BC (30)	40 years	BAD	Samuel
David	1010–970 BC (16)	40 years	VERY BEST	Samuel, Nathan
Solomon	970–930 BC (12)	40 years	GOOD to BAD	Nathan

KINGDOM OF JUDAH (and Benjamin)

KING	REIGN (age crowned)	CHARACTER	PROPHETS
1. Rehoboam	931–913 BC: 17 years (41)	Mostly Bad	Shemaiah
2. Abijah	913–911 BC: 3 years	Mostly Bad	
3. Asa	911–870 BC: 41 years	Good	
4. Jehoshaphat	870–848 BC: 25 years (35)	Good	
5. Jehoram	848–841 BC: 8 years (32)	Bad	
6. Ahaziah	841 BC: 1 year (22)	Bad	
7. Athaliah (Queen)	841–835 BC: 6 years	EVIL	
8. Joash	835–796 BC: 40 years (7)	Good to Bad	
9. Amaziah	796–767 BC: 29 years (25)	Good to Bad	
10. Uzziah	767–740 BC: 52 years (16)	Mostly Good	
11. Jotham	740–732S BC: 16 years (25)	Good	Isaiah, Micah
12. Ahaz	732–716 BC: 16 years (20)	EVIL	
13. Hezekiah	716–687 BC: 29 years (25)	BEST	
14. Manasseh	687–642 BC: 55 years (12)	WORST	Nahum, Habakkuk, Zephaniah
15. Amon	642–640 BC: 2 years (22)	WORST	
16. Josiah	640–608 BC: 31 years (8)	BEST	
17. Jehoahaz	608 BC: 3 months (23)	Bad	Daniel, Ezekiel, Jeremiah
18. Jehoiakim	608–597 BC: 11 years (25)	EVIL	
19. Jehoiachin	597 BC: 3 months (8)	Bad	
20. Zedekiah	597–586 BC: 11 years (21)	Bad	

When Athaliah heard that Ahaziah had been killed, she had his children (her grandchildren) put to death and made herself queen. Ahaziah's sister took his son, baby Joash, and hid him in Jerusalem's temple for six years while Jehoida, the high priest, cared for him. David's only remaining offspring, Joash, was made king at seven. If he had died, there would have been no heir to the Davidic throne, eliminating the Messianic lineage. God providentially protected Joash!

KINGDOM OF ISRAEL (Ten Northern Tribes)

KING	REIGN	CHARACTER	PROPHETS
1. Jeroboam I	931–910 BC: 22 years	Bad	Abijah
2. Nadab	910–909 BC: 2 years	Bad	
3. Baasha	909–886 BC: 24 years	Bad	
4. Elah	886–885 BC: 2 years	Bad	
5. Zimri	885 BC: 7 days	Bad	
6. Omri	885–874 BC: 12 years	EVIL	Elijah, Micaiah
7. Ahab	874–853 BC: 22 years	WORST	
8. Ahaziah	853–852 BC: 2 years	Bad	
9. Joram	852–841 BC: 12 years	Mostly Bad	Elisha
10. Jehu	841–814 BC: 28 years	Good and Bad	
11. Jehoahaz	814–798 BC: 17 years	Bad	
12. Jehoash	798–782 BC: 16 years	Bad	Jonah, Amos, Hosea
13. Jeroboam II	782–753 BC: 41 years	Bad	
14. Zechariah	753–752 BC: 6 months	Bad	
15. Shallum	752 BC: 1 month	Bad	
16. Menahem	752–742 BC: 10 years	Bad	
17. Pekahiah	742–740 BC: 2 years	Bad	
18. Pekah	740–732 BC: 20 years	Bad	
19. Hoshea	732–712 BC: 9 years	Bad	

EZEKIEL 21:25: (spoken by King Zedekiah, Israel and Judah's last king; the next king is Yeshua, the Messiah) "Now to you, O profane, wicked prince of Israel, whose day has come, whose iniquity shall end, thus says the Lord GOD: 'Remove the turban, and take off the crown; Nothing shall remain the same. Exalt the humble, and humble the exalted. Overthrown, overthrown, I will make it overthrown! It shall be no longer, until He comes whose right it is, and I will give it to Him.'"

HEROD THE GREAT IS ONE OF THE most significant individuals in Jewish history. Although he was not Jewish, Herod was appointed by Rome as king of Judea. He reigned from 37 BC until his death in 4 BC—an era of unprecedented growth and construction due to his obsession with massive and elaborate building projects.

Herod the madman: Herod became known as a "madman who murdered his own family and a great many rabbis." Herod had such a paranoia of his throne being seized that he had at least six relatives killed, whom he suspected of conspiring against him. This number included his own two sons, his wife's brother, Aristobulus, and even his Jewish wife, Miriam—whom he murdered in a fit of jealousy. Later, Herod went on to murder many prominent rabbis whom he perceived as threats to his power and hindrances to the mass Hellenization (Greek cultural influence) of the Jews.

Herod the builder: Herod the Great was one of the greatest builders in all of history. He had a huge ego which thrived on impressing others with his ostentatious building projects. Some of his renowned projects included:

- Caesarea Maritima (p. 93)
- Masada (p. 236)
- Reconstruction of Jerusalem's Second Temple and construction of the adjoining Antonia Fortress
- Herod's Jerusalem palace (presently the Tower of David; see p. 178)
- Herodium (p. 206)
- Three winter palaces and a hippodrome at Jericho
- Cave of the Patriarchs enclosure (p. 210) in Hebron (photo above)

Herod, the first enemy of Jesus: Upon hearing a report that the true King of the Jews had just been born in Bethlehem, Herod's paranoia got the best of him. He gathered the Sanhedrin together and inquired as to the location of this "Anointed One." They quoted Micah 5:2, which specified Bethlehem, so Herod the Great ordered the killings of all the boys in Bethlehem two years and under (Matthew 2:16).

Herod's lineage: Herod the Great's lineage included the other five Herods in the Bible—all of whom significantly influenced Jewish history and New Testament events. After Herod's death, his three sons, **Herod Archelaus, Herod Antipas,** and **Herod Philip** split control of Israel. **Herod Archelaus** tyrannically reigned over Judea for ten years, then was replaced by Caesar Augustus. Joseph was warned to take his family to Galilee to escape his rule of terror (Matthew 2:22). **Herod Antipas** was a *tetrarch* (one of four rulers) of Galilee. Antipas had John the Baptist beheaded to fulfill an oath he had made to his daughter Salome. **Herod Agrippa I,** grandson of Herod the Great, was respected by both Sadducees and Pharisees. However, he had James killed and Peter imprisoned; the Lord struck him down (Acts 12:21–23). **Herod Agrippa II** was the last of the Herodians to rule over Israel. He inquired of Paul, "In a short time would you persuade me to be a Christian?" Agrippa II found Paul guiltless (Acts 25–26).

In the Talmud it is recorded,
"He who has not seen Herod's building, has never in his life seen a truly grand building."

JESUS CHRIST AND THE CALENDAR: The birth, life, and death of Jesus all took place under Roman rule. The two prominent calendars (Gregorian and Julian) both center around the birth of the Messiah, Jesus Christ—the only person in history to achieve this eminence. "AD" stands for *anno domini*, Latin for "in the year of the Lord"—referring specifically to the birth of Jesus Christ. "BC" signifies *before Christ*.

THE GREAT REVOLT (AD 66–70): For four years, a faction of Jews known as *Zealots* sporadically waged war against the oppressive Roman rule in Jerusalem. However, this was a huge mistake! In AD 70, the **Siege of Jerusalem**, led by Titus, resulted in the total destruction of Jerusalem and the Second Temple, while masses of Jews were either slaughtered or became slaves. Others fled to Europe, Asia, and Africa—leading to the culmination of the **Jewish Diaspora**, or dispersion.

BAR KOCHBA REVOLT (AD 132–135): Simon Bar Kochba, who many believed to be the messiah, organized a revolt against Roman rule. As a result, an independent Jewish state was established for over two years, but eventually the Romans decimated the Jewish stronghold, seized Jerusalem, and sent most of its Jews into exile.

ISRAEL BECOMES "PALESTINE" (AD 135): Roman Emperor Hadrian resolved to obliterate Jewish identification with the land of Israel by renaming it "Syria-Palestinia." *Palestinia* is a Latinized version of *Philistine*—the historic archenemy of the Jews. In reality, there never was a true *Palestine* or *Palestinian* people. The Bible consistently referred to the land as "Caanan," "Judah," or "Israel." "*And he arose,…and came into the land of Israel*" (Matthew 2:21).

ISAIAH 53'S "MESSIAH" REINTERPRETED TO BE "THE NATION OF ISRAEL" (AD 1050): The original and only Jewish view for over 2000 years was that the suffering servant of Isaiah 53 was the Messiah. No exceptions were made to this interpretation until the eleventh century, when Rabbi Rashi reinterpreted the passage to mean the nation of Israel.

"All the ancient Jewish writings—the Mishnah, the Gemara, the Midrashim and many others—all regard this portion of Scripture (Isaiah chapter 53) as relating to the Messianic Person. The first rabbi to suggest otherwise was Rashi, around AD 1050. Every rabbi prior to Rashi, without exception, viewed this passage as describing Messiah. When Rashi first proposed that this passage spoke of the nation of Israel, he sparked a fierce debate with his contemporaries. The most famous of these was the Rambam, perhaps better known as Maimonides. Rambam stated very clearly that Rashi was completely wrong in going contrary to the traditional Jewish viewpoint… this was to go contrary to all rabbinic teaching of that day and of the preceding one thousand years. Today, Rashi's view has become dominant in Jewish and rabbinic theology. But that is not the Jewish view. Nor is it the traditional Jewish view."

– ARNOLD FRUCHTENBAUM, *Messianic Christology*

ZIONIST MOVEMENT—JEWISH/CHRISTIAN COLLABORATION (1890s): Zionism is the belief that the Jews are entitled to their own national homeland of Israel.

William E. Blackstone, an American evangelist and Christian Zionist, is known by many Jews as the **"Father of Zionism."** He authored the **Blackstone Memorial Petitions of 1891 and 1916,** which called upon America to actively return the Holy Land to the Jewish people. Blackstone began the dialog that would lead to the modern State of Israel as he mobilized Christian support for a Jewish national homeland. Blackstone was also a founding trustee and the first dean of Biola University. He is remembered for his devotion to God's people Israel, his longing for Jesus' return, and his deep humility. Today, he is commemorated in Jerusalem in the "Blackstone Grove" in the Jewish National Forest.

Theodor Herzl, a successful Jewish journalist and playwright from Austria-Hungary, was the founder and president of the Zionist Organization, the political movement that worked to establish an independent Jewish state. Herzl published his Zionist manifesto *The Jewish State* in 1896 and went on to convene the **First Zionist Congress in 1897.** Herzl is the only individual mentioned by name in Israel's Declaration of Independence, which refers to him as the **"author of the vision of the Jewish state."** As he told the assembled delegates at the First Zionist Congress, "Zionism is a return to Judaism even before there is a return to the Jewish land." Herzl established hundreds of chapters of the Zionist Organization throughout Europe and in America. He also established a Jewish national bank and the Zionist newspaper *Die Welt.* Herzl was pivotal in bringing hundreds of thousands of Jews to "Palestine," leading to the establishment of Israel as an independent Jewish state in 1948. Mount Herzl cemetery is named after Theodor Herzl.

Blackstone and Herzl collaborated in diplomatic negotiations with leadership in various countries for the purpose of issuing a formal charter for a Jewish state. **The Israel State** Archives in Jerusalem possesses a Hebrew Bible given by Blackstone to Theodore Herzl. Blackstone had marked for Herzl's reference all the passages concerning the future fulfillment of the spiritual promises and blessings of a restored Israel in their own homeland when they recognize their Messiah. The Bible was said to have been prominently displayed on Herzl's desk for many years.

ISRAELI FLAG (1891): The Israeli flag was designed for the Zionist Movement in 1891, and the Star of David symbol in its center was adopted by the First Zionist Congress in 1897. The flag officially became the national flag of Israel on October 28, 1948, five months after the establishment of the State of Israel.

BALFOUR DECLARATION (1917): The Balfour Declaration, a formal appeal issued by the British government, was the first major political triumph of Zionism. The appeal favored the establishment of a national homeland for the Jewish people. The British cooperated with the League of Nations to appeal to Jews worldwide to return to Palestine (Israel). However, the Balfour Declaration, spurred the Arabs to revolt and claim *their* control over Israel.

The end result for the Jews was enormous conflict and a massive reduction of land. Britain declared the land west of the Jordan River would be "Palestine," and the land east of the Jordan River would belong to Jordan—**Transjordan.** In the end, "Palestine" encompassed 23% of the Mandate territory, and Transjordan 77%.

Wooden beds in barracks,
Birkenau concentration camp

1933 MARKED THE BEGINNING OF the **Holocaust,** known by the Jews as the *Shoah.* It began with Adolf Hitler's rise to power, seeking supremacy of the "perfect race" and world domination. Adolf Hitler was a German politician and leader of the Nazi Party who ultimately implemented the "**Final Solution**"—the plan to annihilate all European Jews who he saw as a demonic and powerful force that would destroy Germany. Under his regime, the segregation and persecution of the Jews was systematically implemented in stages, beginning in 1933 with state-sponsored anti-Jewish legislation and economic boycotts.

KRISTALLNACHT (1938): Persecution escalated with *Kristallnacht*, or "Night of Broken Glass." In just two days, German Nazis torched synagogues, vandalized Jewish homes, schools and businesses, killed nearly 100 Jews, and arrested about 30,000 more—sending them to Nazi concentration camps.

GHETTOS (1939–1944): In 1939, Jews began to be deported to ghettos, while their Jewish schools and synagogues were being closed down and their property confiscated. The purpose of the ghettos was to segregate Jews from the rest of the population. They were ordered to wear identifying badges or armbands, typically a yellow Star of David inscribed with the word "Jew." Some ghettos lasted only a few days or weeks, others several years. Over 1,200 ghettos were set up in German-occupied Poland and the Soviet Union alone. Poland's Warsaw ghetto had more than 400,000 Jews packed into just 1.3 square miles (3.4 sq km). Their living conditions were horrific—overcrowded and unsanitary, with critically inadequate food and shelter. Most Jewish men were sentenced to forced labor for the German Reich.

THE FINAL SOLUTION (1941–1945): In June 1941, with the German invasion of the USSR, the Germans began systematically

Cremation ovens in Auschwitz

murdering the Jews throughout the occupied areas in the East. This annihilation plan was accomplished through special operational units of Germany's SS, police, and armed forces, as well as local collaborators. By December 1941, over 700,000 Jews had been murdered. The shooting of Jews continued until May 1945, the last hours of WWII. An estimated 1,800,000 Jews were shot by these collaborating units.

EXTERMINATION CAMPS (1942–1944): Extermination camps were designed implicitly for efficient mass killing through asphyxiation by poison gas. Auschwitz-Birkenau was the infamous camp where nearly one million European Jews lost their lives. Altogether, over 2,700,000 Jews died in the six extermination camps: Chelmno, Belzec, Sobibor, Treblinka, Majdanek and Auschwitz.

HOLOCAUST CONCLUSION (1945): On May 8, 1945, the Allied powers led by Great Britain, the United States, and the Soviet Union, finally defeated the Nazis and brought this horrific event to an end. However, six million Jews had lost their lives; 1.5 million of them were children. In 1945, this number represented about one-third of the world's Jewish population and two-thirds of all European Jewry.

Thanks to Ephraim Kaye of Yad Vashem's International School for Holocaust Studies for his expert input.

PARTITION PLAN (1947): On November 29, 1947, a special commission of the United Nations unanimously agreed that "Palestine" should be granted her independence. The majority of the UN General Assembly (33-13) supported a partition of the land into two separate states, a Jewish state and an Arab state—comprised of three Jewish sections, four Arab sections, and an international administration of Jerusalem. However, six Arab nations walked out in protest; the Partition Plan was never implemented.

DISCOVERY OF DEAD SEA SCROLLS (1946–1956): The Dead Sea Scrolls, primarily dating back to 152–63 BC, were discovered in eleven different caves in the vicinity of Qumran, all within a radius of about 3–4 miles (5–6 km). On the same day as the Partition vote for Israel to be recognized as a nation (November 29, 1947), some of these manuscripts, which included the Book of Isaiah, were for the first time seen in public—in the hands of a dealer in Bethlehem. God was on the move!

CIVIL WAR (1947–1948): Murders, retaliations and counter-retaliations resulted in numerous deaths to both Jews and Arabs. The Civil War lasted from November 30, 1947, through May 14, 1948.

ISRAEL BECOMES A STATE (1948): On May 14, 1948, a miracle happened. After 2900 years, Israel officially became a state—fulfilment of biblical prophecy that the nation would be reborn in a day (Isaiah 66:8). Jewish leaders gathered under the leadership of David Ben-Gurion, who would become Israel's first Prime Minister. They declared the creation of the sovereign State of Israel.

Hatikvah, "The Hope" in Hebrew, was unofficially proclaimed Israel's national anthem. Its final lyrics are moving and powerful: *"Our hope is not yet lost, the hope of two thousand years, to be a free people in our land, the land of Zion and Jerusalem."* Hatikvah was inspired by the "Vision of the Dry Bones" in Ezekiel 37.

LAW OF RETURN (1950): Israel's new Declaration of Independence clearly stated its unprecedented Law of Return,

The State of Israel will be open to Jewish immigration and to the ingathering of the exiles. It will foster the development of the country for the benefit of all its inhabitants. It will be based on freedom, justice and peace as envisioned by the prophets of Israel…

Since 1948, over three million Jews from 90+ countries have immigrated to Israel. According to the 2019 Central Bureau of Statistics, of Israel's nine million current residents, over six-and-a-half million (75%) are Jews. These figures reflect staggering growth since 1900, when only 12,000 Jews were living in Israel, a number which represented a mere 8% of Israel's total population. *Read more about the history of Israel's immigration and population on pp. 56–57.*

WAR OF INDEPENDENCE OR ARAB-ISRAELI WAR (1948–1949): Only one day after Israel's declaration of statehood, the collective armies of Iraq, Egypt, Syria, and Jordan launched an invasion on the new nation, igniting the War of Independence. Although outnumbered 100 to one, Israel was the decided victor and the land of Israel was increased by almost 50%. However, the Jews were brokenhearted, as their beloved Old City Jerusalem fell under Jordanian control.

REDISTRIBUTION OF LAND (1950): Jordan (formerly Transjordan) officially annexed East Jerusalem and the "West Bank" (biblical Judea and Samaria), while Egypt seized the Gaza Strip.

PREDECESSORS TO THE ISRAEL DEFENSE FORCES

(1907–1948)

THERE HAVE BEEN THREE PRIMARY paramilitary defense organization in Israel's history—which were precursors to Israel's present-day Israel Defense Forces. The first evolved during the Ottoman rule from two small groups of less than 100: the **Bar-Giora** (1907–1909) which developed into the **Hashomer,** which was responsible for protecting Jewish settlements (1909–1921).

HAGANAH (1921–1948): The Hashomer gave birth to the Haganah defense forces. Its average membership was 21,000 (60,000 at its height). The Haganah was critical in defending Jewish settlements. They fought in the Arab Revolt (1936–1939), World War II (1942–1946), the "Civil War in Mandatory Palestine" (1947–1948), and the first two weeks of the 1948 Arab-Israeli War (prior to disbanding on May 28, 1948).

IRGUN (1931–1948): In 1931, many Haganah fighters held adamant convictions that Israel should be able to initiate counterattacks against militant Arab factions, which the Haganah did not allow. This group splintered off and formed the Irgun, also known as *Etzel.* According to Howard Sachar, a professor of Modern History at George Washington University, who specializes in Israeli history, *"The policy of the new organization was based squarely on Jabotinsky's teachings: every Jew had the right to enter Palestine; only active retaliation would deter the Arabs; only Jewish armed forces would ensure the Jewish state."* As the years passed, the Irgun was increasingly viewed by many as a terrorist organization. The Irgun was intolerant of the British presence in Israel, whom they regarded as illegal occupiers of their Jewish homeland. One of their most notorious acts of terrorism was the bombing of the King David Hotel in 1946, which housed the British administrative headquarters and symbolized the British Mandate in Palestine; more than 90 British were killed. The present-day **Likud** political party stems from the Irgun.

PALMACH (1941–1948): On May 14, 1941, the Palmach (or "strike forces") was established. Six of their elite "special forces" units generated from the Haganah, and it became both operationally and financially responsible for all Haganah operations. The Palmach became the underground army of the Jewish community during British rule. At one point, Palmach members arrested dozens of the Irgun and handed them over to the British, while they banished others to Africa until the conclusion of the British mandate.

According to the Palmach Museum's website, some of the Palmach's most prominent operations included the Battle of Mishmar Ha´emek (which extended the borders of Jerusalem), the conquest of Tiberias, the capture of Haifa, the freeing of the Upper Galilee, the conquest of Safed and Beit She´an, the surrender of Jaffa, and the release of the Western Galilee.

From 1945–1947, the Palmach actively opposed the "British blockade" committed to preventing the immigration of Holocaust survivors. Palmach members both accompanied and commanded most of the 60 "illegal" immigration ships carrying Holocaust survivors with tens of thousands of immigrants from throughout Europe, ultimately bringing them to Israel in defiance of the British blockade.

By 1948, the Palmach had grown to over 2,000 men and women in three brigades. Upon formation of Israel's national army (the Israel Defense Forces) on May 26, 1948, the

Palmach brigades were disbanded. However, many of their heroes would subsequently become leaders in the IDF.

ISRAEL DEFENSE FORCES (1948–Present): The Israel Defense Forces (IDF) are the present-day military forces of the State of Israel, consisting of the ground forces, the air force, and the navy. The IDF is the sole military division of Israel's security forces. According to GlobalSecurity.org, the number of wars and border conflicts in which the IDF has been involved in during its short history makes it one of the most battle-trained armed forces in the world. There are approximately 175,000 active IDF personnel and 450,000 mandatory reservists. Most reservists are under the age of 40 with past IDF service.

ELI COHEN (1961–1965): This Israeli national hero is known as the greatest spy in the history of Israel. From 1961–1965, Cohen provided extensive, vital intelligence information to the Israeli Army.

Born an Egyptian Jew to Syrian parents, Cohen was recruited by the Mossad to infiltrate the Syrian government. He was given the false identity of *Kamel Amin Thaabet*—a Syrian businessman born in Lebanon to Syrian Muslim parents. Cohen moved to Damascus in 1962, where he was soon loved and trusted by Syria's elite leadership. He was even appointed chief advisor to Syria's Minister of Defense. This esteemed position made Cohen privy to Syria's covert political and military secrets.

Cohen is best known for his remarkable work in the Golan Heights, where he accompanied top-ranking Syrian military personnel. Here he memorized comprehensive intelligence details of every Syrian fortification, which he promptly transmitted to Israel. Cohen advised the Syrian army to plant eucalyptus trees at each fortification so their soldiers would be protected from the sun. Syria complied, and these trees became targets for Israel's military during the Six-Day War, effactually enabling Israel to capture the Golan Heights in just two days. In 1965, Syrian authorities caught Cohen sending a transmission to Israel.

Convicted of espionage, Eli Cohen was publicly hanged in Damascus. The film, *The Impossible Spy*, is a depiction of his life.

SIX-DAY WAR (1967): By and large, Israel enjoyed peace for ten years. Then, in the spring of 1967, nine nations (Egypt, Jordan, Syria, Lebanon, Algeria, Kuwait, Sudan, Saudi Arabia, and Iraq) declared war on Israel—declaring the imminent extermination of every Jew. Again, Israel's troops and artillery were vastly outnumbered by her Arab neighbors. June 5 was the first day of the Six-Day War, a war in which Israel achieved one of the greatest military feats in history. In the end, this small, minimally-armed nation seized the Gaza Strip, the Sinai Peninsula, the "West Bank," and the Golan Heights. Most importantly, Israel recaptured her beloved Old City Jerusalem.

Approximately one million Arabs from these territories fell under Israel's authority; barbed wire and concrete barriers were torn down. Jewish losses and casualties were great, but minimal considering the projections. Jews across the world celebrated as they gave praise to God for a miraculous victory—once again in the face of incredible odds.

GOLDA MEIR (1948–1974): Known as the "Iron Lady" of Israel politics, Golda Meir was one of the two female signers of the Israeli Declaration of Independence as well as a key contributor to the strong historic US–Israel bond. In 1969, after she had served as Israel's ambassador to the Soviet Union, Minister of Labor, and Foreign Minister, Golda became the fourth Prime Minister of Israel. She held this position until her resignation in 1974, following the Yom Kippur War. Golda lived for four more years and was ultimately buried in Jerusalem's Mount Herzl Military Cemetery.

YOM KIPPUR WAR (1973): The Yom Kippur War took place in October of 1973 while Golda Meir was Israel's Prime Minister, Moshe Dayan was Israel's Minister of Defense, and Anwar Sadat was the President of Egypt. Syria and Egypt held alliances with Iraq, Jordan, Libya, Morocco, Saudi Arabia, Lebanon, and the Soviet Union, while Israel possessed only one ally—the United States, who provided support in the form of weapons and intelligence. The Arab Allies unified for the purpose of recovering the territory lost in the 1967 war. Their plan was to catch Israel off-guard and overpower her limited resources; hence, their initial assault took place on the Jewish holy day of Yom Kippur. Israel had only 500 soldiers to Egypt's 80,000, and 150 tanks to Syria's 1,400. Egyptian troops forged ahead into the Sinai Peninsula while Syrian troops descended into the Golan Heights. However, Israel counterattacked and successfully recaptured both the Sinai Peninsula and the Golan Heights.

RAID ON ENTEBBE (1976): While Americans were celebrating the bicentennial on July 4, 1976, about 140 Israeli commandos were undertaking one of the most daring missions in the history of the Israel Defense Forces: **Operation Thunderbolt**, a counter-terrorist hostage-rescue assignment at the Entebbe Airport in Uganda.

A week earlier, an Air France plane departing Tel Aviv had been hijacked by two members of the Popular Front for the Liberation of Palestine and two members of the German Revolutionary CZ Cell. The plane was flown to Libya and then to Uganda, where the hijackers and additional terrorists held the Israeli and Jewish passengers, along with the 12-member flight crew, hostage at the airport.

The Israeli government, after unsuccessful negotiations, decided to send 140 commandos on a 2,500-mile journey to carry out a night-time rescue operation that freed 106 hostages in 90 minutes. Four hostages were killed as well as all the terrorists. Four Israeli commandos were wounded and one, Lt. Col. Yoni Netanyahu (brother of Prime Minister Benjamin Netanyahu), was killed.

RESTORATION OF THE SHEKEL (1980): The shekel is first mentioned in the Bible in Exodus 30:24. This **"shekel of the sanctuary"** was used to calculate the precise measurements of ingredients for the Temple's holy anointing oil. Additionally, according to Jewish law at this time, whenever a census of the Jewish people was conducted, every person that was counted was required to pay a *half-shekel* for his atonement. During the Second Temple period, Jews were required to offer a *half-shekel* into the Temple treasury for its upkeep and maintenance.

The **Jerusalem shekel** was issued from AD 66–70 amid the First Jewish Revolt—symbolizing the independence of Judea from Roman rule. The last recorded ancient shekel was the **Bar Kochba Shekel**—issued between AD 132–135 during the Bar Kochba Revolt.

Only in recent times has the **Israeli shekel** been restored, replacing the Israeli *lira* or *pound* in 1980. The current **New Israeli Shekel** (NIS) replaced the Israeli shekel in 1985.

GOD'S PROTECTION AND DELIVERANCE: Considering all the nations and civilizations that have attempted to eradicate the Jewish people—the nation of Israel is nothing short of a miracle! In almost every war, Israel began on the defensive and concluded as the military victor. This is the work of a God who unconditionally loves this nation and continues to perform wonders on her behalf. Over 2,500 years ago, Isaiah 31:5 records the prophet Isaiah's declaration:

"Like birds hovering, so the Lord of hosts will protect Jerusalem; he will protect and deliver it; he will spare and rescue it"
(Isaiah 31:5).

Hostages arriving safely home in Tel Aviv

"In Israel, in order to be a realist, you must believe in miracles."
– DAVID BEN GURION

MIXED ETHNICITY AND INSUFFICIENT surveying have made it nearly impossible to accurately specify the number of Jews in the world. However, in 2017, the Berman Jewish Data Bank estimated the world's Jewish population at 14.5 million—less than 0.2% of the total world population.

According to the Jewish Virtual Library, as of May 2019, approximately 6.7 million (46%) of the world's Jews were living in Israel and 6.7 million (40%) were living in the United States (2.1% of the U.S. population).

Remarkably, Israel is a nation created from over 80% immigrants who do not even share a common language, only a common religious heritage and a yearning for their own common homeland. The Hebrew term, **Aliyah**, refers to Jews immigrating to their homeland from the Diaspora. Since 1948, when Israel became a state, more than three million Jews from over 90 countries have "made Aliyah" and immigrated to Israel.

PRE-STATE ALIYAH

The **First Aliyah** (1882–1903) took place prior to the Zionist movement. Most of these new immigrants came from Russia and Yemen.

The **Second Aliyah** (1904–1914), which took place prior to World War I was composed almost exclusively of Russian Jews. Pogroms and anti-Semitism, along with the rise of Socialism and Jewish nationalism, motivated immigration to Israel. This group conceived the first kibbutz and revived the Hebrew language!

The **Third Aliyah** (1919–1923), also from Russia, arrived after the establishment of the British Mandate and the Balfour Declaration. This group was able to create a sustainable agricultural economy by strengthening and building the kibbutz movement.

The **Fourth Aliyah** (1924–1929) originated from Poland and Hungary. These immigrants fled anti-Semitism. Many were middle-class families who went on to establish small businesses and give a major boost to Israel's economy.

The **Fifth Aliyah** (1929–1940) was born out of the rise of Nazism in Germany and extreme nationalism across Eastern Europe. This wave of Aliyah consisted of nearly 250,000 immigrants—many of whom were professionals, doctors, lawyers and artists. They contributed to a thriving economy, while developing a focus on the arts and architecture.

POST-STATE ALIYAH

Operation Magic Carpet (1949–1950) was Israel's first mass Aliyah after becoming a nation. This effort's nickname was **Operation "On Wings of Eagles,"** an operation that brought 49,000 Yemenite Jews to the new state of Israel. Although most of them had never even seen an airplane before, they possessed a strong belief in the biblical prophecy of Isaiah 40:31, in which God promised to return the children of Israel to Zion on "wings" like eagles. Alaska Airlines, an airline owned by Christians, conducted the airlift over a seven-month period. 48,000 Yemenite Jews were relocated to Israel by 28 Alaska Airlines pilots and a total of 380 flights. Not a single death or serious injury occurred during the airlift. Many of the pilots had spent up to 270 hours a week in the air, three times what they were allowed to fly in the United States.

The **Arab Aliyah** (1948–early 1970s) took place after Israel had become a nation. Anti-Zionism and anti-Semitism had drastically escalated in the Arab world. The Arab-Israeli War triggered many Jews living in Arab countries to flee to Israel for safety. Close to

900,000 Jews from various Arab nations either fled or were expelled; many were forced to abandon all their belongings. In 1951, 114,000 Jews came from Iraq through the efforts of **Operation Ezra** and **Operation Nehemiah**. Today, only a few very small Jewish communities remain in the Middle East outside of Israel.

Operation Moses (1984) was the covert evacuation of Ethiopian Jews from Sudan during a civil war that caused a serious famine. Trans European Airways airlifted approximately 8,000 Sudanese Jews to Israel via Brussels over a seven-week period. This operation required over 30 flights with about 200 passengers at a time. Unfortunately, an estimated 4,000 lost their lives on their long trek to Sudan.

Operation Solomon (1991) was a phenomenal undercover Israeli military operation that airlifted over another 14,324 Ethiopian Jews to Israel in only 36 hours! 34 El Al planes, with seats removed to maximize capacity, were utilized to successfully complete the mission.

Russian Aliyah (early 1990s) took place during the Cold War. Soviet Jews were being denied their rights to practice Judaism or emigrate for many years. Finally, under the leadership of Mikhail Gorbachev, nearly one million Jews from the Soviet Union were allowed to emigrate to Israel.

Current Aliyah (2014–present) to Israel is roughly 25,000 new immigrants per year, most from the Ukraine.

LEADING JEWISH IMMIGRATION TO ISRAEL

NUMBER OF ISRAELI IMMIGRANTS	COUNTRIES OF ORIGIN
80,000+	Iran
91,000+	Ethiopia
100,000+	United States, Iraq
200,000+	Morocco
500,000	Africa and Asia
1,000,000+	Soviet Union

Wikipedia

POPULATION STATISTICS OF ISRAELI JEWS

YEAR	# OF JEWS IN ISRAEL	% JEWS IN ISRAEL	% OF TOTAL WORLD'S JEWS
1882	24,000	8%	.3%
1918	60,000	8.1%	.6%
1946	543,000	30%	4.9%
1950	1,203,000	87.8%	10.6%
1955	1,590,500	88.9%	13.5%
1980	3,282,700	83.7%	25.6%
2019	6,738,500	74.8%	46%

Online (2014), www.jewishvirtuallibrary.org

PROPHECY	OLD TESTAMENT REFERENCE	NEW TESTAMENT FULFILLMENT
King enters Jerusalem on a donkey.	"…See, your king comes to you, righteous and victorious, lowly and riding on a donkey, on a colt, the foal of a donkey." (Zechariah 9:9)	"Jesus found a young donkey and sat on it, as it is written: 'Do not be afraid, Daughter Zion; see, your king is coming, seated on a donkey's colt.'" (John 12:14–15)
Crowds shout blessing.	"Blessed is he who comes in the name of the Lord…" (Psalm 118:26)	"Blessed is the king who comes in the name of the Lord!.." (Luke 19:38)
Jesus cleansed the temple.	"Has this house, which bears my Name, become a den of robbers to you?" (Jeremiah 7:11)	"When Jesus entered the temple courts, he began to drive out those who were selling. 'It is written,' he said to them, 'My house will be a house of prayer; but you have made it a den of robbers.'" (Luke 19:45–46)
Jesus speaks in parables with hidden meaning.	"I will open my mouth with a parable; I will utter hidden things, things from of old." (Psalm 78:2)	"He said, 'The knowledge of the secrets of the kingdom of God has been given to you, but to others I speak in parables, so that, though seeing, they may not see; though hearing, they may not understand.'" (Luke 8:10)
Rulers take council against him.	"The kings of the earth rise up and the rulers band together against the LORD and against his anointed…" (Psalm 2:2)	"While he was still speaking, Judas, one of the Twelve, arrived. With him was a large crowd armed with swords and clubs, sent from the chief priests and the elders of the people." (Matthew 26:47)
Jesus is betrayed by his close friend.	"Even my close friend, someone I trusted, one who shared my bread, has turned against me." (Psalm 41:9)	"Jesus replied, 'The one who has dipped his hand into the bowl with me will betray me.'" (Matthew 26:23)
Jesus is sold for 30 pieces of silver.	"I told them, 'If you think it best, give me my pay; but if not, keep it.' So they paid me thirty pieces of silver." (Zechariah 11:12)	"Then one of the Twelve — the one called Judas Iscariot — went to the chief priests and asked, 'What are you willing to give me if I deliver him over to you?' So they counted … thirty pieces of silver." (Matthew 26:14, 15)
Jesus is deserted by his followers.	"…Strike the shepherd and the sheep will be scattered…" (Zechariah 13:7)	"Then Jesus told them, 'This very night you will all fall away on account of me, for it is written: I will strike the shepherd, and the sheep of the flock will be scattered.'" (Matthew 26:31)
False witnesses rise up against him.	"…for false witnesses rise up against me, spouting malicious accusations." (Psalm 27:12)	"The chief priests and the whole Sanhedrin were looking for evidence against Jesus so that they could put him to death, but they did not find any. Many testified falsely against him, …." (Mark 14:55–56)
Jesus kept silent.	"…and as a sheep before its shearers is silent, so he did not open his mouth." (Isaiah 53:7)	"Then the high priest stood up before them and asked Jesus, 'Are you not going to answer? What is this testimony that these men are bringing against you?' But Jesus remained silent and gave no answer." (Mark 14:60–61)
Jesus was beat and spit upon.	"I offered my back to those who beat me, my cheeks to those who pulled out my beard; I did not hide my face from mocking and spitting." (Isaiah 50:6)	"Then some began to spit at him; they blind-folded him, struck him with their fists, and said, 'Prophesy!' And the guards took him and beat him." (Mark 14:65)
The potter's field was bought with the 30 pieces of silver.	"And the LORD said to me, 'Throw it to the potter — the handsome price at which they valued me!' So I took the thirty pieces of silver and threw them to the potter at the house of the Lord." (Zechariah 11:13)	"…what was spoken by Jeremiah … was fulfilled: "They took the thirty pieces of silver, the price set on him by the people of Israel, and … used them to buy the potter's field, as the Lord commanded me." (Matthew 27:9–10)

*All prophecies were proclaimed between
500 and 900 years prior to the birth of Jesus.*

PROPHECY	OLD TESTAMENT REFERENCE	NEW TESTAMENT FULFILLMENT
He was mocked and insulted by many.	"All who see me mock me; they hurl insults, shaking their heads." (Psalm 22:7)	"After they had mocked him, they took off the robe and put his own clothes on him. Then they led him away to crucify him." (Matthew 27:31)
They divided his garments and cast lots for them.	"They divide my clothes among them and cast lots for my garment." (Psalm 22:18)	"When...soldiers crucified Jesus, they took his clothes, dividing them, ...'Let's decide by lot who will get it.' ...happened...scripture might be fulfilled...'" (John 19:23–24)
Onlookers shake their heads at him.	"I am an object of scorn to my accusers; when they see me, they shake their heads." (Psalm 109:25)	"Those who passed by hurled insults at him, shaking their heads." (Matthew 27:39)
Family and friends watch from a distance.	"My friends and companions avoid me because of my wounds; my neighbors stay far away." (Psalm 38:11)	"But all those who knew him, including the women who had followed him from Galilee, stood at a distance, watching these things." (Luke 23:49)
Jesus is mocked and told to save himself.	"He trusts in the LORD," they say, 'let the LORD rescue him. Let him deliver him, since he delights in him.'" (Psalm 22:8)	"The people stood watching, and the rulers even sneered at him. They said, 'He saved others; let him save himself if he is God's Messiah, the Chosen One.'" (Luke 23:35)
Onlookers stare and gloat.	"All my bones are on display; people stare and gloat over me." (Psalm 22:17)	"When all the people who had gathered to witness this sight saw what took place, they beat their breasts and went away." (Luke 23:48)
Jesus is numbered with transgressors.	"...because he poured out his life unto death, and was numbered with the transgressors..." (Isaiah 53:12)	"...they crucified him there, along with the criminals — one on his right, the other on his left." (Luke 23:33)
"My God, my God, why have you forsaken me?"	"My God, my God, why have you forsaken me?..." (Psalm 22:1)	"...Jesus cried out in a loud voice, 'Eloi, Eloi, lema sabachthani?' (which means 'My God, my God, why have you forsaken me?'" (Mark 15:34)
"Into your hands, I commit my spirit."	"Into your hands I commit my spirit; deliver me, LORD, my faithful God." (Psalm 31:5)	"Jesus called out with a loud voice, 'Father, into your hands I commit my spirit...'" (Luke 23:46)
Jesus thirsts.	"My mouth is dried up like a potsherd, and my tongue sticks to the roof of my mouth;...." (Psalm 22:15)	"Later, knowing that everything had now been finished, and so that Scripture would be fulfilled, Jesus said, 'I am thirsty.'" (John 19:28)
Jesus is offered vinegar and gall.	"They put gall in my food and gave me vinegar for my thirst." (Psalm 69:21)	"There they offered Jesus wine to drink, mixed with gall; but after tasting it, he refused to drink it." (Matthew 27:34)
None of his bones are broken.	"He protects all his bones, not one of them will be broken." (Psalm 34:20)	"But when they came to Jesus and found that he was already dead, they did not break his legs...so that the scripture would be fulfilled..." (John 19:33, 36)
Jesus is buried with a rich man.	"He was assigned a grave with the wicked, and with the rich in his death, though he had done no violence, nor was any deceit in his mouth." (Isaiah 53:9)	"As evening approached, there came a rich man from Arimathea, named Joseph...took the body, ...and placed it in his own new tomb...." (Matthew 27:57–60)
Jesus does not remain dead.	"...my body also will rest secure, because you will not abandon me to the realm of the dead, nor will you let your faithful one see decay." (Psalm 16:9–10)	"The angel said..., 'Do not be afraid, for I know that you are looking for Jesus, who was crucified. He is not here; he has risen, just as he said....'" (Matthew 28:5–6)

MESSIANIC GENEALOGY

❧ FROM ADAM TO CHRIST ❧

ADAM
(4004 BC – 3074 BC)

Seth
Enosh
Kenan
Mahalalel
Jared
Enoch
Methuselah
Lamech

NOAH
(2948 BC – 1998 BC)

Shem
Arphaxad
Shelah
Eber
Peleg
Reu
Serug
Nahor
Terah

ABRAHAM
(1996 BC – 1821 BC)

Isaac
Jacob
Judah
Perez
Hezron
Ram
Amminadab
Nahshon
Salmon
Boaz
Obed
Jesse

KING DAVID
(1085 BC – 1015 BC)

LINE OF JOSEPH

Solomon
Rehoboam
Abijah
Asa
Jehoshaphat
Joram
Ahaziah
Joash
Amaziah
Uzziah
Jotham
Ahaz
Hezekiah
Manasseh
Amon
Josiah
Jehoiakim
Jeconiah
Shealtiel
Zerubbabel
Abiud
Eliakim
Azor
Sadoc
Achim

LINE OF MARY

Nathan
Mattatha
Menna
Melea
Eliakim
Jonam
Joseph
Judah
Simeon
Levi
Matthat
Jorim
Eliezer
Joshua
Er
Elmadam
Cosam
Addi
Melchi
Neri
Shealtiel
Zerubbabel
Rhesa
Joanan
Joda
Josech
Semein
Mattathias
Maath
Naggai
Hesli
Nahum
Amos
Mattathias
Joseph
Jannai
Melchi
Levi
Matthat
Eli
Mary

JESUS CHRIST
(5 BC – 33 AD)

Joseph
Jacob
Matthan
Eleazar
Eliud

For additional information and to answer questions about this chart, visit www.AnswersInGenesis.org/go/messianic-genealogy

TRIP TIPS

*My goal is that they may be encouraged in heart and united in love,
so that they may have the full riches of complete understanding,
in order that they may know the mystery of God,
namely, Christ, in whom are hidden all the treasures
of wisdom and knowledge*

COLOSSIANS 2:2-3

TRIP PLANNING TIPS

YOUR TWO INITIAL DECISIONS: "WHEN" AND "HOW" TO VISIT ISRAEL

WHEN IS THE BEST TIME TO VISIT ISRAEL?

THE TIMING OF YOUR VISIT CAN greatly affect the overall quality of your trip. The best time for *you* may be when you have time off and/or when your favorite church or ministry group is going to Israel. If you have some flexibility, consider your preferences of cost, weather, and/or number of daylight hours available to sightsee.

Regarding cost, prices are more affordable during low season, December through March, March being a bit higher. The fall high holy days, Passover, and the months of July and August are high season—hence, elevated hotel and airfare costs and larger crowds.

If weather is important to you, the most pleasant months overall to visit Israel are October, November, March, April, and May. July and August tend to be uncomfortably hot for the more "mature" travelers. June and September are also hot – but a bit more comfortable than July and August. December is starting to get cold with increased rainfall. Although unpredictable, January and February can be dismal with cold weather, increased wind storms, and significant rainfall. Keep in mind, these months also have fewer daylight hours for sightseeing.

If you want to get the most "bang for your buck" and don't mind longer days of sightseeing, the months with the most daylight hours are April through August. Outdoor water sports, like kayaking down the Jordan River or snorkeling in Eilat, are viable options in these longer, warmer days.

March is popular because it's somewhat more affordable and not quite as crowded, with a bonus of experiencing Israel's vibrant spring flowers and lush green hillsides. However, March does have shorter days and typically a fair amount of rainfall.

Bottom line, what are *your* travel needs and preferences and those of your traveling companion(s)?

HOW DO YOU WANT TO TRAVEL?

You have two options: join a tour or visit "on your own." If you've never been to Israel before, I highly recommend that you join a reputable tour. Traveling on your own in a new country can be daunting. Driving in Israel is risky, as Israeli drivers are typically quite aggressive. Additionally, it's very easy to get lost. Even with a good GPS system, you don't know how to predict traffic (which is very congested in Tel Aviv and Jerusalem). Getting around Israel on your own can be emotionally exhausting. Joining a formal organized tour will allow you to sit back and enjoy the trip, while gaining a broad overview and understanding of the sites, should you want to return in the future. Plus, you generally pay more if you hire your own tour guide and driver because you do not have a busload of travelers to share the costs. *Note: Tour guides are not allowed to drive for tourists unless they have their own state-approved special car and license—which few possess.*

If you have the resources, a nine- or ten-day guided tour of Israel, followed by renting a car for several additional days is ideal. Following the tour, you will have the opportunity to visit places where you wished you could have spent more time and visit new places that your tour didn't include.

OPTION ONE: JOIN A TOUR

A plethora of Israel tours are offered. Make sure the tour you choose has the following:

Reputable travel agency which focuses primarily on Christian tours to Israel

Reputable tour guide: If possible, check for online reviews.

Comfortable pace: Do you want to spend more time at fewer sites or do you want to see as much as you can?

Reasonable cost with optimal amenities: When comparing tour costs, make sure you're comparing apples to apples. Ask the following questions:

- **Does the tour cost include airfare?** If so, does that include the airfare fuel?

- **Is it a reputable airline?** Does the airline have ample leg room for a long trip, friendly service, decent meals with options for food intolerances and allergies, etc.?

- **What is the flight itinerary?** How many layovers and how long? A maximum of one stop of three hours or less is optimal for the comfort and convenience of most travelers. Arriving in Tel Aviv in the morning and/or departing in the middle of the night adds touring time without having to pay for additional nights of lodging.

- **Does the cost include tips for hotels, guides, and bus drivers?** If not, add about $15 a day to your total trip cost.

- **What is the total number of days/nights in the land?** Expect to pay $250–$350 for each extra day with an overnight.

- **Does it include an overnight at the Dead Sea?** (very nice perk)

- **What are the hotel ratings?** Are they three, four, or five stars? *If the brochure doesn't say, ask the travel agent.* Four stars generally fits the bill for both comfort and affordability; anything less may be disappointing—unless accommodations are not that important to you. *You can check hotel reviews on Tripadvisor.*

- **What meals are included?** All tours include breakfasts and most include dinners as well. *Lunches average $10–$15, plus about 12% tip; dinners: $25–$35 plus tip.*

- **What season and month is the trip scheduled? Can you live with the weather?**

- **How many and what types of sites/activities are included?** Israel offers an abundance of sites to visit. If you study various online itineraries, you will notice that the vse majority of the included sites are the same. Agencies and tour leaders want to be sure that if you visit Israel only once in your life, you will visit the most important places. Understand up front that most tours keep a quick pace. You *run* where Jesus walked! You'll probably be very tired at the end of each day and you may feel like complaining, but that will just drain you and others around you. And when you get home, chances are, you will be *very grateful* that you were able to see everything you did! **From a strictly monetary context, the more sites/activities—the more bang for your buck!**

- **Does the tour include interaction with Israelis?** Most tours visit only the historical and biblical sites across Israel. However, interaction with the Israeli people is often the highlight of a trip to Israel! This could mean sharing a Shabbat meal in a home, talking to Messianic believers about their experience living in the land, hearing a lecture from a local ministry leader or military official, or joining Israelis for the Friday evening festivities before sundown at the Western Wall—praying, singing, and dancing to bring in the Shabbat!

- **Does the tour include service?** There are many opportunities to bless Israel by serving. For instance, you may want to pick up trash around the Galilee, serve a meal to Holocaust survivors, or distribute food to the needy. generates double blessings—for the recipients and for you!

OPTION TWO:
CUSTOMIZE YOUR OWN TOUR

If you're not part of an organized tour, you have the flexibility to customize your itinerary and set your own pace. Here are some awesome options for activities and day tours.

Deerland Zipline

- Jeep ride in the Golan Heights (p. 121)
- Kayaking on the Jordan River in the Golan Heights (Check out Kfar Blum online)
- Magic of the Golan (p. 123)
- Living Stones (p. 115) OR Shabbat of a Lifetime (p.151)
- Friends of Zion Museum (p. 148)
- Jerusalem Prayer Tower (p. 148)
- Tower of David Night Spectacular (152)
- Temple Mount Sifting Project (archaeology p. 151)
- Caliber 3 Shooting Adventure with IDF (p. 208)
- Deerland Zipline (p. 209)
- The Arad Experience (p. 238)
- Camel ride: If you can't go to Genesis Land (p. 140), make sure to have a camel ride before you leave Israel. Camels rides are available on the roadside while travelling past Jericho to the Dead Sea, at the top of Mt. of Olives, or at Kfar Hanokdim in Arad (half-hour inland from Masada: p. 241).

AFFORDABLE DAY TOUR OPTIONS

For those on a tight budget with only a day or two in Israel, check out Sandemans tours. Just type "Sandemans Jerusalem" into your online search bar. Register online for these popular tours before the tour is full—at least one month prior to arrival, if at all possible.

At the time of this writing, Sandemans offers two FREE two-hour walking tours:

- Old City, Jerusalem
- Old Jaffa

You can also participate in any of their other affordable tours:

- Three-hour walking tour of Mt. of Olives
- Four-hour walking tour of the Old City including the Temple Mount
- Two-hour Friday walking tour of the Jewish Quarter of the Old City and Shabbat at the Western Wall
- Full-day tour: Masada at sunrise, Ein Gedi, Dead Sea float
- Two-and-a-half hour walking tour of Tel Aviv

NINE-DAY ITINERARY FOR FIRST-TIMERS

Recommendations from travel agents specializing in Israel tours

DAY 1: TEL-AVIV-JAFFA (early arrival)
- Jaffa and Jaffa Tales
- Independence Hall or Palmach Museum

DAY 2: NORTHERN ISRAEL
- Caesarea
- Mt. Carmel
- Megiddo
- Nazareth Village
- Drive by Cana

DAY 3: CENTRAL GALILEE
- Magdala Excavations
- Mt. of Beatitudes
- Capernaum
- St. Peter's fish lunch
- Galilee boat ride
- Jesus Boat Museum (only if time)

DAY 4: GOLAN HEIGHTS
- Magic of the Golan
- Mt. Bental
- Drive by Mt. Hermon
- Caesarea Philippi
- Tel Dan
- Longer days—Kayaking on the Jordan River

DAY 5: GALILEE TO JERUSALEM
- Beit She'an
- Qasr el Yahud (where John was baptized by Jesus)
- Genesis Land (camel ride)
- Mt. Scopus Observation Point

DAY 6: JERUSALEM
- Mt. of Olives, Gethsemane
- Garden Tomb
- Damascus Gate
- Lions' Gate
- St. Anne's Church, Pool of Bethesda
- Walk Via Dolorosa; visit Lithostratos (Ecce Homo Convent) and Church of the Holy Sepulchre
- Old City Marketplace
- Jaffa Gate

DAY 7: JERUSALEM
- City of David, Hezekiah's Tunnel
- Pool of Siloam, Zion Gate
- Southern Wall Excavations, Southern Steps (Davidson Center)
- Yad Vashem Holocaust Museum
- Israel Museum—model of second Temple period Jerusalem and Dead Sea Scrolls
- Drive by Knesset

DAY 8: DEAD SEA
- Qumran
- Ein Gedi
- Masada
- Dead Sea Float

DAY 9: JERUSALEM AND BETHLEHEM
- Western Wall and Western Wall Tunnels
- Jewish Quarter (Cardo, Temple Institute) OR Caiaphas' House
- Bethlehem, Shepherds' Fields

SUGGESTIONS FOR FEWER TOURING DAYS
Numbers are from itinerary days above

ONE DAY	TWO DAYS	THREE DAYS	FOUR DAYS	FIVE DAYS	SIX DAYS	SEVEN DAYS	EIGHT DAYS
6	6, 7	3, 6, 7	3, 6, 7, 8	2, 3, 6, 7, 8	2, 3, 6, 7, 8, 9	2, 3, 4, 6, 7, 8, 9	2, 3, 4, 5, 6, 7, 8, 9

TRIP PREP TIPS

DEPARTURE COUNTDOWN!

You've chosen *when* and *how* you are going to travel; now start preparing!

YOU ARE ABOUT TO EMBARK ON A trip of a lifetime! A trip to Israel is like no other; it is a unique spiritual journey, a pilgrimage. You've made a substantial *financial* investment for this trip; now take that a step further and maximize your investment by also investing your *time* to prepare. This step will yield invaluable rewards. Prepare yourself in all ways: spiritually, mentally, practically, and physically. In the following pages, you will find some time-honored recommendations.

WITHIN TWO WEEKS OF YOUR INITIAL TRIP DEPOSIT

Seriously consider travel insurance—which is generally NOT included in your tour price. Good travel insurance will cover trip cancellations, trip interruptions, all of your medical needs; and loss of or damage to your luggage. There are a number of reputable travel insurance companies; do your homework. Personally, I have had excellent coverage and stellar service with **Travel Guard.** You could potentially be out a substantial sum of money if you forego purchasing travel insurance and need to cancel your trip, even a couple of months prior to your departure date.

PLEASE NOTE: Many insurance policies allow you to include a Pre-Existing Medical Condition Exclusion Waiver when you purchase your insurance 10–14 days of your initial trip deposit.

TWO MONTHS (OR MORE) PRIOR TO DEPARTURE

Check your passport: Ensure you have an up-to-date passport—one that **will not expire within 6 months after your trip!** There is no need for a visa if you have a U.S. passport. If you don't have a passport, visit the U.S. Department of State/Bureau of Consular Affairs website at Travel.State.Gov. You can make a passport appointment at your local post office, and Costco is one of several places that offers quality, inexpensive passport photos. Allow six to eight weeks for passport processing; expedited service is available for an additional fee at locations listed at Travel.State.Gov.

Arrange transportation to and from your airport of origin: What is the most stress-free and cost-effective option for you? If your group is taking a bus to the airport, that simplifies your decision! Other options include: 1) Arrange for a family member or friend to take you to the airport for your departure and pick you up when you return. 2) Drive your car with or without others and pay for long-term parking either at the airport or at a facility close to the airport that will shuttle you to the airport. *Research online for prices and reviews; you can find some good deals at cheapairportparking.org.* Keep in mind that popular Park and Rides fill up quickly, so if this is your choice—reserve a space early. 3) Take a one-way rental car. 4) Take a shuttle or taxi.

Start walking daily to build stamina: Tours involve quite a bit of walking and you don't want to be the straggler keeping your group behind schedule. Walk at a good clip at home. Climb stairs as much as possible and if you can, try walking on uneven ground (which you will find at many sites in Israel).

Break in your primary walking shoes: Walk at home in your new shoes as often as possible; you don't want blisters!

Start learning about Israel: Read your travel guide. Complete as much of the accompanying study guide as you can, track your itinerary on a map, and avail yourself of the recommended resources.

Prepare spiritually through prayer (pp. 70–71) **and Bible reading** (journal pp. 64–65).

Start your packing list. See pp. 72–77.

Plan tour group get-togethers. You will appreciate getting to know fellow travelers before the trip. You can discuss the itinerary, share packing tips, and initiate lifelong friendships. Share a lunch, grab some coffee, take a walk, or have a potluck and movie night!

ONE MONTH PRIOR TO DEPARTURE

Purchase all necessary supplies.

Start a folder with important papers. Include your itinerary, flight schedule, important contacts, travel insurance documents, health information (including medications), a copy of your passport and driver's license, (also take a cell phone snapshot of each), health information (including medications), etc.

Make sure your clothes and backpack or purse are comfortable. They need to be comfortable for walking, stooping down, hiking uphill, etc. This is the time to figure out how you will *comfortably* carry everything.

This is a great time to start a journal!

Learn some Hebrew. Start with a few words and phrases. See pp. 20–21.

Increase your water intake. If you are not already drinking water in abundance, now is the time to start. Hydrate yourself before the trip even begins.

If you are using a SIM card for your phone, make sure your smartphone is unlocked and order one now. See p. 11.

Let your bank and credit card providers know the dates you will be in Israel. Write down each applicable **PIN code**; you will need them for use in Israel.

ONE TO TWO WEEKS PRIOR TO DEPARTURE

Begin the packing process. Try to be fully packed a couple of days early so you're not totally stressed out the day before departure. Pack your carry-on baggage efficiently for a stress-free flight; you can relax knowing you have just what you need at the convenience of your plane seat.

Ensure your passport is in a safe place.

Make sure your camera is working and fully equipped. You will need a fully-charged camera with ample memory, a charger, and extra batteries if required. *Not necessary if you are using your smartphone.*

Attend to your flight needs. Contact your airline or travel agent regarding any special dietary needs or requests.

Print out your boarding pass up to 24 hours prior to departure.

Need caffeine to stay awake? You may want to have something with caffeine to enable you to stay up all night before your next-day departure. This will likely help you sleep better on the plane and be more acclimated to Israel time when you arrive. Read about tips to minimize jet lag on the following page.

Dress for the long flight. Wear your most comfortable clothes and socks; you'll be sleeping in them! Also, bring your heaviest jacket and shoes to reduce check-in luggage weight. Additionally, you will appreciate having a watch.

Pack your carry-on items efficiently. You want to have easy access to everything you will need during your flight. See p. 74.

Prepare your airport documents. Passport holders are convenient to hold your boarding pass, passport, and driver's license. Those that hang around your neck are quite handy!

YOU ARE NOW EMBARKING ON YOUR TRIP OF A LIFETIME!

TIPS TO MINIMIZE JET LAG AND MAXIMIZE GOOD SLEEP

Jet lag is debilitating fatigue and other physical effects caused by crossing several time zones. Here are some tips:

- Change your watch to Israel time when you board the plane; this will psychologically help you to transition to Israel time.

- Control your sleep time. Using California as an example: there is a 10-hour time difference between Israel and California. If you are serious about wanting to reduce jet lag, consider drinking as much caffeine as needed (using wisdom for your system) to stay up all night and throughout the next day until you board your plane. Calculate the time you would need to go to sleep by 9:00 PM (Israel time) and sleep through until 6:00 or 7:00 AM the next day (Israel time). Use doctor-approved, safe doses of sleep aids as needed to get good sleep. If you wake up too early, take the minimum amount you need to fall back to sleep. Note: limit your caffeine intake several hours before you plan to sleep.

- One helpful over-the-counter sleep aid is melatonin, which is naturally secreted in our bodies to help regulate our circadian rhythms for sound sleep. One doctor suggests taking three milligrams of melatonin an hour or two before your destination's bedtime; then try to sleep for ten hours. *Check with your doctor before using.*

- An eye mask or earplugs may help you sleep on the plane (and at your destination).

- Stay hydrated. Drink water before, during, and after your flight.

- Before sleeping, avoid alcohol and caffeine. They can interfere with your sleep and may contribute to dehydration.

- High carbs and fatty food close to bedtime can disrupt your sleep; avoid them.

- On the flight, get up and walk around periodically, do static exercises, and stretch.

AFTER YOU ARRIVE IN ISRAEL

- Avoid heavy exercise near bedtime; it can delay sleep.

- Try your hardest *not* to allow yourself to take a nap or fall asleep before your regular bedtime!

- A hot bath before bedtime can ease sore muscles from travel and help you relax and wind down. The bath causes your body temperature to drop, which can help make you sleepy.

- Try to eliminate distractions in your room at bedtime. If light is shining in through a window, close the shades.

- Starting with your first touring day, wake up on time, stay alert, and get as much sunlight as possible in the early morning hours. The light helps shift your body's circadian clock so that you will feel rested and be awake at appropriate times.

- A good sleep machine with white noise (and/or other comforting sounds) masks background sounds which might otherwise prevent you from either falling asleep or staying asleep. Sleep sound apps are available for smartphones as well. If you purchase a sleep machine, make sure it is either 220 volt or dual voltage.

PRAYER

Prayer is the most important part of your trip preparation.

Try to set aside a few minutes each day to pray for various aspects of the trip. Be aware that most pilgrims experience a significant degree of spiritual warfare prior to departure, with many almost having to cancel. Don't give in (unless you're certain of the Lord's leading); persevere in prayer and move forward! Stand on the Word of God, review Ephesians 6:10–18. The following are some topical daily prayer suggestions. Do whatever works for you—just PRAY!

SUNDAY: SPIRITUAL WARFARE

But the Lord is faithful, and he will strengthen you and protect you from the evil one.

(2 THESSALONIANS 3:3)

- Pray for you and your team to have the discipline to spend daily time in prayer, praise, and the Word—before and during the trip.

- Pray that any schemes of the Enemy to keep people from visiting the Holy Land would be thwarted, and all spiritual opposition would be met with prayer and praise. Quote Ephesians 6:10–18 out loud.

- Pray for provision of faithful group intercessors in the land. Be aware that Satan wants to rob you of the Lord's blessings in Israel and bringing striving and contention within your group. Be proactive! Even with the best intentions, it's difficult to find time to pray before or after the day's activities when you're rushed and fatigued. However, your tour leader can lead the group in prayer on the bus; a faithful group of intercessors praying at the back of the bus first thing every morning would be awesome!

MONDAY: TRIP PREPARATIONS

The plans of the diligent lead surely to abundance... (PROVERBS 21:5)

- Pray for efficient, stress-free planning to complete all necessary tasks prior to departure.

- Pray for efficient and prudent packing.

- Pray for financial provision for everyone the Lord has called to join your team.

- Pray for exceptional provision and smooth operations for everyone's charges and responsibilities back home: church, home care, business, pets, children, elderly parents, etc.

- Pray for built-in time to study the Bible, review the itinerary, and to become intimately acquainted with Israel through various resources prior to the trip.

TUESDAY: TRAVEL MERCIES

The Lord will keep you from all harm— he will watch over your life; the Lord will watch over your coming and going both now and forevermore.

(PSALM 121:7, 8)

- Pray for safe and reliable travel with all modes of transportation (car, bus, and plane) both at home and in Israel.

- Pray for minimal jet lag upon arrival in Israel and the return home.

- Pray for good sleep and comfortable sleeping arrangements on the plane and at all hotels; pray that all hotel reservations will be in order.

- Pray for seamless airport processes: timely check-in, no lost or damaged luggage, smooth customs and safekeeping of all required paperwork and important documents.

- Pray for weather that enhances, as opposed to distracts from, the tour itinerary and opportunities to bless others.

WEDNESDAY: GROUP DYNAMICS

And be ye kind one to another, tender-hearted, forgiving one another, even as God for Christ's sake hath forgiven you.

(EPHESIANS 4:32)

- Pray for unity in the group—for humility, the ability to consider others' needs more important than personal needs and wants.

- Pray that each member will be punctual and considerate of others, so sites and activities aren't missed.

- Pray for grateful spirits and joy; no "Debbie the Downer" complainers in the group (1 Thessalonians 5:16–18).

- Pray that all "glitches" (that inevitably *will* come) will be encountered with patience, understanding, and prayer.

- Pray for close knit fellowship with rich and lasting friendships forged in Christ.

- Pray for excellent teamwork and relationships between the tour leaders, tour guide, bus driver, and group members.

THURSDAY: HEALTH/SAFETY

Beloved, I pray that you may prosper in all things and be in health, just as your soul prospers.

(3 JOHN 2 NKJV)

- Pray for safety and health throughout the flight and trip—no accidents, unexpected health crises, food poisoning, etc.

- Pray for absence of health issues with those with unique medical needs, and that they would bring all their necessary medication and/or supplements.

- Pray for all special dietary needs addressed without glitches or unnecessary stress.

- Pray for wisdom to effectively and compassionately assist those with mobility challenges, without negatively affecting others.

- Pray for energy and stamina, especially for those with mobility challenges—that all may fully experience and enjoy the trip.

FRIDAY: SPIRITUAL GROWTH

...so that you may live a life worthy of the Lord and please him in every way: bearing fruit in every good work, growing in the knowledge of God...

(COLOSSIANS 1:10)

- Pray for spiritual inspiration, transformation, and increased faith.

- Pray for teachable spirits to glean what the Holy Spirit is impressing on each heart.

- Pray for a greater understanding of the Bible and of individual personal callings.

- Pray for growth in spiritual wisdom and discernment.

- Pray for growth in the fruit of the Spirit through daily group interactions.

- Pray for hearts of adoration and praise.

SATURDAY: HEART FOR ISRAEL

I will make you into a great nation, and I will bless you... I will bless those who bless you, and whoever curses you I will curse; and all peoples on earth will be blessed through you.

(GENESIS 12:2–3)

- Pray for a greater understanding of Israel's history, Bible history, God's heart for Israel, and the Jewish roots of the Christian faith.

- Pray for a greater understanding of anti-Semitism (both past and present) and the age-old, critical wound of the Jewish people that keeps them from faith in Yeshua.

- Pray for a deeper appreciation of the Israeli culture and all people groups in the land—Jews, Arabs, and Christians, as well as potential God-given callings of future service to one or more of these people groups.

- Pray for an increased desire to be a light and witness to Israelis and Jews back home.

- Pray for a passion to pray for Israel upon returning home, learn more about Israel, support Israeli ministries, and solidly stand for Israel.

PACKING TIPS

LUGGAGE

Strong, sturdy, and durable luggage is a necessity. Your luggage will be tossed around on flights, pulled through airports, thrown under the tour bus multiple times, and repeatedly repacked—resulting in substantial wear and tear! Lightweight luggage is helpful to accommodate the weight of everything you'll want to pack. Make sure your luggage securely and easily opens and closes and has wheels in good working order; nothing is as frustrating as a suitcase that keeps falling over! Also, make your luggage easily identifiable. You can either choose a print or a color other than black, tie a brightly colored ribbon or scarf to the handle, attach a bright luggage tag, secure it with a luggage strap, add a bright handle grip, use a strip of *washi* tape (tape with colorful designs), or even paint a design on your suitcase. Sturdy and identifiable luggage will facilitate smooth sailing at the airport and throughout the trip.

Allowable Baggage (*no extra cost*)

Check with your airline; airlines are increasingly beginning to charge for all check-in baggage. The current "norm," which may not be accurate for all airlines is as follows:

- One CHECK-IN bag, max 50 lbs: 62" total (L + W+ H)
- One CARRY-ON bag, max 17 lbs (10" x 17" x 21.5")
- One PERSONAL ITEM such as purse or computer

Baggage Tips

- Check your airline's website for a list of restricted or prohibited items for both carry-on and checked baggage. Valuable information can be found on the *US Transportation Security Administration* website.
- Checked baggage must remain unlocked unless you are using a TSA-approved lock (recommended).
- TSA currently allows travel-sized 3.4-oz containers (100 ml) or less per item of liquids, aerosols, gels, creams and pastes in your carry-on bag and through the checkpoint. Place them in a quart-sized Ziploc at the top of your bag. Fill no more than three-quarters full for expansion. Larger sizes should be transferred to checked baggage. Exceptions include medications and baby formula—each of which are required to be declared for inspection at security.
- Do not wrap bungee cords, ties or straps around baggage.
- Remove old airline tags from your luggage.
- For an extra measure of security, attach identification tags to the inside and outside of your bag, noting your destination and home address, as well as any other relevant contact information.

LAUNDRY

It's best to pack enough clothes for five to seven days (seven if you'll be gone close to two weeks or more). Most travelers like to wash their clothes at least once a week. You can wash your own laundry in your hotel sink or bathtub and hang it out to dry in your hotel room over the next touring day. A plastic bag is handy for damp clothes that need to be packed. If you're in Jerusalem, you can call *Superclean Laundry* at 02-566-0367. Superclean is a reputable laundromat offering pickup, wash, dry, fold, and delivery services at a very affordable cost. You pay by weight and number of bags, so place all your dirty clothes in one bag if you can; most hotels have laundry bags in the closet. Superclean closes early on Friday for the Shabbat and re-opens on Sunday morning.

PACKING YOUR PURCHASES

Tourists frequently come back with more souvenirs and gifts than they had planned on, which can create a predicament of excessive suitcase weight and/or insufficient suitcase space. One way to solve this dilemma is to have several people pack their gifts together in one additional suitcase and share its cost for the return flight home. The cost of an extra piece of checked-in luggage currently averages $100. Have one or more on your tour group bring a lightweight, strong, rolled-up duffel bag in their suitcase for this express purpose. Or *underpack* so you will have extra room in your suitcase to pack your souvenirs and gifts.

CLOTHING CONSIDERATIONS

Bring comfortable, breathable, lightweight, and durable clothing. Comfort and flexibility are more important than fashion; tour sites are typically very informal with no need to dress up. Lightweight shoes and clothing allow you to pack more items while keeping your suitcase light—a welcome advantage when you're repacking several times. Comfy pants, such as "cargo" pants with a zipper pocket, is a great way to easily and securely access essentials like your phone, paper and pens, sunglasses, sunscreen, etc.

Include "modest dress" options. You never know when a change in schedule will unexpectedly land you at a religious site, necessitating modest dress for entrance. Many religious sites require shoulders, heads, and legs to be covered. **Make sure you bring pants or a skirt that at least covers your knees and a shirt or shawl that covers your shoulders.** Layering will keep you from having to stop at a facility for a change. Keep it simple by storing a bag on the tour bus with easy clothing changes. For men, either a loose-fitting pair of pants or zip-off pants work well; baggy pants can easily be pulled over shorts and zip-off pants can instantly turn into shorts. For women, a lightweight, calf-length wrap/skirt and shawl will come in handy. Wraps or skirts can be thrown over shorts, and a shawl or scarf can quickly be wrapped around bare shoulders. It is important to be respectful and courteous of others' customs and values—even when it's outside your comfort level. Be a stellar representative of your group, your country, and your Lord!

Take seasonal weather into account when packing. The best way to accommodate variable changes in weather throughout the day (which is common in Israel) is to LAYER your clothes! Bring multiple light layers as well as a lightweight windbreaker or jacket for all seasons and a warm jacket for colder weather. Since Israel tends to be dry, breathable and quick-drying clothing is preferable.

FOOTWEAR

SOCKS: Find out if your socks are too hot, too tight, or too uncomfortable *before* the trip—while you still have an opportunity to replace them. If you have a propensity toward blisters or foot odor, wear hiking socks over liner socks. Bring additional warm socks for cold feet while sleeping.

SHOES: Depending on your itinerary, you'll want to bring a minimum of three pairs of shoes: sturdy walking shoes, casual shoes, and water shoes for Hezekiah's Tunner, the Jordan River, and the Dead Sea. A pair of flip flops can come in handy as well.

WALKING SHOES: Sturdy, comfortable walking shoes are a must! Many sites in Israel have uneven surfaces, including the prolific cobblestone streets in the Old City. For the majority, tennis shoes with durable rubber soles, good traction, and a thick tread will provide adequate comfort and stability. Some may find a thinner sole provides better balance. Adequate ankle support is important; you may want to check with a sports company shoe specialist about a boot with higher ankles. An additional consideration for rainy season is a quick drying, water-resistant shoe, or plastic booties to cover your shoes. *Whatever your preference, test out your primary walking shoes before the trip: walk on different types of terrain, up and down stairs, and on various types of inclines.*

SHOE INSERTS: You can minimize your chances of foot pain by investing in a good shoe insert for your primary walking shoes. *Powerstep*, found on Amazon, offers good quality shoe inserts.

CASUAL SHOES: Sometimes after a long day of being on your feet, simply changing into a different pair of shoes can be revitalizing. A simple, lightweight, somewhat dressier shoe is great for evenings out!

WATER SHOES: Hidden rocks or other objects on the sea floor can quickly turn your exciting dip in Israel's beautiful waters into an agonizing adventure. You won't regret bringing a pair of simple strap-on water shoes for the Red Sea, Med Sea, Dead Sea, Galilee, or the Jordan River! Flip-flops fall off easily under moving water, so be sure to bring something with a strap. Old, lightweight tennis shoes that you can throw away are a great option!

PACKING TIPS

CARRY-ON BAGGAGE

Suggestions for a stress-free flight; customize as needed

- Keep your passport, plane ticket, debit and credit cards, cash, driver's license, SIM card, etc. close to you in a money belt or secure zippered compartment.
- Wear your watch.
- Good travel pillow—essential for getting good sleep on the plane
- Comfy throw blanket from home for extra warmth to help sleep
- Earplugs
- Eye mask
- Sleep aids (most travelers need them)
- Decongestants and other medication as needed
- Chewing gum to "pop" plugged ears
- Snacks
- Small, empty plastic bottle to fill with water before boarding your flight
- Israel travel guide
- Map of Israel
- Books/materials you'd like to read on the plane
- Pens, highlighters
- Paper
- Business cards
- Glasses and cleaner
- Hand sanitizer or sanitary wipes
- Kleenex
- Breath mints
- Toothbrush and toothpaste
- Small makeup case and brush for women

The following items can remain in the overhead compartment of the plane:

- Car/house keys
- High-value items such as cameras, jewelry and electronic devices
- Pajamas and one change of clothes (in the unfortunate event your bag is "lost in transit")
- Toiletry case
- Supplements and medications not needed at seat
- Camera
- Notebook or folder with itinerary, security info, copies of important papers (flight info, passport, phone numbers/ addresses, prescriptions, medical diagnoses)

CHECKED BAGGAGE

- Copies of passport, plane ticket, and prescriptions buried at bottom of suitcase
- An extra pair of glasses or contacts at bottom of luggage (if applicable)
- Extra pair of walking shoes, flip flops, and water shoes
- Sweater or lightweight jacket
- Between two and four pairs of jeans or casual pants, one nicer pair of pants

- "Modest" dress for men: baggy pants or zip-off pants
- "Modest" dress for women: lightweight calf-length wrap/skirt and shawl or scarf
- Protein bars and snacks that don't melt or crumble
- Reading material/Bible
- Dirty clothes bag; plastic bag for wet clothes
- Assorted sizes of zippered plastic bags— useful for a wide variety of travel needs
- Items on following two pages

SUGGESTIONS FOR GROUPING OF PACKED ITEMS

Pack only the items you need; less is more! You may want to organize your packing with packing cubes, re-closeable plastic bags of various sizes, and/or customized pouches. The following are ideas for those who might benefit from some efficient packing groupings. Use as needed.

MORNING/NIGHTTIME GEAR

- Medications and supplements
- Toothbrush and toothpaste
- Mouthwash
- Deodorant
- Night and day skin care
- Hand and body lotion
- Sunscreen
- Safety pins and lint roller
- Jewelry
- Makeup
- Eye drops, contact lenses with solutions and cleaners
- Nail clippers/file/tweezers

HAIR

- Brush, comb
- Hair products and accessories
- Flat iron or curling iron
- Blow dryer (220 volt or dual voltage)

SHOWER

- Shampoo & conditioner (most hotels have these; but you may want your own)
- Body wash or soap
- Washcloth (many hotels do not have them)
- Razor
- Shower cap

TOPS AND OUTERWEAR

*Rolled-up tops take up less room
and tend to be more wrinkle-resistant.*

- Two nicer blouses or shirts
- Six to eight weather-appropriate tops
- Two sweatshirts (cooler weather)
- Sweater or light jacket

INTIMATE APPAREL AND MORE

- Five to seven pairs of socks
  and underwear
- Two to three bras for women
- Tank tops, warm undershirt for layering
- Tights and/or leggings (cooler weather)
- Pajamas
- Belt(s)
- Swimsuit and cover

COOL WEATHER

- Scarves and gloves
- Small umbrella
- Parka and waterproof shoe covers
- Rain hat, warm hats, ear muffs
- Hand and/or feet warmers (HotHands)
- Moisture-control socks or wool socks

WARM WEATHER

- Insulated water bottle and sling
- Sunscreen and sun glasses
- Wide-rim sun hat
- Reusable cooling cloth for neck

NIGHT ELECTRONICS

- Travel alarm clock
- Adapters, extension cord
- Camera, batteries (include extras),
  charger, cable, memory cards
- Phone charger
- Laptop or tablet charger (extra cables?)

FIRST AID

- Ibuprofen, Tylenol, and/or aspirin
- Pain-relieving creams
- Prescribed antibiotics
- Medications as needed: decongestant,
  antacid, cold relief, cough lozenges,
  constipation, diarrhea, nausea, Benadryl,
  electrolytes for rehydration, athlete's foot
- Bandaids and blister treatments
- Wound cleanser
- Cotton balls
- Antibiotic ointment
- Any brace you may have need of
  (back, neck, elbow, knee, ankle, etc.)

LAUNDRY (optional)

- Laundry detergent
- Stain treatment
- Clothesline
- Collapsible hangers
- Towel to absorb moisture
- Small sewing kit

"IN THE LAND" TIPS

Above all, be prepared and respectful.

PLAN AHEAD. YOU WILL MOST LIKELY be rushed and scattered if you wait to prepare for your touring day on the same morning. **Prepare each evening for the next day.** Take the time you need to lay out your clothing (wash or iron clothes, if necessary), organize your belongings, and recharge your electronics: cell phone, computer, camera batteries, etc. Be aware that most hotels do *not* have clocks in the rooms. If you don't have your own alarm clock, make sure the front desk wakes you up at whatever time you need to be on time! **Five minutes early to the bus is on time!** Give yourself extra time before the day's departure time to insure you've used the restroom, packed your day bag for the bus, and taken care of all your personal needs.

Show respect to your fellow participants, leaders, and tour guide. This is a group experience; make every attempt to be supportive, considerate, and sensitive to the needs of each and every group member. **Be present and courteous to those around you. Use your phone and internet only for emergencies when with the group. Better yet, leave your phone in your hotel room or on the bus.** It's the little, yet important things like being prepared, being punctual, and following instructions that make a tour successful. While you may feel like you're rushing through some sites, remember you're having a once-in-a-lifetime experience! You won't regret being tired on the tour; you will regret missing sites. *Tourists run where Jesus walked!*

It is critical to stay with your group. Individuals who lag behind for sightseeing or photo-taking affect the entire group. They inadvertently cause missed itinerary sites and annoyingly rushed comrades, while placing undue pressure on those who are physically challenged to keep up the pace. The tour can only move as fast as the slowest person; don't be that person!

Love your neighbor as yourself and exercise the fruit of the Spirit. "*But the fruit of the Spirit is love, joy, peace, forbearance, kindness, goodness, faithfulness, gentleness and self-control...*" (Galatians 5:22–23). "*Anyone who wants to be first must be the very last, and the* servant *of all*" (Mark 9:35). How can you be a servant of Christ? Be a servant to your fellow travelers, especially your leaders. Let others go before you and show patience and kindness to those who have challenges or are slower than you. What an amazing tour it would be if each participant resolved each day to love their neighbor as themselves and to make a point of assisting even one leader and/or fellow traveler! Ask yourself how you can encourage and build up one another. **Decide to be a "Joyful Judy" instead of "Debbie the Downer!"**

Resolve to have NO PART of these three destructive practices and mindsets:

1) COMPLAINING—instead give thanks and praise.

2) GOSSIPING—instead, go directly to the person you have issue with.

3) A SENSE OF ENTITLEMENT—instead, expect nothing; be a servant to all.

Respect others in the land. Be actively alert and mindful to those around you—your travel partners, native Israelis, and international visitors. Israel is an international melting pot. Let your dress, your actions, and your words show respect for other cultures and belief systems.

Be flexible. Respect others by deciding beforehand to hold your tongue and not complain if a visit is cut short, if your bus is caught in heavy traffic, or a scheduled site is unable to be accommodated. Israel is very different than the United States and Canada. **Schedule changes are the norm.** Go with the flow.

UTILIZE THE BUS!

A small "day" tote bag that you can hold on your lap and leave on the bus is especially useful. Items you may want to include are your travel guide, a map, extra batteries, a lightweight jacket, a spare shirt and pair of socks, your modest dress (a pair of baggy pants for men or a wrap and scarf for women), deodorant, sunglasses, hat or visor, sunscreen, snacks, etc. This tote bag is also handy for the days you will need your water shoes.

PACK YOUR PURSE OR BACKPACK RESOURCEFULLY

Items may include the following, some of which could already be in your tote bag:

- Phone
- Travel guide and journal
- *Lap Map for the Christian Traveler*
- Small, wire-bound notepad for taking notes
- Several pens and highlighters
- Business cards
- Sunscreen
- Sunglasses (on a lanyard?)
- Glasses, cleaner
- All necessary medications and supplements
- Protein bar(s) or other snacks
- Hand sanitizer or sanitary wipes, toilet paper, tissue
- Comb and/or brush
- Chapstick, breath mints, hand lotion, nail file
- Women: makeup and hair accessories
- Shekels for restrooms and dollar bills for small purchases
- Small flashlight for tunnels and nighttime outdoors

KEEP YOUR PASSPORT AND PERSONAL BELONGINGS SAFE

While traveling through Israel, you'll want to have your passport readily available, secure, and close—either on your person (in a belly bag) or in your purse. You'll need it for emergency medical care and checkpoints. Also, keep a *copy* of your passport in a secondary safe location (like the bottom of your suitcase); this is essential if your passport is lost or misplaced. Always keep your valuables safely on you or in your hotel safe-deposit box.

Israel is full of pickpockets in Jerusalem, especially at the Mt. of Olives, Mt. Scopus, and the Old City. You may want to leave your credit card and wallet in your room on these days and bring only necessary currency (unless you are in need of your credit card). Don't place anything of value in a back pocket or backpack; you can use a money belt under your clothes. Strap your purse or bag across your body and secure it under your arm, covering it with your hand. Pickpockets—many of whom are children—will often deliberately bump into you with a sweet apology, then quickly reach into your bag and take their loot. Be alert and stay with your group at all times. With these precautions, your valuables should be adequately protected.

WATER

The total solar radiation in Israel is among the highest in the world, making it essential to **stay hydrated**. Increase your normal water intake and drink small amounts of water throughout the day. Try to carry a water bottle around with you. Even though Israel's tap water is high quality and safe, it does have a high mineral content. You may prefer to buy bottled water, which is sold "chilled" on most tour buses for one dollar a bottle. Bring a few dollar bills with you daily. If you have difficulty drinking plain water, try a powdered drink mix or Mio.

SNACKS

Your body needs fuel to adapt to the new time zone and exercise regimen. Although most meals in the hotels are all-you-can-eat, long days and exercise can stimulate your appetite. You may need to eat protein and/or carbohydrate-rich healthy snacks throughout the day to keep your energy levels elevated. You'll probably want to pack something from home to munch on between meals, on the bus, or in the middle of the night. Try not to bring messy snacks that could melt or crumble all over you and those around you!

RESTROOMS

Take advantage of the time your tour guide gives you to use the restroom! If you feel like you are not being allotted enough time, let your guide know. It is not uncommon for restrooms to be out of toilet paper or paper towels. Carrying hand sanitizer and a partial toilet paper roll with you is highly recommended. Helpful hint: a toilet paper roll will fit better in your bag or purse if you pull out the cardboard tube. **Many sites in Israel have started charging anywhere between one and three shekels to use their restrooms. Make sure you carry extra one-shekel coins with you for these stops!**

SHOPPING AND SOUVENIRS

There is no lack of souvenirs for purchase across Israel! Rest assured; English is widely spoken at most shops. While you'll find endless souvenirs for sale at gift shops across Israel, often the best souvenir is an item from a site that helps tell its story. You can gather small rocks and sand from significant locations like the Dead Sea or Valley of Elah (David and Goliath), pick up a piece of Jerusalem stone or a polished marble chip from the beach at Caesarea, or even bring small bottles from home to fill with water from the Jordan River. *See other shopping tips on pp. 15, 149–150.*

JOURNALING

The accompanying journal is tailor-made for taking notes across Israel. If it's difficult for you to write fast and neat simultaneously, you may want to write on an inexpensive wire-bound notepad and transfer the most important information to your official journal later in the evening—when you have time to focus on aesthetics as well as content. Be sure to jot down the date and each site name as you go.

Journaling back at your hotel will allow you to process your spiritual insights, thereby increasing your faith. Try to make this a daily habit—in the morning or evening, whichever is less rushed for you. You can journal so many things—lessons learned, interesting new information, questions you would like answered, inspirations, prayers, Scripture, trip highlights, amusing adventures, new revelations. The ideas are endless! You want to especially journal answers to prayer and God's "surprise" blessings!

DEVOTIONAL TIMES

If you have the energy in the evenings, read about tomorrow's sites in this guide, along with their applicable scriptures. Ask the Lord to open your eyes to the significance of each site, as well as His lessons, new insights, and special blessings just for you.

If you push yourself to rise early, you can have an awesome time of prayer and worship while taking in a breathtaking sunrise, perhaps over the Mediterranean Sea, the Sea of Galilee, or the Dead Sea. Or while the sun begins to rise in Jerusalem, gaze down upon the city atop the Mt. of Olives or Mt. Scopus. This can be a moving experience—breathing in the air of the very city where our Lord suffered, died, and rose from the dead on our behalf. Our biblical heritage in this city dates back to the days of Abraham, Isaac, and Jacob; you are literally standing on "holy ground." Allow the Lord to give you a glimpse of what that means. These are moments in time that stand still, never to be forgotten.

PHOTOGRAPHY TIPS

Following a few simple guidelines will ensure great photos! A point-and-shoot or smart-phone camera is more than adequate. Here are some tips:

- **Invest in a memory card with plenty of memory.** This will facilitate high-resolution, high-quality photos.

- **Stay with the group at all times, preferably toward the front.** If you pause to take a photo, you'll quite likely end up at the back of the group or possibly even left behind! Be especially alert to stay with your group in crowded places. Save your photo-taking time for *after* the tour guide has finished his or her teaching, and make sure you know where and when to meet the group; don't linger.

- **Keep track of your photos.** When you arrive home with hundreds of photos, many will look similar and you'll likely be frustrated and confused! Since itineraries typically change for various reasons, **you will make your life much easier by writing in the times as well as the dates of each destination in your journal—as you go.** With this valuable data, you will be able to match your itinerary date and time with your camera's photo date and time (technology included in most newer cameras), provide accurate photo ID, and save yourself literally days of work and incalculable stress!

  Additionally, most of today's smart-phones, tablets, and newer cameras have built-in GPS systems which allow you to "geotag" your photographs. Geotagging helps you to keep track of your geograph-ical location through latitude and longi-tude. If you need tech support for this feature, get it before leaving home. Another way to keep track of "which photos were at which sites" is to have the first photo of each site be a sign with the site's name or the last photo of each site on the bus, showing your transition.

- **Take fewer, more intentional photos.** You'll be tempted to take a picture of almost *everything*; don't give in! You'll miss valuable teaching from your tour guide and miss precious sights and sounds—of places you may never see again. And the reality is, you'll end up *deleting* most of those photos when you return home. You never hear others say they didn't get *enough* photos—only whining over being inundated with too many photos! **Focus on photos that can't be purchased—photos that incorporate you, your fellow travelers, and new friends you meet along the way.** Limit yourself to a specific number of photos per site—perhaps fifteen or twenty; you will be forced to deliberate whether to click that button or wait for something more important. When you get home, you'll be rewarded for your self-control.

- **Take your best shot!** Some of the photos you'll appreciate the most are those where you stood back at a distance or zoomed out to include more of the surroundings. These photos provide context. On the other hand, zoom in for photos with detail—such as flowers, wildlife, or interesting faces.

- **It's all about your position.** Capture a unique perspective by stooping down low or climbing up on something (with wisdom) to shoot from above. These photos really stand out!

- **Exercise cultural discretion.** Some Israelis are not willing or able to have their photos taken; always ask permission of Orthodox Jews, Muslims, and especially military personnel (many are prohibited from having their pictures taken).

- **Outside photographers:** At some sites, like the Mt. of Olives, a local photogra-pher may take your group photo. They are usually good-quality and reasonably priced, but don't feel pressured into buying; you are under no obligation to purchase the photo.

TIPS FOR GROUP LEADERS

IF YOU ARE THE GROUP LEADER, YOU are critical to the success of the tour. You are the practical and spiritual shepherd of your tour group. You set the pace, you raise the spiritual bar, and you keep the group operating smoothly in unity and harmony. Your responsibility is to keep track of all group members, work with the tour guide to communicate instructions and protocols, and inform the group of changes in a timely fashion. Specific group leader responsibilities will differ from tour to tour, but may include the following:

■ **Pre-trip meetings:** Organize at least one meeting of the participants prior to going to Israel. This will be the beginning of group bonding and the time for tour details, expectations, and a Q & A session. Potlucks are great!

■ **Flight Prep:** Check with the travel agent the week before departure to confirm all flight meal preferences related to dietary needs. Make sure each person flying with the group has possession of his or her plane ticket at the airport.

■ **Tip allocation:** Prior to departure, your travel agent will give you tip money. Prepare cash envelopes to disperse to the appropriate parties in a timely manner (your tour guide, bus driver, and each hotel maître d' upon checking out of the hotel). Keep the tip money secure in a hotel safe. This task can be delegated to another, but you are ultimately responsible.

■ **Emergency communications:** It is immensely helpful to have at least two people in the group with working phones that are available to take calls 24/7.

■ **Hotel arrival:** Make sure each hotel has a complete and accurate room list with proper beds assigned, and everyone has his or her room key.

■ **Meeting first night in the land:** Co-lead a meeting with your tour guide at your hotel the first night. If time permits, allow for one-minute introductions. Make sure everyone has a current itinerary with pertinent phone numbers and hotel names. Name tags in plastic inserts on a lanyard are very helpful. You can also fold up a paper inside the insert with your "Personalized Group Info" from pp. 6–7 in the journal, so they will know what to do if separated from the group. Discuss the itinerary, other important information, and clearly spell out all expectations and requirements for a smooth-running, God-honoring tour.

Encourage them to **write down the date, time, and place on the "My Itinerary" pages** of the accompanying journal, which will assist them in accurately identifying their photos upon returning home. Make it clear that **you alone are the official point person** for all questions and concerns. You will direct them to the tour guide, bus driver, or other appropriate individual as needed.

■ **Wake-up alarms:** Arrange daily wake-up alarms (in collaboration with the tour guide and hotel reception). Let the group know that if they need a different wake-up time (or none at all), it is their responsibility to make alternative arrangements with the hotel reception.

■ **Punctual departure:** You are responsible for keeping the group on schedule. To get everyone on the bus on time each morning is typically a challenge. One proven method is to charge everyone one dollar each time he is late—but only up to five minutes. After five minutes, the bus departs, and the late individual(s) must take a taxi to meet up with the group. Yes, this policy is strict, but usually just one person has to take a taxi and the tour stays on schedule!

- **Adequate time for personal needs:** Work with the tour guide to ensure the group has built-in personal time after concluding teaching at each site. You may want to allot up to twenty minutes for individual needs such as taking photos, lingering at interesting displays, using the restroom, engaging in a short time of reflection or prayer, etc.

- **Tracking the group:** After each site, make sure everyone is on the bus. Assigning numbers to each member and counting off is one proven way to know if someone is missing. An additional safeguard is the "buddy system"—each person keeps track of his "buddy." The same rules as morning hotel departure can apply at the sites—one dollar for being late; catch a taxi to the next site if you are more than five minutes late.

- **Daily bus announcements:** At the end of each touring day, announce the following day's schedule: time of wake-up alarm, time of departure, and time to place their packed luggage outside of their rooms for pick-up when checking out of a hotel.

GROUP VOLUNTEERS

Group volunteers can facilitate an anointed, smooth-operating tour. These individuals need to be willing and able to execute their specific responsibilities well. You can decide if the position, number of volunteer hours, and tour budget allow a tour discount.

Worship Leader: Generally, this person is a spirit-led vocalist who plays the guitar (or another instrument) and has previously led worship. He/she would need to bring the musical instrument on tour. You would direct the worship leader regarding specific sites as well as days and times allotted for worship. At the pre-assigned times, the worship leader should check with you to confirm how much time there is for worship. Collaborate beforehand on songs. Songbooks can greatly enhance the worship time!

Prayer Facilitator: This vital role serves as the forerunner to keep the Enemy at bay, while keeping the group under God's protection, guidance, and blessing. The prayer facilitator needs to be a true prayer intercessor with leadership ability. Prayer needs would be given to this person. Optimally, the prayer coordinator would be sending out prayer requests to the group weeks before the tour begins, while drawing their attention to "Prayer Preparation" on pp. 70–71. Since concentrated prayer time before and after tour days is quite challenging, the facilitator could lead the group in prayer on the bus, first thing each morning. After this, until arrival at the first site of the day, the prayer coordinator may consider leading a faithful group of intercessors in prayer at the back of the bus.

Group Photographer: A professional photographer is awesome, but a gifted, aspiring photographer is more than adequate. This person will take many photos across Israel, focusing on shots that include group members and shots of unique, special events or experiences. Many sites across Israel lend themselves to exceptional group photos. Some of these include: Mt. of Olives, Mt. Scopus, Caesarea, Mt. of Precipice, Megiddo, Abraham's Gate at Tel Dan, Masada, Southern Steps of the Temple Mount, Western Wall plaza, in front of the Garden Tomb door, and in front of one of your hotels. **The group photographer would be responsible to upload the tour photos to a group photo share site within the first week of returning home.**

Group Videographer: This position isn't essential but very much appreciated for capturing and preserving precious trip memories, as well as providing loved ones back home with a "real-time" tour of the Holy Land. If the videographer enjoys posting on Facebook, the group participants and those back home can enthusiastically follow the trip by viewing daily posted videos.

Bus Assistants: Have different people assigned to give a two or three-minute scripture encouragement first thing each morning (especially encouraging good attitudes and thinking of others) and someone assigned to ensuring everyone is on the bus (like counting off).

Medical Assistant: If you have a doctor or nurse in the group, hopefully that person will be willing to serve as your official medical assistant, giving support to those who are injured, administering first aid, and when necessary, directing the injured party to the nearest urgent-care facility or hospital.

Rear Guard(s): Rear Guards are critical to an efficiently-run tour group. Their job is to herd the group when leaving each site, remind them of the time, and get them on the bus in a timely manner! You can count on "lost" stray members—taking photos, using the restroom, talking to a new friend, etc. Optimally, rear guards are highly organized and cognizant of time, natural motivators, and pleasant, yet firm.

Dietary Manager: Typically, several members in each tour group have food allergies, food sensitivities, gluten-intolerance, or other special dietary needs. Most hotels are already prepared for these needs. The dietary manager should be a responsible and compassionate person who will bring a written list of these individuals and their specific needs. This person might want to call the restaurant manager of each hotel before arrival and confirm with them how each need will be accommodated. *Hotels may even need to prepare special food.* When arriving at a hotel, the dietary manager should introduce themselves to the restaurant maître d' at the very first meal. Have him or her show you what foods these individuals should avoid and what foods accommodate their needs. Then promptly pass this information on to the applicable individuals.

Crisis Intervention: If you have a person who is skilled in counseling and/or coming aside others in crisis for prayer, they would be very helpful. Every tour can expect some type of unforeseen, critical need.

Laundry Organizer (optional): If you would like to have your laundry done as a group, you will need a laundry organizer. This individual needs to be highly responsible and reliable, gifted in organization, and proficient in math! The job entails the following:

- Call the laundromat the day before it needs to be done (no later than Friday morning for Sunday pick-up). Let them know the date and time of pick-up and delivery, your hotel name and phone number, and the number of people in your group. Be sure to confirm prices.

- Superclean Laundry in Jerusalem has been very reputable for groups. Their phone number is 02-566-0367.

- The day prior to "laundry day," give instructions on the bus as to how to pack the dirty clothes and what to write on each laundry bag. They should write their name, the hotel name, and their room number. Inform the group of laundry prices and suggest a two-dollar tip.

- Arrange with hotel reception where the bags should be left, which is usually at the front desk. Instruct the group to leave their bags at this location prior to tour departure the next morning.

- On the bus ride home at the end of laundry day, remind everyone to pick up their laundry at the agreed-upon location.

- When you return from touring that day, an invoice from the laundromat with individual charges should be there. Let everyone know how much they owe (including the tip) and collect money from each person that evening. Check off their names on the invoice after payment.

- Give the hotel front desk an envelope with payment for the laundromat rep. The complete invoice total including tips should be included. An accompanying brief thank you note is a considerate gesture. This can be dropped off at the front desk that evening or before tour departure the following morning.

TIPS FOR RETURNING HOME

JET LAG: FOR MOST TRAVELERS, JET lag is more of an issue upon returning home than arriving in Israel. If possible, allow yourself at least one day to do *nothing*—simply relax, sleep, and de-stress! Don't even unpack—unless you have to. Then try to adjust your sleep to your original schedule. One of the best things you can do is to take an early morning walk, allowing the early morning light exposure to penetrate your skin, helping your body adjust to your former circadian clock and morning wakeup time. Try to keep naps to a minimum.

Journal: If you didn't journal very much but want to remember your most impactful experiences, try to write them down within three days of returning home. It's amazing how fast important lessons, inspirations, and life-changing events can be forgotten!

Photo sharing: Most photo share sites do not give members the ability to download photos that have been uploaded to the site. Two great share sites that allow group members to both upload their best photos *and* download others' photos are the Cluster app (currently free) and the Zenfolio share site (a minimal fee for the group host).

Photo memories: If you procrastinate, you'll likely forget where many of your photos were taken, and you may never make the time to properly organize the photos to share with others. Additionally, your enthusiasm and zeal will diminish—along with that of your friends and family back home. Seize the moment and work while the motivation is high! Photobooks from companies like Shutterfly and Costco are easy to create and make wonderful keepsakes.

Israel—a uniquely unforgettable experience with memories that will last a lifetime!

MEDITERRANEAN COASTAL PLAIN

Every place where you set your foot will be yours:
Your territory will extend from the desert to Lebanon,
and from the Euphrates River to the Mediterranean Sea.

DEUTERONOMY 11:24

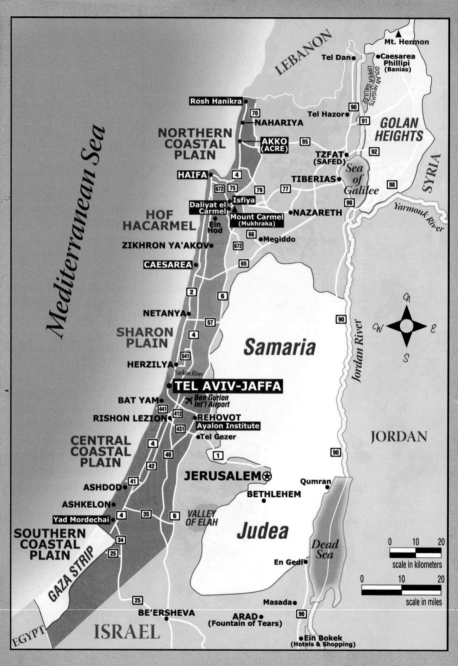

Mediterranean Sea

LEBANON

Mt. Hermon ▲

Tel Dan ●
Caesarea Phillipi (Banias) ●

Rosh Hanikra
NAHARIYA
70
Tel Hazor ●
90
91

NORTHERN COASTAL PLAIN

AKKO (ACRE)
85

TZFAT (SAFED)
92

Sea of Galilee

GOLAN HEIGHTS

SYRIA

HAIFA
4
672 75
79
TIBERIAS
77

Daliyat el Carmel
Isfiya
98
90

HOF HACARMEL

Ein Hod
Mount Carmel (Mukhraka) ▲

NAZARETH

Yarmouk River

ZIKHRON YA'AKOV
66
672
Megiddo ●

CAESAREA
65

2
6

NETANYA ●
90

SHARON PLAIN
57
4

Samaria

Jordan River

HERZILYA ●
541

Yarkon River

TEL AVIV-JAFFA

BAT YAM ●
✈ Ben Gurion Int'l Airport

441 412

JORDAN

RISHON LEZION ●
431
REHOVOT
Ayalon Institute
Tel Gezer ●

CENTRAL COASTAL PLAIN
4
40
1
90

ASHDOD ●
42

ASHKELON ●
41

JERUSALEM ⊛
Qumran ●

BETHLEHEM ●

Yad Mordechai ●
4
35
6
VALLEY OF ELAH

SOUTHERN COASTAL PLAIN
34

Judea

Dead Sea

25

GAZA STRIP

En Gedi ●

25

Masada ●

BE'ERSHEVA ●
ARAD (Fountain of Tears) ●
90

EGYPT

ISRAEL

Ein Bokek (Hotels & Shopping) ●

N
W E
S

0   10   20
scale in kilometers

0   10   20
scale in miles

View additional site info online: Akko, Haifa,
Tel Aviv, and Yad Mordechai.

Go to WalkAboutZion.com; click on Inspiration Israel.

THE MEDITERRANEAN COASTAL plain, Israel's western border, is comprised of five regions. **Most tour groups visit Tel Aviv, Jaffa, Caesarea, and Mount Carmel** (pp. 91–98).

The **Northern Coastal Plain** begins at Israel's northernmost point on the Mediterranean. It includes the grottoes of **Rosh Hanikra** (p. 88), **Nahariya, Akko** (p. 89), and the **northern suburbs of Haifa** (p. 90). **Nahariya** is the northernmost coastal city in Israel with a predominantly Jewish population of approximately 56,000. Due to its location just six miles (10 km) south of the Israel-Lebanon border, Nahariya had been a frequent target of cross-border terrorist attacks. A noteworthy destination in Nahariya is the Ghetto Fighters' House, the second Holocaust museum in the world.

Just south of the Northern Coastal Plain is the **Hof HaCarmel** region. Included in this region are **Haifa, Mt. Carmel**, the Druze communities of **Isfiya** and **Daliyat el Carmel** (p. 92), **Mount Carmel**, and **Zikhron Ya´akov** which forms the southern border of Hof HaCarmel as well as the northern border of the Sharon Plain. Zikhron Ya´akov is a small, upscale community located at the southern end of the Carmel mountain range overlooking the Mediterranean Sea. Tourists are drawn to its picturesque setting and historic city center. *Derekh HaYayin* ("Path of the Wine") is the restored main street of Zikhron Ya´akov with historic buildings, coffeehouses, and boutique shops.

Continuing south is the **Sharon Plain** which also includes **Zikchron Ya´akov**, as well as **Caesarea, Netanya**, and **Herzilya**. **Netanya**, capital of the Sharon Plain, is a beautiful coastal city of over 200,000. Many tour groups spend their first night here, prior to visiting Caesarea the following morning. The city of Netanya proudly houses several museums, galleries, and war memorials, including the *Holocaust Train Car* and *Victory Monument*. The "happening place" in Netanya is the *Inter Active Atzmaut Square* which is networked with state-of-the-art advanced technologic systems for interactive games, virtual visits, LED screens, water screens, audio and light events, live broadcasting, and activities for children including fountain water games, story time, plays, folk dancing, etc. **Herzliya**, named after Theodor Herzl, is an affluent and rapidly growing city of about 100,000, located 6 miles (10 km) north of Tel Aviv. Herzliya is recognized for its emphasis on education and its successful start-up and entrepreneurial culture. The city is home to Herzliya Studios, Israel's largest television and film studio. Situated close to the Mediterranean, visitors can enjoy its luxury hotels and beautiful ocean views.

South of the Sharon Plain is the most populated region of the Mediterranean coast, the **Central Coastal Plain**. Its northern border is the Yarkon River. Its primary cities are **Tel Aviv, Jaffa, Bat Yam, Rishon Lezion, Rehovot** (p. 97), **Ashdod**, and **Ashkelon**. **Bat Yam** is a resort city with golden beaches, just a few minutes south of Tel Aviv. Water enthusiasts can enjoy surfing, windsurfing, sailing, kayaking, and snorkeling. Bat Yam also offers a contemporary art museum, a sculpture collection, and an experiential science center for kids. **Rishon LeZion**, founded in 1882 by Jewish Russian immigrants, is Israel's fourth largest city with a population of roughly 250,000.

The **Southern Coastal Plain**, the southernmost region of the Mediterranean Coastal Plain, is predominantly comprised of the **Gaza Strip**, which borders both Israel and Egypt. This region also includes the fascinating **Yad Mordechai** kibbutz that fell to the Egyptians in May of 1948 and was re-captured by the IDF six months later.

ROSH HANIKRA (HEBREW FOR "HEAD of the grottoes") is located in the northwestern corner of Israel, on the border of Israel and Lebanon. Its white chalk cliffs offer a spectacular panoramic view of Haifa Bay, the Galilee hills, and the Mediterranean Sea.

In ancient times, Rosh Hanikra was known as the "Ladders of Tyre," the gateway in and out of Israel. It was positioned along the trade route, connecting Lebanon and Syria to the north with Israel, Egypt, and North Africa to the south. In 1949, the Israeli and Lebanese officials negotiated and sanctioned an armistice agreement at Rosh Hanikra; this agreement ended the Lebanese-Israeli conflict of the 1948 Israeli War of Independence. It was at Rosh Hanikra that the British army invaded Lebanon during both World Wars, as did Israeli forces in the late '70s and early '80s.

Nature lovers flock to Rosh Hanikra to visit its renowned grottoes that were formed by the sea's chipping away portions of the soft chalk rock over thousands of years. In 1968, a tunnel was dug slightly above the sea surface, from the shore to the natural grottoes. This tunnel facilitated the modern-day cable cars which take visitors down to the shoreline where they can explore the spectacular grottoes inhabited by bats, loggerhead sea turtles, sea birds and other diverse wildlife.

Rosh Hanikra, without a doubt, should be on your bucket list!

AKKO (ARABIC), OR ACRE (HEBREW), IS a city on the Mediterranean located at the northern limits of Haifa Bay. It is one of the oldest continuously inhabited sites in the country, home of the country's steel industry, and a renowned World Heritage Site.

Akko is a magnet for tourists. It is a city of intrigue and charm with its highwalled alleys, underground passages, and waves from the Mediterranean Sea continually crashing against its ancient walls. Visitors can experi-ence a Christian monastery, an inn with Turkish baths, fascinating museums, a lively open market, hotels near the beach, a marina, restaurants and a picturesque fishing port.

Akko is considered the holiest city of the Bahá'í Faith for which Baha'u'llah was the founder. A shrine containing his remains is located in Bahjí near Akko. The Shrine represents their "Qiblih," or "direction," that Bahá'í are directed to face while saying their daily compulsory prayers.

UNDERGROUND CRUSADER CITY

Akko is well-known as one of the primary cities of the Crusaders. Beneath its citadel and prison is the entrance to an extensive, subter-ranean Crusader city. Archaeological excava-tions have uncovered numerous halls which were built and utilized by a group called "Hospitallers Knights," of the Order of the Knights of St. John. The complex includes six halls, one recently excavated large hall, resi-dential quarters, a dining room, a market-place, remains of an ancient Gothic church, and a dungeon. The impressive Knights' Hall, which was used by the Hospitallers as a fortress more than 700 years ago, is the main hall used for concerts today.

HAIFA, WITH A POPULATION OF NEARLY 300,000, is the third largest city in Israel, after Jerusalem and Tel Aviv. Located an hour north of Tel Aviv, Haifa is partially situated on Mount Carmel. According to the Israeli Central Bureau of Statistics, its population is about 80% Jewish, 9% Arab, and the remainder primarily Druze, Bahá'í, and "nonreligious." Haifa is home to the country's largest port, Israel's only subway, an exceptionally active beach, and the Bahá'í World Center.

Haifa is a city built of workers and industry. A popular Israeli saying is, "Tel Aviv plays while Jerusalem prays. But Haifa works!" Its main facilities are the port of Haifa and an oil refinery on the bay.

For a beautiful view, drive on **Yefe Nof Street**, also known as Panorama Road. Yefe Nof curves high above the outskirts of the city, providing remarkable views day and night. On a clear day, from any of its several lookouts you can see the port below, Akko across the bay, the cliffs of Rosh Hanikra, and Lebanon at a distance.

BAHÁ'Í SHRINE AND GARDENS

Resting on the slopes of Mt. Carmel is the Bahá'í Shrine and Gardens, a UNESCO World Heritage Site. Haifa is the world center for the Bahá'í faith, a faith that originated in Iran in the nineteenth century. Three core assertions of the Bahá'í Faith, coined the "Three Onenesses," are central to its teachings. They are the "Oneness of God," the "Oneness of Religion," and the "Oneness of

Humanity." Bahá'í teaches that many great prophets have appeared throughout history to reveal divine truths; Jesus is considered to be one of these prophets.

The striking gardens are comprised of 19 concentric landscaped terraces artistically composed of flowers, small trees, waterworks and small sculptures—all surrounded by beautiful, wooded areas. These terraces can be viewed all the way from Yefe Nof Street to the picturesque German Colony. The prominent feature of the gardens is the gleaming **Shrine of the Bab** (burial site of "the Bab," forerunner of Bahá'í). The Shrine was renovated in 2011 with 11,790 gold-glazed porcelain tiles imported from the Netherlands; its brilliantly gilded dome illuminates the skyline of Haifa. Forty-five-minute tours are offered free-of-charge daily. The tours encompass 600 steps, so be sure to wear comfortable walking shoes!

The desert and the parched land will be glad; the wilderness will rejoice and blossom.
Like the crocus, it will burst into bloom; it will rejoice greatly and shout for joy.
The glory of Lebanon will be given to it, the splendor of Carmel and Sharon;
they will see the glory of the Lord the splendor of our God. ISAIAH 35:1–2

THE STUNNING MOUNT CARMEL range is approximately 4–5 miles (6.5–8 km) wide and over 1,500 ft (500 m) high. The name *Carmel* means "Vineyard of God." In ancient times, Mount Carmel thwarted armies and merchants traveling northeast to the **Jezreel Valley**. See pp. 99–100.

In the Bible, Mount Carmel denotes majestic beauty and fertility; it was a blessing to be given the "splendor of Carmel." However, for Carmel to wither was a sign of God's judgment. *"He rebukes the sea and dries it up… Bashan and Carmel wither and the blossoms of Lebanon fade"* (Nahum 1:4).

Muhraka, at the summit of Mount Carmel, is the location of the Church of the Carmelite Sanctuary and Convent. This setting is believed to be the location of the showdown between Elijah and the prophets of Baal depicted in 1 Kings 18:16–40. At that time, much of the nation was worshipping Baal—who they believed was responsible for their fertility and rainfall. *"Elijah went before the people and said, 'How long will you waver between two opinions? If the Lord is God, follow him; but if Baal is God, follow him.'"* (1 Kings 18:21). In spite of the people calling on the name of Baal from morning until evening, even pleading with self-mutilation, there was no answer.

Then Elijah rebuilt the altar of the Lord with twelve stones representing the twelve tribes of Israel. Next, he dug a trench around the altar, and poured four jars of water on the burnt offering and on the wood. Elijah did this three times.

Then he prayed: *"'…Lord, the God of Abraham, Isaac and Israel, let it be known today that you are God in Israel and that I am your servant and have done all these things at your command. Answer me, Lord, answer me, so these people will know that you, Lord, are God…' Then the fire of the Lord fell and burned up the sacrifice, the wood, the stones and the soil, and also licked up the water in the trench. When all the people saw this, they fell prostrate and cried, 'The Lord — he is God! The Lord — he is God!'"* (1 Kings 18:36–39).

In accordance with God's judgment, Elijah seized the 450 false prophets of Baal, took them down to the brook **Kishon** (which can be clearly seen from the balcony of the church), and personally slaughtered each one of them there.

ON THE SLOPES OF MT. CARMEL, JUST A FIVE-MINUTE DRIVE FROM MUHRAKA, are the Druze villages of Daliyat el-Carmel and Isfiya. *You can learn more about the Druze people on p. 39.* In 2003, Daliyat el-Carmel was merged with Isfiya to create "Carmel City." However, in 2008, the communities became separate once again.

DALIYAT EL CARMEL

Daliyat el Carmel, literally "Vine of the Carmel," was discovered by French explorer Victor Guérin in 1870. He found 400 inhabitants living primarily in adobe houses and worshipping inside a cave. Today, Daliyat el-Carmel is Israel's largest and southernmost Druze village with a population of almost 17,000.

This village is famous for its colorful market and warm hospitality. Locals host groups in their homes, serving authentic ethnic food in their traditional Druze garments while sharing captivating stories of the Druze culture. On Saturdays, many locals frequent Daliyat el-Carmel, strolling through their vibrant marketplace with dozens of shops lining the main street. Here they enjoy authentic Druze foods: sweet pastries, pita baked right on the street, olive oil, and locally-produced Labneh cheese. Also worth visiting is the Carmel Center for Druze Heritage on 8th Street. The Center is a hands-on museum dedicated to educating visitors about the Druze people, religion, and culture.

ISFIYA

Built on the ruins of a Byzantine settlement, Isfiya was also discovered by Victor Guérin. He found 600 inhabitants dwelling in old houses surrounded by profuse gardens. Today, Isfiya has a population of over 10,000. The town's inhabitants are primarily Druze, but also include roughly 10% Catholics, 5% Muslims, and even a few Jewish families due to the affordable rent.

Here you can visit the Carmel Center of Isfiya Heritage and the Promotion of Druze Women showcasing the exclusive Druze culture and the story of Isfiya spanning the last 100 years. The presentation includes personal stories of the village pioneer as well as the historical progression of status among Druze women. Visitors can also view an ancient olive press which is located in a cave in order to preserve the quality of both the olive oil and all of the tools used for oil production. A guide is available to provide an explanation about the past and present olive oil industry; the presentation ends with sampling the olive oil.

NATIONS AND FLAVORS
An authentic culinary and cultural experience of Druze hospitality

- Begin with a walk through the old alleys and the village of Isfiya.
- Join a Druze family in their *madpa* (guest home).
- Savor an enormous, all-you-can-eat meal featuring lamb kebab.
- Enjoy pita, hummus, salads, stuffed grapeleaves, baklava, & more.
- Listen to a guide's fascinating accounts and stories of the Druze people.

Request one of the two large homes with breathtaking views of the Jezreel Valley!
Phone: 972-4-839-0125 or 972-52-453-5100 ■ www.el-carmel.co.ii

Then Herod went from Judea to Caesarea and stayed there... On the appointed day Herod, wearing his royal robes, sat on his throne and delivered a public address to the people. They shouted, "This is the voice of a god, not of a man." Immediately, because Herod did not give praise to God, an angel of the Lord struck him down, and he was eaten by worms and died. But the word of God continued to spread and flourish. ACTS 12:19, 21–24

DURING THE TIME OF YESHUA, THE Roman city of *Caesarea Maritima* (Caesarea "by the Sea") functioned as Judea's capital. Herod the Great built Caesarea into one of the largest cities of the Roman world and named it after his patron, Augustus Caesar. In AD 6, Caesarea became the seat of the Roman governors.

The **Caesarea Harbor**, built using materials that would allow concrete to harden underwater, spanned 40 acres and originally held 300 ships. Here, the remains of a two-level building on the harbor reveal the home of a governor, very likely inhabited at one time by Pontius Pilate.

The **Hippodrome**, built right next to the water, was a popular stadium for chariot races and other athletic competitions; it could seat up to 38,000 people.

With a seating capacity of about 4,000, the **Caesarea Theater** was utilized for 500 years. Initially, classic Greek and Roman plays were presented, and later pantomime. The theater has undergone numerous renovations and is a popular Israeli venue today.

The **Aqueduct** (photo to the left) was built in the first century BC and was expanded by the Romans in the second century AD to transport spring water almost 10 miles (16 km) from the foot of Mount Carmel to Caesarea.

Caesarea is cited frequently in the book of Acts. It was the home of both Cornelius the centurion (Acts 10:1) and Philip the Evangelist (Acts 21:8). Also, the apostle Paul was imprisoned here for two years; this is where he made his convincing appeal to King Agrippa (Acts 23:23–Acts 24).

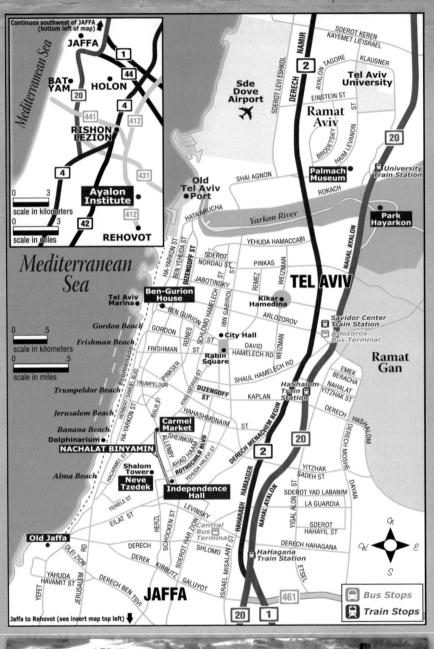

Tel Aviv

I came to the exiles who lived at Tel Aviv... EZEKIEL 3:15

AT THE BEGINNING OF THE 1900s, Tel Aviv was just a sand dune on the outskirts of the ancient port of Jaffa. In 1909, that sand dune became a city; it was founded by sixty Jewish families—including the family of David Ben-Gurion. Tel Aviv became the first all-Jewish city in the world and Israel's second largest city, after Jerusalem. The city was initially named *Ahuzat Bayit*, or "Homestead," and was changed to *Tel Aviv* in 1910. The new name was derived from Ezekiel 3:15. In the Bible, *Tel* denotes "antiquity" or "ruins" and *Aviv* speaks of "spring" or "newness of life." Tel Aviv's flag and city arms include Scripture from Jeremiah 31:4: "*I* [God] *will build you up again and you will be rebuilt.*" In 1948, since Jerusalem was occupied by Jordan, Tel Aviv became the temporary capital of Israel.

In 1914, the Jews of Tel Aviv experienced an enormous setback under Ottoman rule; 16,000 Jews were evicted to Egypt. This event was known as the "Tel Aviv Expulsion." However, one year later—following the defeat of the Turks in World War 1, the British conquered Israel and allowed the Jews to return to Tel Aviv.

When David Ben-Gurion proclaimed the re-establishment of Israel in 1948, he declared Tel Aviv the temporary capital of Israel. Tel Aviv experienced considerable growth from Jewish refugees during this time. Just two years later, Tel Aviv and Jaffa were merged into one single municipality known as "Tel Aviv-Jaffa" with a population of 200,000.

Today, Tel Aviv has a population of approximately 440,000, and is known as "the happening place" in Israel. Tel Aviv not only hosts 86 foreign embassies, it also serves as the national seat of the Stock Exchange and the Diamond Exchange, while being home to the Israel Philharmonic Orchestra, the University of Tel Aviv, and the Shalom Tower—Israel's tallest building. Tel Aviv is recognized as the industrial center of Israel with the highest standard of living in the country. It is known for its technology, textiles, clothing, chemicals, metal working, motor vehicles, and electronic equipment.

Tourists are invited to enjoy Tel Aviv's beautiful, clean beaches, nightclubs, museums, plentiful shopping, world-class entertainment, and wide array of restaurants.

NOTABLE SITES IN AND AROUND TEL AVIV

INDEPENDENCE HALL IS HOUSED IN ONE OF Tel Aviv's first buildings. Meir Dizengoff, Tel Aviv's first mayor, was its first resident. In 1930, after his wife's death, Meir founded an art museum in his home in her memory.

On May 14, 1948, the day before the British Mandate in "Palestine" was to come to an end, members of the Provisional State Council assembled in the museum and signed the Israeli Declaration of Independence. On that day, David Ben-Gurion, then leader of the Zionist movement, sat behind the table and proclaimed the establishment of the new, official Jewish State of Israel. The Hall is still preserved as it was on that remarkable day. That same year, a scroll was signed announcing the establishment of the Independence Hall Museum, under the sponsorship of the Eretz-Israel Museum in Tel-Aviv.

If possible, include Independence Hall in your itinerary. The stories leading up to Israel's independence are poignant and inspirational. Tours are available.

Note: The original Independence Hall will be closed for extensive renovations for several years. Its activities have been relocated to a nearby, temporary visitor center at the Shalom-Mayer Tower. Reservations can be made by phone or email. Phone: 972-3-510-6426; Email: res@ihi.org.il

Tel Aviv's **BEN-GURION HOUSE** was the personal family residence of Israel's first Defense and Prime Minister, David Ben-Gurion. Building began in 1929, expansion in 1946, and renovation in 1960. David and his wife Paula lived in this house until Ben-Gurion retired in 1953—at which time, they resettled in a kibbutz in Sde Boker in the Negev.

The house today is a historic museum, looking just like it did during Ben-Gurion's occupancy. Original furniture, memorabilia, and historical documents speak to the simplicity of Israel's most powerful politician. Visitors can see the simplicity of Israel's most powerful politician through the original furniture, memorabilia, and historical documents. One captivating room served as the "command center" of Ben-Gurion's communication with his chief of staff, Moshe Dayan. From this room, Ben-Gurion received battlefield operation updates.

Also of special interest is a four-room library of over 20,000 books in ancient Greek, Latin, English, Hebrew, French, Turkish, German, Russian and other languages. The library's content is primarily focused on Zionism, history, and various cultures and religions. Also included is an awesome collection of diverse Hebrew Bibles.

In his will, Ben-Gurion bequeathed his home to the State of Israel with a request that it be utilized as a "Reading, Reviewing and Research Center." In 1977, three years after his death, the house was opened to the public for this purpose, as well as to commemorate the legacy of this venerated man.

Visitors at the Ben-Gurion House can experience a sense of the events leading to the State of Israel and the private world of the man known as the "Father of the State of Israel." The museum is open to the public free of charge. Address: 17 Ben-Gurion Blvd., Tel Aviv; Phone: 972-3-522-1010

The **PALMACH MUSEUM** of Tel Aviv is well-known for its impactful presentation of the Palmach, Israel's elite fighting force of the Haganah. In 1920, the Haganah became "Palestine's" national military defense force to secure the Zionist settlement in Israel. The Palmach was established in 1941. By 1948, it consisted of over 2,000 men and women in three fighting units, along with supporting aerial, naval, and intelligence.

The Palmach Museum is an "experiential museum, covering the Palmach legacy through the stories of individuals and groups."

Visitors to the museum become part of the Palmach story—from its inception in 1941 through its conclusion following the 1948 War of Independence. The manner of presentation is "an account of a fascinating personal story accompanied by three-dimensional decor, films, and various effects incorporating documentary materials... The tour commences and ends in the memorial hall for Palmach warriors who died fighting for the establishment of the State of Israel."

Visitors must contact the museum several weeks in advance to secure a place in one of their tours. Address: 10 Lebanon Street, Tel Aviv; Phone: 972-3-545-9800; Email: hapalmach@walla.com

The fascinating **AYALON INSTITUTE** In the city of Rehovot, approximately twenty minutes southeast of Tel Aviv, has been featured on PBS. The institute was a kibbutz (communal living settlement) built in 1945 to disguise an underground bullet factory used by the Haganah defense forces. Kibbutz members ran a 24-hour laundry service that functioned as a cover for the factory; the bullet factory operated under complete secrecy for three years, from 1945-1948.

The Ayalon Institute is a tribute to the forty-five brave men and women who risked their lives under the close watch of the British, while laboring tediously in an unbearable and extremely dangerous work environment. In the end, the factory manufactured more than four million, 9mm bullets for Sten submachine guns, the personal weapons of the Palmach fighters. The Ayalon Institute was a significant contributor to the successful establishment of the State of Israel. Guided tours of the kibbutz and underground factory must be arranged in advance. The tour includes the laundry room, the radiation room, the bullet-testing room, the secret entrance under the washing machine, a reconstructed dining room, an audiovisual show, and more. Address: David Fikes St 1, Rehovot; Phone: 972-8-940-6552; Email: ayalon@shimur.org.il

*Peter sent them all out of the room; then he got down on his knees and prayed.
Turning toward the dead woman, he said, "Tabitha, get up."
She opened her eyes, and seeing Peter, she sat up... This became known all over Joppa,
and many people believed in the Lord. ACTS 9:40–42*

THE QUAINT BIBLICAL TOWN OF *Joppa* (Greek), with its labyrinth of homes and meandering alleyways, is today known as *Jaffa* (Hebrew). Jaffa has a population of about 46,000. Jaffa's harbor is one of the oldest continually-functioning harbors in the world, used for roughly 7,000 years. Today, only small fishing boats and private yachts line the harbor. Joppa is mentioned several times in the Bible. Cedars were floated from Phoenicia to Joppa and then transported to Jerusalem for the construction of King Solomon's temple (2 Chronicles 2:16). Jonah boarded a ship in Joppa and sailed to Tarshish to flee from the Lord (Jonah 1:3). Peter raised Tabitha from the dead in Joppa and stayed at the house of Simon the Tanner (Acts 9:36–43). Jaffa's Church of St. Peter is traditionally considered the site of Peter's vision as described in Acts 10:9–33. While praying on the roof, he saw a vision of a large sheet filled with unclean animals (representative of gentiles) being lowered from heaven—indicating that God's desire was to reach all people, including the Gentiles. The Church, originally built in 1654 and dedicated to St. Peter, was later destroyed. The existing structure was built in the late 1800s and renovated in 1903.

LOWER GALILEE

They are demonic spirits that perform signs,
and they go out to the kings of the whole world,
to gather them for the battle on the great day of God Almighty.
Then they gathered the kings together to the place
that in Hebrew is called Armageddon.
REVELATION 16:14, 16

The Jezreel Valley may be the prophesied location of the gathering of the armies for the end times battle.

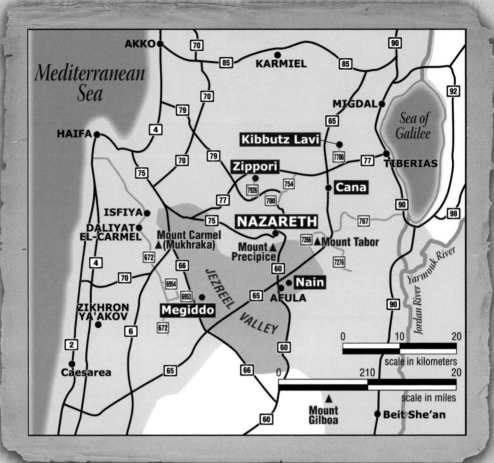

THE LOWER GALILEE IS A BEAUTIFUL, tranquil region within northern Israel. It consists of low mountain ranges and hills, as well as lush green valleys. The Lower Galilee is bordered by the beautiful and fertile Jezreel Valley to the south; the Upper Galilee to the north, the Jordan River and the Sea of Galilee to the east; and the Northern Coastal Plain to the west.

Much of Israel's produce comes from this region, especially from the Jezreel Valley and the Beit She'an Valley. Several sites (Beit She'an, Belvoir Castle, Sachne, Beit Alfa, Mt. Gilboa, and Ein Harod) are technically part of either the Lower Galilee or the Jezreel Valley regions. However, to simplify travel routes, they can be found in Chapter 9—*From Galilee to Jerusalem.*

The Jezreel Valley (also known as the "Great plain of Megiddo" and the "Valley of Armageddon") is Israel's largest valley, covering over 141 square miles (227 square km). The Valley of Jezreel served as an ancient trade route between the Jordan Valley and the coastal plain. The book of Revelation refers to Armageddon as the gathering place of armies for the end time events.

Jezreel was the capital of the northern kingdom of Israel under King Ahab. The first son of the prophet Hosea was named Jezreel, as a reminder of the bloodshed at Jezreel by which King Jehu came into power. "*The LORD said to Hosea, 'Call him Jezreel, because I will soon punish the house of Jehu for the massacre at Jezreel, and I will put an end to the kingdom of Israel'*" (Hosea 1:4).

> *Then they gathered the kings together to the place that in Hebrew is called Armageddon.*
> **REVELATION 16:16**

TEL MEGIDDO OVERLOOKS JEZREEL Valley, a flat, triangular basin between the hills of the Lower Galilee and the hills of Samaria. A *tel* is an archaeological mound from an ancient city. *Megiddo* means "rendezvous or place of troops." The word ***Armageddon*** comes from *Har* ("mountain") and *Megiddo*. This site has faced more battles and bloodshed than any other place on earth, primarily due to its unique, strategic position overlooking the **Via Maris**—a principal route used for international travel.

Megiddo was inhabited continuously from 3,000–300 BC, then abandoned during the Persian rule in 5 BC. Over the years, archaeologists have unearthed 25 layers of settlements, one built on top of another. The layers can be seen behind the **round altar** on the lowest level—the first of 17 temples erected over a period of 2,000 years (photo above). The Megiddo site was a prominent "high place" where the fertility god *Baal* and his "mistress" *Asherah* were worshiped.

Chariots were one of the key instruments of war during King Solomon's reign in the tenth century BC. He rebuilt Megiddo as a royal city with an abundance of **horse stables**. Megiddo was one of his "chariot cities" alluded to in 1 Kings 10:26. In 600 BC, King Josiah was slain by the Egyptians at Megiddo (2 Kings 23:29).

On Megiddo's south side is a large pit, 23 ft (7 m) deep, which was used in the eighth century BC as a **grain silo** for King Jeroboam II. Two narrow flights of stairs lead to the bottom of the pit. This silo could have held over 12,000 bushels of grain.

Megiddo also has a massive **underground water system** (left) that is believed to have been built by King Ahab 2,800 years ago. There are 183 stairs that lead down to a spring under bedrock. This water source was the sole source of water for Megiddo; it allowed its inhabitants to survive long sieges. Its barred and camouflaged underground entrance helped protect the water supply.

He went to Nazareth, where he had been brought up, and on the Sabbath day he went into the synagogue, as was his custom. He stood up to read, and the scroll of the prophet Isaiah was handed to him. Unrolling it, he found the place where it is written: "The Spirit of the Lord is on me, because he has anointed me to proclaim good news to the poor. He has sent me to proclaim freedom for the prisoners and recovery of sight for the blind, to set the oppressed free, to proclaim the year of the Lord's favor."
LUKE 4:16–19, NKJV

THE TOWN OF NAZARETH SITS ON A crest north of the Jezreel Valley. It is divided into **Lower Nazareth**, (home to around 60,000 Arabs) and Upper Nazareth, known as **Nazareth Illit** (home to over 40,000 Jewish residents).

After about two to four years in Egypt, Jesus spent His youth in Nazareth. At about age 30, he moved to Capernaum and returned twice to Nazareth to teach in the synagogue, but He was rejected both times.

Nazareth Village, less than a half-mile (800 m) away from Jesus' childhood home, is located in the lower portion of Nazareth. It is a populare tourist site where visitors can have a taste of the daily life that Jesus would have experienced. Nazareth Village has recreated workshops, farms, and houses that were built using techniques that would have been used in the first century. Men, women, and children are dressed in period costume as they spin and weave yarn, bake bread, operate wine presses, engage in woodwork, till the soil, harvest, and even herd sheep and goats. Visit www.NazarethVillage.com or call 972 4-645-6042.

Mount Precipice, at the foot of Lower Nazareth, offers incredible views of the Jezreel Valley, Nazareth, and Mount Tabor (p 106). Mount Precipice is known as "the Leaping Mountain." This may be the mountain from which Jesus disappeared "in the midst of them" while being pursued by an angry mob intending to throw Him down a cliff.

In the sixth month of Elizabeth's pregnancy, God sent the angel Gabriel to Nazareth, a town in Galilee, to a virgin pledged to be married to a man named Joseph, a descendant of David. The virgin's name was Mary. The angel went to her and said, "Greetings, you who are highly favored! The Lord is with you.... You will conceive and give birth to a son, and you are to call him Jesus." LUKE 1:26–31

THE **CHURCH OF THE ANNUNCIATION,** the largest church in the Middle East, is located in the center of modern Nazareth. It was built over the site believed to be the home of Mary, mother of Jesus, as well as the loca-

tion where the angel Gabriel appeared and announced to her that she would give birth to Jesus—while still a virgin (Luke 1:26–38). The lower church encompasses the *Grotto (or Cave) of the Annunciation,* possibly the remains of Mary's childhood home.

MARY'S WELL is just down the street from the Church of the Annunciation. The well sat on top of an underground spring that for centuries, until 1966, was a gathering place for local Arabs. The present structure

was renovated twice, in 1967 and 2,000. It is essentially a modern water trough built over the ancient trough.

The **SYNAGOGUE CHURCH,** located in the center of the Nazareth marketplace, is traditionally believed to be built on top of the original location of the synagogue where Jesus read from Isaiah 61, declaring that He was the Messiah foretold by the prophet Isaiah—the proclamation that angered the Jews so much that they chased Him from the city.

The **CHURCH OF ST. JOSEPH** is next to the Church of the Annunciation. Tradition places the church over the carpentry work-shop of Joseph and the home of the "holy family." Below the church is an underground crypt with caverns (likely used to store grain, wine, and oil) and a pit with a mosaic floor, possibly a first-century Chris-tian baptistry.

ZIPPORI WAS A PROMINENT ROMAN and Byzantine city, as well as the capital and center of Galilean life. It was a sprawling, sophisticated city with numerous multi-story structures as well as two marketplaces on paved and colonnade-lined streets.

As a predominantly Jewish city, the Talmud records a *Yeshiva* or "Jewish school" and 18 synagogues in Zippori; however, only one has been uncovered. The first *Mishnah*, the written Jewish oral law, originated in the city of Zippori.

Since both Joseph and Jesus were referred to as *tektons* in the Scriptures ("carpenters, stonemasons, and metalworkers" according to Strong's Concordance), they were likely involved in the rebuilding of Zippori. Approximately 10,000 tektons came from surrounding villages for this enormous project. Archaeology indicates Zippori had a population of about 40,000 during the time of Jesus, roughly 100 times the size of Jesus' hometown of Nazareth.

Zippori has unearthed numerous notable artifacts and structures. One of these is the second-century **Roman Theater** carved into the hillside which could seat 4,500 patrons. The theater served only the pagan residents of the city, since the Jewish citizens shunned its performances which they viewed as corrupt.

Elevated on a hillside overlooking the Roman Theater is a **Crusader/Ottoman fortress** (photo below). The upper segment of the fortress was utilized as a school from the early 1900s through 1948. Today the fortress is a museum of archaeological findings.

Another notable discovery, just east of the fortress, is the **Dionysus Building**. This building encloses a large mosaic floor made up of mostly mythological scenes of *Dionysus*, the god of wine and socializing, as well as the gods *Pan* and *Hercules*. The most famous finding in all Zippori is in the center of this mosaic—an impression of a young lady, possibly intended to be Venus. This lady (above) has been dubbed the "**Mona Lisa of the Galilee.**"

What Jesus did here in Cana of Galilee was the first of the signs through which he revealed his glory; and his disciples believed in him. JOHN 2:11

THE TOWN OF CANA, LOCATED FIVE MILES NORTHEAST of Nazareth, has a combined Muslim and Christian population of about 8,500. This is possibly the location of ancient Cana where the first two public miracles of Jesus took place. The first miracle was Jesus' turning water into wine at a wedding (John 2:1–11). At His second visit to Cana, Jesus was met by a distraught official of the court of Herod Antipas who lived 20 miles (32 km) away in Capernaum—where his son lay dying. He came to plead with Jesus for his son's life and, from Cana, Jesus healed his son (John 4:46–54). Also, one of Jesus' disciples, Nathaniel, hailed from Cana (John 21:2).

The **Franciscan Wedding Church** at Cana is a small, two-story church. Artifacts on display include several vessels, a cistern, an ancient winepress, and one of the six stone water jars that Jesus allegedly used for turning the water into wine. The Franciscan Wedding Church is a popular and inspirational venue for tour groups and individual couples to renew their wedding vows. To schedule, call 972-4-651-7011.

NAIN

THE TINY GALILEAN VILLAGE OF Nain is most likely the village referred to in the New Testament as the place where Jesus brought a widow's son back to life as he was being carried through the town gate to be buried (Luke 7:11–17). The Franciscans built a simple, rectangular church here to commemorate this miracle. Nain is located close to both Mount Tabor and Nazareth. Today, Nain is a Muslim village at the top of a steep road overlooking the Jezreel Valley.

IF YOU'D LIKE TO VISIT A WORKING kibbutz, Kibbutz Lavi is a wonderful option. The kibbutz is located on a mountain slope with views of the Sea of Galilee and Golan Heights. It is just a ten-minute drive from Tiberias.

Kibbutz Lavi was founded in 1949 by *Bnei Akiva*, a religious Zionist youth movement from Britain. Many of their members originated from a group of 10,000 German Jewish children who were saved from the Nazi regime by being transported to the United Kingdom.

Kibbutz Lavi has 600+ members. Its main sources of income are agriculture, manufacturing furniture for synagogues, and managing a popular hotel that caters to Orthodox Jews as well as other guests. The spacious and elegant Lavi Hotel, open since 1962, is operated and maintained by kibbutz members, preserving their age-old tradition of hospitality. Lavi Hotel

offers luxury in a unique, relaxing atmosphere of a rural and religious community.

Visitors are invited to stroll through the perimeter path of the kibbutz, surrounded by expansive lawns, trees, flowers, and a fish pond under a bridge. They can visit the milk shed when the cows are being milked, go horseback riding, or sit and study books in their Torah library located in the *Beit Midrash* (Jewish study hall).

MOUNT TABOR

MOUNT TABOR IS LOCATED AT THE EASTERN END OF THE JEZREEL VALLEY, 11 miles (18 km) west of the Sea of Galilee. The prophetess Deborah and Israeli general Barak camped on Mount Tabor with the Israelite army prior to attacking and defeating Sisera, the commander of the pagan Canaanite army (Judges 4–5). Named after Deborah, **Daburiyya** is an Arab village at the foot of Mount Tabor (photo bottom left).

The Franciscan **Church of the Transfiguration**, located at the summit of Mount Tabor, commemorates this event. Some believe Mount Tabor to be the location of the Transfiguration (Luke 9:28–36); others believe it to be Mount Hermon *(page 125)*, near Caesarea Philippi.

SEA OF GALILEE

Jesus went throughout Galilee, teaching in their synagogues, proclaiming the good news of the kingdom, and healing every disease and sickness among the people.

MATTHEW 4:23

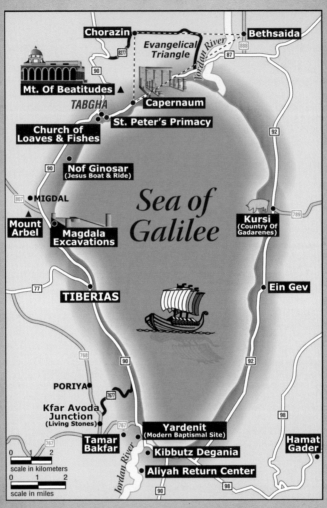

Chorazin
Evangelical Triangle
Bethsaida
Mt. Of Beatitudes
TABGHA
Capernaum
Church of Loaves & Fishes
St. Peter's Primacy
Nof Ginosar
(Jesus Boat & Ride)
MIGDAL
Sea of Galilee
Kursi
(Country Of Gadarenes)
Mount Arbel
Magdala Excavations
Ein Gev
TIBERIAS
PORIYA
Kfar Avoda Junction
(Living Stones)
Yardenit
(Modern Baptismal Site)
Tamar Bakfar
Kibbutz Degania
Aliyah Return Center
Hamat Gader

Jordan River

0 1 2
scale in kilometers
0 1 2
scale in miles

View additional site info online: Bethsaida, Chorazin, Ein Gev, and Hamat Gader,
Go to WalkAboutZion.com; click on Inspiration Israel.

THE SEA OF GALILEE IS ALSO CALLED the *Sea of Kinneret*. Kinneret means "harp," referring to the harp-shape of the Sea of Galilee, which lies roughly 700 ft (213 m) below sea level and is the second-lowest lake on earth, after the Dead Sea. It is 13 miles (21 km) long, up to 7.5 miles (12 km) wide, and 150 ft (46 m) deep.

Jesus performed His "mighty works" and laid the foundation of His ministry in the Galilee region. On the northern shores of the Sea of Galilee, the three ancient cities of Capernaum, Chorazin, and Bethsaida are known as the "Evangelical Triangle." However, these three cities were also ultimately cursed by Jesus because of their lack of faith.

"And He sent away the multitude, got into the boat, and came to the region of Magdala."
MATTHEW 15:39 (NKJV)

THE REGION OF MAGDALA, REFERRED to in Matthew 15:39, is located west of the Sea of Galilee at the foothills of Mount Arbel. All four gospels refer to a follower of Jesus called Mary Magdalene, known as "Mary from Magdala."

In 2009, as workers were digging the foundation of a retreat center, they discovered a first century synagogue and the rest is history. Magdala Excavations is one of the most visited sites in the Galilee region.

Excavations began in 2012; a complete, first century Jewish town was unearthed! The artifacts and remains indicate an influential and prosperous town built upon a successful fishing industry. Magdala's synagogue is currently the oldest excavated synagogue in the Galilee region.

Inside the synagogue is one of the most significant archaeological finds in Israel's last fifty years, the Magdala Stone. Many archaeologists believe this stone may be the earliest known artistic depiction of Second Temple Jerusalem—with intricate carvings of the seven-branched menorah and representations of the Holy of Holies.

Aside from the synagogue, Magdala Excavations encompasses mansions, three mikvahs (ritual baths), a well-designed marketplace with shops lining both sides of the main road, residential areas, and the remains of a large warehouse next to a big stone wharf.

TIBERIAS

IN 1948 AFTER ISRAEL GAINED ITS independence, many Jews migrated to Tiberias, quadrupling its population. Today, Tiberias is the capital of the Galilee region with a population of nearly 45,000. The city is renowned on several accounts:

- Tiberias was a portion of the Promised Land that was bestowed to the tribe of Naphtali.
- In AD 18, Herod Antipas, son of Herod the Great, founded Tiberias.

- Tiberias is one of the four Jewish holy cities mentioned in the Talmud. The other three holy cities are Jerusalem, Tzfat, and Hebron.
- The Sanhedrin (chief Jewish priests and elders) relocated to Tiberias from Zippori in 193 BC.
- Tiberias was home to many Jewish scholars, including those who assembled the Jerusalem Talmud in AD 400.

"The roar of battle will rise against your people,
so that all your fortresses will be devastated—
as Shalman devastated Beth Arbel on the day of battle,
when mothers were dashed to the ground with their children."
HOSEA 10:14

MOUNT ARBEL, LOCATED IN THE lower Galilee region near Tiberias, towers at about 1,250 ft (380 m) above sea level. On a clear day, the view atop the Arbel cliffs is spectacular encompassing almost all of the Galilee region and some of the Golan Heights.

The summit can be reached by either driving or hiking. Trails, which are fairly easy to climb, lead to caves and an ancient synagogue that once served a Jewish community.

The only verse in the Bible that mentions Arbel is Hosea 10:14 above, attesting to its bloody history. Due to its close proximity to the city of Migdal (biblical *Magdala*), Jesus is believed to have preached and performed miracles at the foot of Mount Arbel.

*"When they had crossed over, they landed at Gennesaret. And when the men
of that place recognized Jesus, they sent word to all the surrounding country.
People brought all their sick to him and begged him to let the sick just
touch the edge of his cloak, and all who touched it were healed."*
MATTHEW 14:34-36

NOF GINOSAR KIBBUTZ, SITUATED ON the western shore of the Sea of Galilee, is the ancient historical site of *Gennesaret*. Today, it is the home to the **Yigal Allon Museum and Tourist Center** which encompasses the "**Jesus Boat**" exhibit, a large gift shop, a cafeteria, and a comfortable rest area. Past the center is the boat landing where pilgrims depart on their **boat trips across the Galilee**.

The "Jesus Boat" is a popular destination. As boat conservator Orna Cohen stated, this is a wonderful opportunity to view *"the only authentic object from the period of Jesus on display in its natural habitat."* This kind of boat was referred to approximately fifty times in the gospels. It would have been an integral part of the life and ministry of Jesus. Hence, its name: "Jesus Boat."

Signage in the museum reads, *"During the drought of 1986, the receding waters of the Sea of Galilee yielded hints of a wooden object embedded in the silt a few hundred meters south of Kibbutz Ginosar. After 2,000 years, the ancient vessel emerged from the depths of the sea into the light of day...."*

Archeologists believe the boat was used in the first century by local villagers for fishing and transport. Numerous repairs, the reuse of timbers, and twelve types of wood (including cedar from Lebanon, sycamore, laurel, and tabor oak) indicate a boat that operated over many years and an owner who lived a modest lifestyle.

MOUNT OF BEATITUDES

And seeing the multitudes, He went up on a mountain, and when He was seated,
His disciples came to Him. Then He opened His mouth and taught them, saying.
Blessed are the poor in spirit, for theirs is the kingdom of heaven.
Blessed are those who mourn, for they shall be comforted.
Blessed are the meek, for they shall inherit the earth.
Blessed are those who hunger and thirst for righteousness, For they shall be filled.
Blessed are the merciful, for they shall obtain mercy.
Blessed are the pure in heart, for they shall see God.
Blessed are the peacemakers, for they shall be called sons of God.
Blessed are those who are persecuted for righteousness' sake,
For theirs is the kingdom of heaven.

MATTHEW 5:1–10, NKJV

LOCATED ON A SMALL HILL OVERLOOKING THE SEA OF GALILEE, THE MOUNT of Beatitudes is the traditional site of Jesus' famous *Sermon on the Mount*. The octagonal, Byzantine-style Catholic Church of the Beatitudes stands tall on the hillside's summit. Each of its eight sides artistically displays one of the eight Beatitudes in a stained glass window. The beautiful gardens that overlook the Sea of Galilee and the landscape where Jesus preached create a tranquil atmosphere for prayer and meditation on the Word of God. A favorite of tourists is to walk down the hillside, rest for a Bible teaching part-way down, and end at the road across from nearby Capernaum.

CHURCH OF THE MULTIPLICATION OF LOAVES AND FISHES

THE CHURCH OF THE MULTIPLICATION OF LOAVES AND FISHES COMMEMO-rates the account of Jesus' feeding the 5,000 as described in Mark 6:30–44. Its altar is built on the stone where many believe Jesus stood when He blessed the five loaves and two fishes and then performed the miracle of feeding 5,000 men plus numerous women and children. A restored mosaic of two fish next to a basket of loaves adorns the front of the altar (photo below).

This church is a "daughter-house" of Mt. Zion's Dormition Abbey, a stately monastery located right outside of Jerusalem's Old City.

ST. PETER'S PRIMACY

When they had finished eating, Jesus said to Simon Peter, "Simon son of John, do you love me more than these?" "Yes, Lord," he said, "you know that I love you." Jesus said, "Feed my lambs." Again Jesus said, "Simon son of John, do you love me?" He answered, "Yes, Lord, you know that I love you." Jesus said, "Take care of my sheep." The third time he said to him, "Simon son of John, do you love me?" Peter was hurt because Jesus asked him the third time, "Do you love me?" He said, "Lord, you know all things; you know that I love you." Jesus said, "Feed my sheep." JOHN 21:15–17

ST. PETER'S PRIMACY IS A FRAN-ciscan church located quite close to the Church of the Multiplication of the Loaves and Fishes. St. Peter's memorializes Jesus' asking Peter three times, "*Do you love me?*" and Peter's three-fold response that seemed to cancel out his three-fold denial of Jesus the night before His crucifixion. This dialogue, which directly followed the miraculous catch of 153 fish (John 21:1–14), was the third appearance of Jesus after His resurrection.

CAPERNAUM

When Jesus heard that John had been put in prison, he withdrew to Galilee. Leaving Nazareth, he went and lived in Capernaum, which was by the lake in the area of Zebulun and Naphtali — to fulfill what was said through the prophet Isaiah: "Land of Zebulun and land of Naphtali, the Way of the Sea, beyond the Jordan, Galilee of the Gentiles — the people living in darkness have seen a great light; on those living in the land of the shadow of death a light has dawned." From that time on Jesus began to preach, "Repent, for the kingdom of heaven has come near." MATTHEW 4:12–17

LOCATED ON THE NORTHERN SHORE of the Sea of Galilee is Capernaum, the center of tax collectors during the time of Jesus. The name *Capernaum* is a blend of two Hebrew words: *Kefar* and *Nahum*, meaning "Village of Nahum." Today, a large octagonal Byzantine-style church is built above a house believed to be that of Simon Peter's (photo to the right).

This is the town where Jesus lived during the years of His ministry and where He chose five of His disciples. He healed everyone who was sick, including Peter's mother-in-law and the paralytic who was lowered through a roof. Capernaum is also the location of the synagogue where Jesus delivered the sermon on the "bread of life" and healed the servant of the Roman centurion—the official recognized for building the synagogue. Sadly, Capernaum is one of the three cities condemned by Jesus for its lack of faith (Luke 10:15).

LIVING STONES

IF YOUR GROUP IS VISITING THE Galilee area, you have a unique opportunity to visit the home of Richard and Carolyn Hyde, a "one-new-man" (gentile and Jew) couple of Heart of G-d Ministries. The couple welcomes tourists into their home for a dinner, fellowship, and worship with Carolyn, a messianic worship leader. They also provide Israeli dancing and a short presentation about their lives and ministry in Israel. Friday Shabbat dinners and feast celebrations are options as well.

Richard and Carolyn are located on the southwest side of the Sea of Galilee, where you can enjoy a beautiful view of the sea. Simply ask your group leader or tour operator to exchange one of the evening meals at your hotel for an evening with the "Living Stones Experience." For more information, visit www.heartofg-d.org or call 972-54-660-5408.

TAMAR BAKFAR

THE CAPTIVATING STORY OF EARLY settlers and their family farmstead, Galilean agriculture development, and 100 years of Zionism can be heard, seen, and experienced in the shade of a palm grove near the southern shores of the Sea of Galilee. The Tamar Bakfar Store and Visitor Center is a hidden gem and favorite of both locals and tourists.

Need authentic Israeli gifts for families and friends back home? Tamar Bakfar is a cornucopia of colors and scents. A wealth of products grown and manufactured in the surrounding Galilee area are available: various varieties of sweet and juicy dates, natural palm honey, dried fruits, fresh spices, aromatic tea infusions, chocolates, boutique wines, fine olive oil, natural cosmetics, and a wide selection of choice gifts and baskets that can also be ordered and shipped to you. Ask your tour bus leader if you have time for a short stop! Contact Tamar Bakfar by phone at 972-50-374-8615 or by email at tamar-bakfar2@gmail.com.

DEGANIA, THE FIRST KIBBUTZ IN ISRAEL, was established by twelve Zionist pioneers in 1910 while Israel was under Ottoman rule. The kibbutz was created for the purpose of communal living—their goal was to actively live out equality, freedom, and democracy.

Today, Kibbutz Degania has between 500 and 600 members. Most of what began as communal living is now privatized. Communal meals today include only a lunch served on weekdays and a festive meal served on the Sabbath and holiday eves. Degania manages a clothing store, a laundry service, a grocery store, an electrician's shop, a metalwork shop, and a bicycle repair shop.

As a side note, the second child to be born in Degania was **Moshe Dayan**, the legendary Israeli military leader and politician, whose famous eye patch made him a symbol of Israel.

Strolling the kibbutz grounds gives you a feel of early kibbutz life. You can visit the **Gordon House Museum** or the **Founder's Museum,** stay at their lovely guesthouse, dine at their top-rated **Restaurant 1910,** or visit the popular **Galita Chocolate Farm.** At Galita, you can watch an informative, 15-minute film on the history and origin of Galita chocolates, participate in a 45-minute workshop, and make your own unique, delectable chocolate creation. Phone: 972-2-534-7650

KURSI NATIONAL PARK

KURSI, ON THE EASTERN SHORE OF the Sea of Galilee, is referred to as the "country of the Gadarenes" in the Bible. The national park encompasses the ruins of a fifth to sixth century AD restored church and monastery. Kursi is believed to be the site where Jesus found the demoniac, drove out his demons, and sent them into a herd of swine that "ran violently down a steep place into the sea and were choked in the sea." One Talmud text lists towns with pagan worship during the time of Jesus; Kursi (a town of Gentiles) is included in that list. This inclusion would make sense as pigs were raised only on Gentile farms. This site could have possibly been where Jesus disembarked from the boat to heal the madman (Luke 8:26-27).

ALIYAH RETURN CENTER

IF YOU HAVE TIME, BE SURE TO VISIT the Aliyah Return Center (ARC) where Galilean history is still being made! The ARC is located just south of the southern tip of the Sea of Galilee (in the community of Beit Zera), along the shores of the Jordan. ARC is a 14-acre (5.7 ha) property being developed by local and international people of faith, in partnership with Israel's Jewish Agency.

They are currently housing over 100 Israelis in need, both Arabs and Jews, including IDF lone soldiers. ARC practically shows God's love to local Israelis, while building lasting relationships. They provide food, clothing, shelter, and job training. The dedicated ARC staff believe they are fulfilling the biblical mandate to raise ambassadors and advocates for Israel, develop strategic, global kingdom partnerships, and rally the community of faith to be part of the biblical plan for the people of Israel to return to their land and thrive.

ARC welcomes short-term and long-term volunteers. Call ARC at 972-50-326-8850 or e-mail at watchaliyah@gmail.com.

BLESS LOCAL BELIEVERS AND BE BLESSED!

*Need a central place for your family or small group to stay
while exploring the Galilee and northern Israel?*

EXPERIENCE THE "SHALOM OF THE Galilee" at the **Galilee Getaway** in a serene Galilean village on the Poriyah mountain ridge near Tiberias. Hosts Yosef and Gabriela Danieli would love nothing more than to

with two single beds, and a sleeper couch for two. Amenities include a fully-equipped kitchen, a cozy living and dining area, a bathroom with jacuzzi, a spacious balcony with a spectacular view as well as a gas grill, AC, Wi-Fi, TV, and more.

spoil you for your stay in the Galilee region. Their beautiful home offers breathtaking views of the Sea of Galilee, the Jordan Valley, the Golan Heights and the Gilead mountains. Two accommodations are available, each with a separate entrance providing complete privacy.

Experience your visit from an insider's perspective and get to know the people of the land. Yosef, a native Israeli and Messianic believer, is a dynamic author and teacher of the Hebraic/Jewish roots of Christianity, the biblical and historical sites of Israel, and the political climate of Israel. Gabriela is a gifted ceramic artisan, songwriter, and worship leader. She also plays the harp beautifully and produces worship CDs.

The **Moroccan Hideaway** is a romantic studio apartment surrounded by a beautiful, tropical garden. Its unique Moroccan décor with warm lighting creates a serene atmosphere. The Moroccan Hideaway is the perfect retreat for a couple, a family, or a group up to four individuals. This apartment features

The tranquil **Lake View Escape** is a spacious rooftop apartment ideal for a couple, family, or small group up to six. This beautifully-decorated space features a private bedroom with a queen-size bed, an open loft area

a queen-size bed and sleeper couch for two (separated by a curtain partition), a living and dining area, a convenient kitchenette, a bathroom with a shower, a garden sitting area, AC, Wi-Fi, and TV.

For more information, visit www.GalileeGetaway.com or call 972-52-802-1701.

THE L'CHAIM EXPERIENCE

*Bless Holocaust Survivors
and Be Blessed!*

*Sponsored by the Israel Now Project, a non-profit foundation. in cooperation with
Israeli Helping Hands Coalition and the Radiant Group.*

The remaining 120,000+ Holocaust Survivors living in Israel
today will only be with us for a few more years; their average age
is 88 years old. These resilient souls have survived unspeakable
suffering and loss, which they will carry with them to their grave.
L'Chaim in Hebrew is a toast meaning "to life." You can help
bring life, joy, and hope to some of these precious people.

COMING SOON:
An opportunity for tour groups to interact with local Galilean Holocaust Survivors.

Plans are in the works for shared meals and fellowship twice a week.

TENTATIVELY, THIS WILL ENCOMPASS:

- A dinner and fellowship shared between a tour group and local Holocaust Survivors
- A brief introduction to the Holocaust and Israeli Holocaust Survivors today

- A Survivor testimony
- Israeli music and folk dancing
- An opportunity to interact with and "adopt" a Survivor as part of your extended family

Email Joan@IsraelNowProject.com for updates and reservations.
Visit www.IsraelNowProject.com

GOLAN HEIGHTS & UPPER GALILEE

But I will bring Israel back to their own pasture, and they will graze on Carmel and Bashan (Golan); their appetite will be satisfied on the hills of Ephraim and Gilead. In those days, at that time," declares the Lord, "search will be made for Israel's guilt, but there will be none, and for the sins of Judah, but none will be found, for I will forgive the remnant I spare.

JEREMIAH 50:19–20

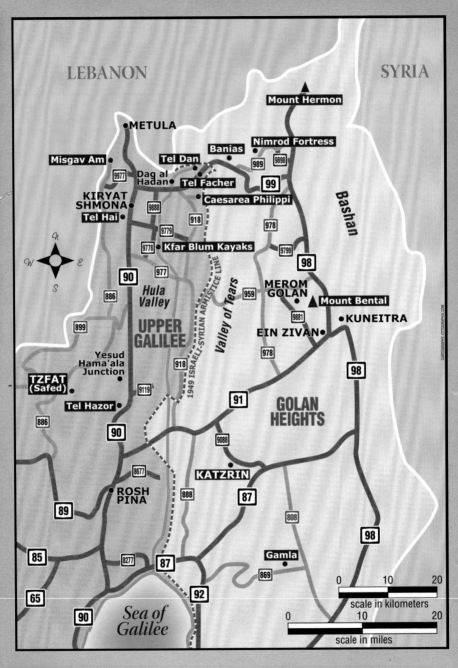

LEBANON

SYRIA

▲ Mount Hermon

● METULA

Banias
Nimrod Fortress

Misgav Am
Tel Dan
989
9898

9977
Dag al
Hadan
Tel Facher
99

KIRYAT
SHMONA
Caesarea Philippi

Tel Hai
9888
918
978

9779

9778
Kfar Blum Kayaks
9799

Bashan

90
977
98

886
Hula
Valley
959
MEROM
GOLAN
Mount Bental
KUNEITRA

899
UPPER
GALILEE
9881

EIN ZIVAN

Yesud
Hama'ala
Junction
918
978

TZFAT
(Safed)
9119
91
GOLAN
HEIGHTS

Tel Hazor
886
9088

90
8677
KATZRIN
87

808

89
ROSH
PINA
888

98

85
8277
Gamla

65
92
869

90
Sea of
Galilee
87

1949 ISRAELI-SYRIAN ARMISTICE LINE

Valley of Tears

CARTOGRAPHY: OTTOGRAPHIX.COM

0   10   20
scale in kilometers

0   10   20
scale in miles

**View additional site info online: Tel Facher, Tel Hai,
Misgav Am (Lebanon border), and Kfar Blum.**

Go to WalkAboutZion.com; click on Inspiration Israel.

GOLAN, OR "BASHAN" IN THE BIBLE, was one of six cities that God provided as a city of refuge for a person accused of murder. *"The Levite clans of the Gershonites were given: from the half-tribe of Manasseh, Golan in Bashan..."* (Joshua 21:27).

The Golan Heights is the region Israel captured from Syria in 1967. Its western border, the **1949 Israeli-Syrian Armistice line**, divides northern Israel into two regions—the **Upper Galilee** to the left (west) and the **Golan Heights** to the right (east). Relics of Syrian military bases and mosques can be seen scattered throughout the area.

Golan's current population base is comprised of both Druze (p. 39) and Israeli Jews. Currently 32 Jewish settlements with an estimated 20,000 settlers and an additional 22,000 Druze inhabitants reside in their respective settlements.

In biblical times, the Golan Heights was heavily forested (Ezekiel 27:5-6). Today the Golan is composed of two geologically distinct areas: the slopes of Mount Hermon and Golan Heights "proper." While the Mt. Hermon range is mostly limestone, the Golan Heights "proper" is comprised predominately of basalt and other types of volcanic rock, which form an immense plateau; it is a natural fortress created by God.

The Golan Heights is of critical importance to Israel due to its strategic location between the borders of Lebanon, Syria, and Jordan. If the Golan Heights were to be taken over by a hostile country, Haifa (one of Israel's largest cities located only 60 miles from the Golan) would be an easy target. Israel would again suffer serious repercussions as it did when the nation was under Syrian control from 1948-1967. During these years, Israelis lived in constant fear for their lives. Syrian troops randomly shot Israeli civilians in the Upper Galilee's Hula Valley, forcing children to sleep in bomb shelters at night. They further tormented Israelis by planting minefields on many of the roads in northern Israel.

To gain an appreciation of the strategic importance of the Golan Heights, visitors can partake in an affordable two-hour jeep tour of the Upper Golan where they will walk through former Syrian bunkers and experience firsthand the view that snipers had of the Israelis in the valley below. This jeep tour below is highly recommended!

NESTLED IN A MOUNTAIN IN THE lower Golan Heights, east of the Sea of Galilee, are the remains of the ancient town of Gamla known for its strong defense against the Romans in the Great Jewish Revolt of AD 66–67. The city was incredibly well-secured against invaders and completely fortified by deep **wadis** (valleys) on all sides except for its eastern side. In AD 66, Jewish rebels reinforced the weaker, eastern wall in the expectation of an anticipated Roman invasion.

In spite of Gamla's strong fortification, three Roman legions attacked the city and penetrated its defenses in just one month. Due to their strong defense, the Jews of Gamla were able to slay many of the attackers and the Romans withdrew for a period of time. However, that defeat proved to be only a temporary victory. Only a few days later, the Romans returned for a second invasion; this time, they captured Gamla. Roman historian Josephus recorded the tragic end of Gamla: 4,000 Jews were massacred and another 5,000 were either trampled to death, fell off the cliff, or threw themselves off the mountain into a ravine—thus the nickname, "the Masada of the North."

Today Gamla Nature Reserve is a symbol of heroism for the state of Israel as well as an important archaeological site. From an observation terrace, visitors can view the ancient town of Gamla as well as a collection of **domens** (Bronze Age burial mounds made of huge boulders). Nature lovers can appreciate the nesting colony of birds of prey, the imposing cliffs of the Gamla Stream canyon, and its majestic waterfall that flows year-round. Gamla Nature Reserve is just 15 minutes from the Sea of Galilee, 3 km from road 869. Phone: 972-4-682-2282

KATZRIN IS LOCATED ABOUT 20 minutes north of Gamla. With a population of roughly 6,700, Katzrin serves as the capital of the Golan Heights.

The **Golan Heights Winery**, one of Israel's leading wineries, and the **Golan Olive Oil Mill** are both located in Katzrin.

Katzrin is best known for **Golan Magic**—a large complex encompassing a coffee shop, a boutique, and brewery. Its main feature is the **Magic of the Golan**, an educational presentation which includes a spectacular movie and a precise, scaled-down replica of the Golan Heights. The movie's multisensory effects allow the viewer to see, feel, and hear the breath-taking scenery of the region. The model is the focus of a captivating audiovisual narration of the Golan Height's history from biblical times to the present. *An excellent introduction to your day in the Golan Heights!*

In the industrial section of Katzrin are the reconstructed remains of an authentic **Talmudic Village** and synagogue. The village encompasses an authentic ancient olive oil press, rooms and courtyard, and many genuine articles and tools that were used in daily Talmudic life. The village has an open-air museum and an audio-visual show that explores the ancient sages of this era. Phone 972-4-696-2412

DE KARINA CHOCOLATE FACTORY

- Delicious, gourmet chocolates, chocolate-spiked coffees, and liqueurs
- Founded by a third-generation chocolatier from Argentina
- Chocolate-making workshops and factory tours
- Favorites: pralines and the "Mt. Hermon"—a milk chocolate cone topped with white chocolate "snow"

30 minutes north of Katzrin — the perfect stop on your way to or from the Northern Golan Heights!

Ein Zivan ▪ Call in advance for hours, tours, and workshops: 972-4-699-3622

MOUNT BENTAL, CLOSE TO THE northern edge of the Golan Heights and just 37 miles (60 km) west of Damascus (Syria's capital), is one of a series of dormant volcanic mounds. Mount Bental towers over the region at almost 4,000 ft (1,170 m) above sea level. This elevation has rendered the mountain a key strategic center for Israel's defense. During the 1973 Yom Kippur war, Mount Bental was the site of one of the largest tank battles.

Drive to the top of the mountain and enjoy the stunning, panoramic views of the Golan, Mount Hermon, Druze villages, and even portions of Lebanon and Syria. At Bental's summit, you will find a charming café and a fascinating visitor's center encompassing an automated information system, an engaging sculpture garden made of scrap-iron, and a reconstructed IDF military post complete with a dark, winding underground network of trenches and deserted bunkers. Definitely worth a visit!

VALLEY OF TEARS

Blessed is the man whose strength is in You, whose heart is set on pilgrimage.
As they pass through the Valley of Baca ["Tears"], they make it a spring;
The rain also covers it with pools. They go from strength to strength;
Each one appears before God in Zion. PSALMS 84:4-6

THE LONG STRETCH OF VALLEY between Mount Bental and Mount Hermon has become known as the "Valley of Tears" in remembrance of the 1973 Yom Kippur war. As in the Psalm above, tears have turned into springs of blessings. While old army tanks can still be seen strewn across the hillsides, the old Israeli-Syrian battlefield now flourishes with fields of grain and produce!

On Yom Kippur 1973, massive Syrian and Egyptian forces launched a surprise attack on the State of Israel. Israel was greatly outnumbered by the Syrian tanks and arsenal; the outcome for Israel appeared dismal. On the fourth day of battle, the Syrians unleashed an extensive strategic assault with hundreds of state-of-the-art Arab tanks. They came from the bottom of a valley north of **Kuneitra** (Syria's former capital of the Golan that came under Israeli control after the 1967 war). Had this maneuver been successful, the Syri-ans would have gained access to the plateau above the valley (located along today's Route 98). The Syrians could have easily deployed their forces to further infiltrate Israeli terri-tory and Israel would have lost possession of the Golan Heights.

Due to supernatural intervention, this pre-meditated occupation never transpired. In the end, only seven out of one hundred Israeli tanks remained and Israel suffered many casualties. However, the Syrians mysteriously retreated and over 500 of their destroyed tanks and transportation vehicles *were aban-doned on the battlefield.*

This battlefield became known as the "Valley of Tears." Today, a memorial site with audio narration tells the story of the battle. Visitors can view one of the T62 Syrian tanks that spearheaded the Syrian attack as well as a grove of trees planted in memory of the fallen, valiant soldiers of the 77th Brigade.

MOUNT HERMON, 9,230 FT (2,813 M) tall at its summit, is the highest point in Israel; its peak straddles the border between Syria and Lebanon. Several demilitarized zones with UNDOF (United Nations Disengagement Observer Force) supervision serve in this region. Snow-capped half of the year, the lower slopes are used for skiing and snowboarding in winter.

In the narration of the Transfiguration (Matthew 17:1–9), Jesus and three apostles are on top of a mountain, Jesus becomes radiant, and they are visited by Moses and Elijah. The Transfiguration may very well have taken place on Mount Hermon, as it was in the "region of Caesarea Philippi" (Matthew 16:13) located at Mount Hermon's base.

NIMROD FORTRESS

DRIVING THROUGH THE NORTHERN Golan on the way to Caesarea Philippi, one can catch a glimpse of the towering Nimrod Fortress, or "Castle of the Large Cliff." Located on the slopes of Mount Hermon (Road 989) near the town of Kiryat Shmona and above the Banias Spring, the fortress complex encompasses more than fifteen acres (six hectares) of land framed with large, meticulously squared stones and rectangular towers. Nimrod "castle" is, in reality, the remains of an extraordinary medieval fortress 2,600 ft (800 m) above sea level. The fortress was named after the hunter Nimrod (mentioned in Genesis 10:8-9) who, according to local belief, dwelt on this very hilltop.

The fortress was initially built in the Middle Ages around AD 1229 by the governor of Banias. Its purpose was to defend the city of Banias in the valley below. The site changed hands and was expanded in subsequent years as Muslims and Christians contended for control of the region. Today, Nimrod Fortress is a part of the Israeli national park system.

Nimrod Fortress offers magnificent, panoramic views and sparks fascination for all ages—especially children; it is full of wonders to explore! Visitors will discover a large "keep" or dungeon-fortress, a sizeable moat built to separate the keep from the main fortress, a secret passageway made of massive stones (with an exit doorway indistinguishable from the outside to assist in surprise attacks), a ladder leading down to an underground cistern, a mysterious spiral staircase, and numerous veiled niches.

A visit to Nimrod Fortress would definitely be a highlight of any trip to the Golan Heights! Phone: 972-4-694-9277

TWENTY-FIVE MILES NORTH OF THE Sea of Galilee, at the base of Mount Hermon, is Caesarea Philippi—a city built at the base of an enormous rock. It is believed that **Peter's great confession** in Matthew 16:13-18 occurred in this region of the Golan.

Philip, the son of Herod the Great, established the city as the capital of his territory and named it Caesarea in honor of Rome's emperor, Caesar. Caesarea Philippi was originally called *Panion* or *Panias* (which later morphed to the modern *Banias*). This term, as well as the word *panic*, originated from the Greek god *Pan*—the god of nature, fields, forests, shepherds, and rustic music. Pan's presence was believed to instill fear due to his half-man/half-goat appearance. (Ancient Pan worship is still evident today in *Pantheism* which views nature as divine.)

Pan Grotto was a sacred precinct that encompassed temples of Zeus, a deep pool of water from a spring, dancing goats, court- yards, a grotto, and sacred niches carved into the mountain for the inhabitants' many idols. The large cave in the mountain became the center of pagan worship in the third century BC. Sacrifices were cast into its pool as offerings to Pan, whom the Greeks believed lived in its underground waters and decided which sacrifices were acceptable. If the ritual sacrifice disappeared in the water, Pan had accepted the offering. However, if signs of blood appeared nearby, the sacrifice had been rejected.

BANIAS

ADJOINING CAESAREA PHILIPPI ON Road 99 is the beautiful Banias Nature Reserve enveloped in lush green woodlands—made possible by its abundant water supply from the Banias Stream. A suspended, wooden boardwalk, known as the "hanging trail," leads to the breathtaking Banias Waterfall—the largest, most powerful waterfall in all of Israel.

Dan shall judge his people, as one of the tribes of Israel. GENESIS 49:16, ESV

TEL DAN, BOTH A NATURE RESERVE and national park, is located just west of the Golan Heights in the Upper Galilee region. *Tel* means "ancient mound" and *Dan* means "judge," referring to the Israeli tribe of Dan, the fifth son of Jacob. This northernmost city and capital of the ancient northern Kingdom of Israel spans 50 acres (20 ha). Tel Dan was a large and powerful Canaanite city dating back to 18 BC. From the era of the Judges through the reigns of Israel's first three kings (Saul, David, and Solomon), the biblical phrase *"from Dan to Beersheba"* represented the entirety of the United Kingdom of Israel (Judges 20:1; 2 Samuel 24:2; 1 Kings 4:25).

Tel Dan is the headwaters of the Jordan River as well as its largest source of water. (The word *Jordan* is a contraction of the Hebrew words *Yored* and *Dan* meaning "descending from Dan.") The Dan River emerges from the snowmelt at the base of Mount Hermon, where it flows for four miles before joining the Banias Spring—Jordan River's second largest source of water.

Archaeologists believe the area referred to as the **High Place of Jeroboam** at Tel Dan was the temple built by King Jeroboam where he housed the golden calf and built an altar, essentially challenging the temple in Jerusalem as Israel's religious center (1 Kings 12:28-31).

Tel Dan's **Middle Bronze Gate** is the world's oldest known gated archway, constructed more than 1,500 years before the Romans claimed to invent the arch. Abraham and his 318 servants would have passed through this gate while pursuing the kings of the north to rescue Abraham's nephew, Lot, who had been taken hostage (Genesis 14:14).

TZFAT, ALSO KNOWN AS *SAFED*, IS located just southwest of Tel Hazor (also in the Upper Galilee). Tzfat, sits atop a hill over ½ mile (.8 km) high, yielding magnificent views. In fact, it is Israel's *highest* town and most likely its *coldest* town! In the sixteenth century, many renowned Jewish scholars and mystics moved to Tzfat, fleeing from the horrors of the Spanish Inquisition. This wave of immigrants marked the beginning of the town's growth.

Tzfat is well-known on several accounts. The first printing press in the Middle East was in Tzfat, and in 1578, the first Hebrew book printed in Israel was published here. During this period, Tzfat was a thriving trade center. However, over several decades, the town suffered severe devastation from earthquakes, plagues, and attacks by Arabs. The restoration of Tzfat did not come until the 1948 War of Independence. This long-awaited liberation was celebrated as a powerful victory!

Jewish mysticism's foremost practice, **Kabbalism**, also originated in Tzfat. You can read more about Kabbalism on p. 31. The "bible" of the kabbalists, the **Zohar**, was credited to Rabbi Shimon bar Yochai, better known as the legendary "**Rashbi.**" The Rashbi was a second-century Galilean sage and mystic who believed every single word and line of the Torah held a "higher meaning." Additionally, he was a star pupil of **Rabbi Akiva** and a notable contributor to the **Talmud** (the oral law developed as a "manual" for interpreting the written Law—the Bible). The Rashbi was laid to rest in a grave in Tzfat; admirers regularly visit his grave to pay their respects.

Known for its "Jewish soul," many of Tzfat's Jewish men immerse themselves in Torah study daily. A significant number of **Tzaddikim** (righteous, holy men) are buried in the vicinity, due to the belief of Jewish sages that "a Tzaddik never dies." Today, Tzfat is considered one of the four holy cities in Israel, along with Jerusalem, Hebron, and Tiberias.

Thousands of immigrants from Russia and Ethiopia have made Tzfat their home in the past decade, contributing to the current population of roughly 27,000. Experiencing this lovely, quaint town with its cobble-stoned streets, outdoor cafés, synagogues on almost every corner, small guest houses, and myriad of art galleries is definitely an "off the tour route" highlight of a trip to Israel. Tzfat is located west of Highway 90 and is reached by passing through the intersection of Highway 91.

THE HULA VALLEY OF THE UPPER Galilee boasts an abundance of fresh water springs, marshes, rivers, and lakes, while encompassing numerous nature reserves and archaeological sites. Within the valley is the **Hula Nature Reserve** which spans 786 acres (3,180 dunams). Hula is Israel's central location for the preservation, rehabilitation and restoration of its flora and fauna. Upon entrance to the reserve is the **Hula Valley Lookout** which provides tremendous views of the Hula Valley, the Hills of Naftali, and the slopes of the Golan and Mount Hermon.

Hula attracts a variety of flora and wildlife, including many rare and endangered species. It is located on the worldwide bird migration route; its diverse water birds are a draw for bird watchers year-round, even though the "official" migrating season is July through March. An estimated 500 million birds of 400 species fly over Hula each year.

The reserve's **"Euphoria" Visitors Center** offers a 3D interactive presentation of Hula Valley's fauna and flora, with a focus on the migrating birds. On display are bird migration maps and a variety of specimens of bird species that come to the valley. *Hula Trivia*, an interactive, trivia quiz about wildlife within the reserve is a favorite to many!

Bird-watching stations are integrated into Hula's many biking and walking trails. On the main trail, a three-story **Observation Tower** provides an unobstructed view of the marsh and the lake, enabling bird watchers to observe the activities of the migrating birds who winter at Hula.

Guided tours for groups leave every twenty minutes; you may want to call to confirm. Hula Nature Reserve is located almost 2 miles (3 km) north of the Yesud Ha'Ma'ala junction and about 1½ miles (2½ km) east of Highway 90. Phone: 972-4-693-7069

TEL HAZOR

"Hazor will become a haunt of jackals, a desolate place forever. No one will live there; no people will dwell in it." JEREMIAH 49:33

JUST SOUTH OF THE HULA VALLEY IS the archaeological site of ancient Tel Hazor, encompassing an upper tel of 30 acres and a lower tel close to 200 acres. In 2005, Tel Hazor was designated a World Heritage Site by UNESCO.

In the Bible, Tel Hazor was known as "the head of all those kingdoms"; it was the seat of the evil and powerful Canaanite King Jabin who had harshly oppressed the Jews for twenty years. In obedience to the Lord's instruction, Joshua burnt Hazor to the ground (Jeremiah 49:33).

Archaeological finds, resembling those found at Tel Megiddo and Tel Gezer, include a massive water system, stables (quite likely built for King Solomon's royal cavalry), and a six-chambered gate. It is possible that all three tels were built by King Solomon, as described in 1 Kings 9:15.

Some of the most significant findings at Hazor date back to the era of the Canaanites. Many pagan artifacts and structures were discovered in the lower tel, including figurines and standing stones—indicative of a community immersed in idol worship. A four-room "pillared" style house was also unearthed. Pillared houses, common in Israeli settlements, had either one or two rows of pillars separating the central court from the surrounding rooms.

Tel Hazor findings are housed in a nearby museum at Kibbutz Ayelet HaShahar. Address: 90, Rosh Pina; Phone: 972-4-693-7290

Banias (Caesarea Philippi)

FROM GALILEE TO JERUSALEM

He said to the Israelites, "In the future when your descendants ask their parents, 'What do these stones mean?' tell them, 'Israel crossed the Jordan on dry ground.' For the Lord your God dried up the Jordan before you until you had crossed over. The Lord your God did to the Jordan what he had done to the Red Sea when he dried it up before us until we had crossed over. He did this so that all the peoples of the earth might know that the hand of the Lord is powerful and so that you might always fear the Lord your God."

JOSHUA 4:21–2

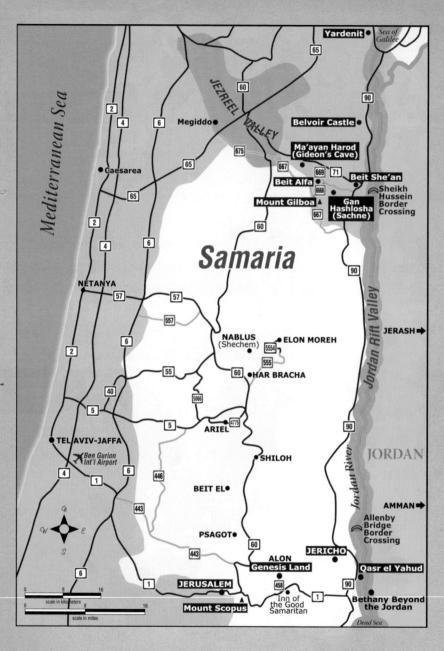

View additional site info online: Belvoir Castle and
Beit Alfa archaeological site.

Go to WalkAboutZion.com; click on Inspiration Israel.

THE JORDAN RIVER IS ISRAEL'S LONG-est river. Measuring straight from north to south, its distance is about 70 miles (113 km); its total length is roughly 200 miles (322 km) including its curves. The Jordan's width fluctuates from 90 ft to 100 ft (27 m to 30 m), and its depth 3 ft to 10 ft (1 m to 3 m). The river begins at Israel's northern tip, Mount Hermon, and flows south through the Sea of Galilee and the tropical Jordan valley before emptying into the Dead Sea. The name *Jordan* means "flowing or descending downward."

The Jordan River is mentioned approximately 175 times in the Old Testament. Most notably, in Joshua Chapter 3, the Lord instructed Joshua to lead the Israelites into their Promised Land by crossing the Jordan River—during flood season! When the feet of the priests carrying the ark of the covenant touched the water, the river stood up like a wall. God's people were miraculously able to cross over and claim their Promised Land. Forty years prior to this (a frequently repeated number in Scripture), God had parted the Red Sea, allowing the Israelites to flee from Egypt. Years later, another notable event in Scripture took place at the Jordan River: a servant of Elisha told the Syrian general, Naaman, to wash seven times in the Jordan to cure his leprosy. When Naaman reluctantly obeyed, God kept His promise and cured his leprosy.

In the New Testament, the Jordan River is mentioned fifteen times. John the Baptist preached and baptized his followers in the Jordan River. He also baptized Jesus in these same waters—officially initiating the public ministry of Jesus that would continue until His death three years later.

MOUNT GILBOA

MOUNT GILBOA (ACTUALLY A RIDGE) sits on the southeastern side of the Jezreel Valley. Every year from February to April, throngs of visitors come to see its beautiful display of wildflowers including its renowned purple Gilboa Iris. Mount Gilboa's summit provides a magnificent view.

It is on this mountain where King Saul and his sons died fighting the Philistines (1 Samuel 31:8). Reflecting sorrowfully on the deaths of those he loved dearly, David cursed the mountain: "*Mountains of Gilboa, may you have neither dew nor rain, may no showers fall on your terraced fields…*" (2 Samuel 1:21).

GIDEON'S CAVE

AT THE FOOT OF MOUNT GILBOA SITS **Ma'ayan Harod National Park**, also known as **Gideon's Cave** (or Gideon's Spring), from which flows the Spring of Harod. The park encompasses a memorial for local war casualties, a small museum, and Gideon's Cave.

This spot is renowned as the place where the Lord reduced **Gideon's army** from 22,000 men to 300 fearless men who drank water from the spring by means of their cupped hands (Judges 7:2–7). This same site is where armies would gather and train prior to battle, and where great battles were fought. The Spring of Harod served as one of the first training bases for the **Palmach**, a special strike force within the underground army, which ultimately led to the establishment of the Israel Defense Forces (IDF).

*There is a river whose streams make glad the city of God,
the holy place where the Most High dwells. PSALM 46:4*

WHEN TRAVELING SOUTH TOWARD Jerusalem, five notable sites in the Lower Galilee are in close proximity to one another: Beit She´an, Gan Hashlosha National Park, Mount Gilboa, Gideon's Cave, and Bet Alpha Synagogue.

Named by *Time Magazine* as one of the most beautiful parks in the world, Sachne's highlight is its beautiful waterfalls and spring-fed pools that flow through the park, sur-

rounded by green lawns and lush palm trees. The Amal Stream crosses the park and widens into its renowned, refreshing pools. The waters serve as a natural jacuzzi with a constant, year-round water temperature of 82°F (28°C).

A variety of interesting sites are available to visit. The Museum of Regional and Mediterranean Archaeology houses a display of rare Greek tools and artifacts from excavations in the Beit She´an valley. A 1936 life-size reconstruction of a "Tower and Stockade" settlement, set up by some Jewish pioneers who opposed the rule of the British Mandate, features an exhibit of daily articles used by the pioneers. In another room, children have the opportunity to construct a model of a settlement. A ten-minute film in the restored dining hall depicts life during the time of the Arab Revolt (1936–1939). Climb to the top of the tower for a great view!

The next day, when the Philistines came to strip the dead, they found Saul and his three sons fallen on Mount Gilboa... They put his armor in the temple of the Ashtoreths and fastened his body to the wall of Beth Shan. When the people of Jabesh Gilead heard what the Philistines had done to Saul, all their valiant men marched through the night to Beth Shan. They took down the bodies of Saul and his sons from the wall of Beth Shan and went to Jabesh, where they burned them. Then they took their bones and buried them under a tamarisk tree at Jabesh, and they fasted seven days. 1 SAMUEL 31:8,10–13

BEIT SHE'AN IS LOCATED 17 MILES (27 km) south of the Sea of Galilee. In the Bible, Beit She'an was a major administrative center of Solomon's kingdom. Its most well-known biblical event followed the death of King Saul and his three sons on Mt. Gilboa; the Philistines hung their bodies on the walls of the city. Beit She'an was rebuilt by Pompey and the Romans in 63 BC and renamed **Scythopolis**, but it was leveled by a massive earthquake in AD 749, laying in ruins until a series of archaeological excavations beginning in 1921.

Beit She'an is one of the world's largest archaeological sites. The foremost finds were a series of temples from the Middle and Late Bronze Ages. One large Roman temple is believed to have been dedicated to

the Greek god Dionysus. Additionally, remains of elaborate fourth- and fifth-century villas displaying mosaics were found in the western part of the city, along with a large, elaborate bathhouse complex.

Many excavated churches attest to a significant Christian population at some point during Beit She'an's history. Ruins of both a Jewish and a Samaritan synagogue were found here as well.

Three hundred evenings a year, a spectacular, award-winning multimedia sound and light show is displayed onto the ruins of Beit She'an. Visitors walk along the dirt roads, while the multisensory special effects make the entire ancient city come to life! Call 972-4-658-7189 for current showings.

Then the Lord said to Joshua, "See, I have delivered Jericho into your hands, along with its king and its fighting men." JOSHUA 6:2

JERICHO, THE "CITY OF PALMS," IS A rich oasis of greenery amid a desert landscape. Located near the Jordan River in the "West Bank," Jericho holds the distinction of being the lowest city in the world, sitting 825 ft (255 m) below sea level. Jericho is also one of four cities claiming to be the oldest city in the world, based on its continual occupation for nearly 3,500 years. Nearby in Jordan are the biblical kingdoms of Ammon and Moab and the peak of Mt. Nebo, from which Moses viewed the Promised Land before his death.

Jericho today consists of the sites of the Old Testament and New Testament Jericho—separated from each other by about a mile; the nearby modern city of Jericho has a population close to 19,000.

The city was occupied by Jordan from 1948 to 1967 and then fell under Israeli control until 1994, when its jurisdiction was switched to the Palestinian Authority. Israeli citizens are prohibited by law from entering Jericho because of security concerns; however, tourism continues to flourish. One of Jericho's primary sources of income is Christian tourism to its biblical sites.

Jericho is mentioned 70 times in the Old Testament. The location is most famous for the miraculous account (Joshua chapter 6) of the **Battle of Jericho**, in which the walls of Jericho fell down, becoming the first city conquered by the Israelites after Joshua led them into Canaan.

Below Ancient Jericho is **Elisha's Spring** (photo above) named after the prophet Elijah's water purification miracle in 2 Kings 2:19–22. Jar sculpture has been placed around the spring to commemorate this event. Drinkable water still comes up from the ground today—delivering 1,000 gallons of water per minute, providing a substantial amount of water for Jericho's citizens and irrigation needs.

Across the road from Elisha's Spring is **Tel Jericho**, a large artificial mound 69 ft (21 m) high and covering about one acre. Archaeologists believe this to be the site of the biblical city of Jericho, which survived and flourished for more than a thousand years before being demolished by nomadic groups toward the end of the second millennium BC. Jericho is the second most exca-

vated city in Israel, second only to Jerusalem. Twenty-three layers of ancient civilizations have been uncovered at Tel Jericho.

Towering above Tel Jericho is the mountain known as the **Mount of Temptation**. This mountain is widely believed to be the location where Jesus spent forty days and forty nights praying and fasting throughout His encounter with Satan and his accompanying temptation.

Toward the summit of the mountain, rising 1148 ft (350 m) above sea level, is the **Monastery of Temptation**. The monastery was built in a rather precarious position along a cliff overlooking Jericho and the Jordan Valley. The path leading up to the monastery is quite steep and challenging to climb. However, a modern cable car is available to transport tourists from Jericho to the Monastery and back. The short five-minute ride features spectacular views of the Jordan Valley.

Carved out of the rock and tucked into the cliffs is the picturesque **St. George's Monastery** (photo above). The monastery began in the fourth century with a few monks who were seeking the desert experiences of the prophets and settled around a cave where they believed Elijah had been fed by ravens (1 Kings 17:5–6).

Visitors can also view the "**Zacchaeus Tree**," a huge, gnarled old sycamore tree that some believe was the tree mentioned in Luke 19:1–10, climbed by the wealthy (and short) tax collector to get a better view of Jesus.

The **Inn of the Good Samaritan** is a nineteenth-century Turkish building located on the Old Jericho Road. The property is surrounded by limestone cliffs, providing thieves an easy access to hiding out—aptly fitting Jesus' parable about the Good Samaritan found in Luke 10:30–37. The **Museum of the Good Samaritan**, which opened on the premises in 2009, houses one of the world's largest mosaic museums.

> *When He had been baptized, Jesus came up immediately from the water; and behold, the heavens were opened to Him, and He saw the Spirit of God descending like a dove and alighting upon Him. And suddenly a voice came from heaven, saying, "This is My beloved Son, in whom I am well pleased."* MATTHEW 3:16–17, NKJ

YARDENIT

YARDENIT IS LOCATED AT THE SOUTHern end of the Sea of Galilee. From here, the water flows into the southern section of the Jordan River and then another 60 miles (100 km) into the Dead Sea. *Yarden* is the Hebrew word for "Jordan"; *Yardenit* means a "little Jordan."

Due to the closure of Qasr el Yahud in 1968, Israel's Ministry of Tourism launched Yardenit in 1981 as a replacement baptismal site (primarily financed by Calvary Chapel under the direction of Pastor Chuck Smith). Today this baptismal site accommodates nearly 400,000 visitors each year. Its tranquility and beauty make it an ideal setting for meditation and prayer, accompanying baptism.

QASR EL YAHUD

LOCATED ON THE JORDAN RIVER IN the "West Bank," near Jericho and the Dead Sea, is *Qasr el Yahud* or "Castle of the Jews." This traditional baptismal site is where the New Testament narrative of the baptism of Jesus occurred. This site is also believed to be in the vicinity where the Israelites crossed the Jordan and where Elijah the prophet ascended up to heaven in a fiery chariot (2 Kings 2:1–11).

In 1968, following the Six-Day War, Qasr el Yahud became part of a closed military zone and access to the site was prohibited. However, it was completely renovated and reopened in 2011 under the management of the Israel Parks Authority, becoming a very popular place for group baptisms.

In those days Jesus came from Nazareth of Galilee and was baptized by John in the Jordan. And when he came up out of water, immediately he saw the heavens opened and the Spirit descending upon him like a dove, and a voice came from heaven; "Thou art my beloved Son; with thee I am well pleased."

MARK 1.9-11

IF YOU'RE HEADING SOUTH FROM the Galilee toward Jerusalem, you may have visited Beit She'an or some of its nearby sites. If you visited Jericho or Qasr el Yahud for a baptism, you are now departing the region of Jericho, at 846 ft (258 m) *below* sea level—for Jerusalem, the "city on a hill," at 2,500 ft (762 m) *above* sea level. The phrase "up to Jerusalem" originated from those who made this trek. You are officially starting the "**Ascent of Adummim,**" cited in Joshua 15:7, which means "ascent of the red places," most likely due to the abundance of red rocks in the landscape on the way up to Jerusalem.

In the time of Jesus, the journey by foot was made on the spectacular 17-mile (27 km) **Old Jericho Road** built by the Romans (photo above). This road, landscaped with hills and valleys, stretches from Jericho, near the Dead Sea, across the Judean desert—all the way to Jerusalem. Running parallel to the Old Jericho Road is **Wadi Qelt,** a natural rift in the midst of the hills and valleys, surrounded by high, sheer rock walls. *Wadi* is Arabic for "creek bed" or "ravine."

The Old Jericho Road would have been the location of David's flight from Absalom (2 Samuel 15–16), and Jesus and the disciples probably walked this road often. This jour-ney was routinely made by tens of thousands of pilgrims traveling to Jerusalem for the feast days—a very difficult uphill journey!

If you're with a group, it takes on special meaning to trade off reading the **Psalms of Ascension** (Psalms 120–134) on this uphill trek. These psalms were likely recited or sung by both the captives returning from Babylon and the pilgrims preparing for the feasts. This would have been an emotional, joy-filled "Homeward March" to Jerusalem!

Driving west on highway 90, you will see a number of Bedouin settlements among the hills. Soon the hills will open up to the spec-tacular city of Jerusalem, the **Mount Zion** "of old," and the "**City of the Great King!**" If you have time, make your first stop the Mount Scopus overlook for a breathtaking view of Old City Jerusalem (photo below).

IF YOU HAVE TIME, AN AWESOME stop prior to reaching Jerusalem is Genesis Land. Driving west on Highway 90, Genesis Land is located in the town of Alon on the edge of the Judean desert, roughly a 30-minute drive from Jericho and then another 30–40 minutes to Jerusalem (depending upon your specific destination in Jerusalem).

Genesis Land is an oasis of biblical adventure located in the midst of the magnificent desert setting where Abraham and Lot parted ways (Genesis 13). Prepare for a biblical and geographical education regarding Abraham's journey!

Numerous activities and hands-on workshops are offered. Visitors can:

- Ride a camel
- Enjoy Abraham's "hospitality" in his tent with a choice of either light fare (teas and dried fruit) or King David's Royal Dinner!
- Participate in a workshop: pita bread baking, pottery, mosaics, shepherds, desert drummers, or ancient Hebrew writing.
- Camp overnight in a tent in the wilderness (with some modern comforts).

Genesis Land is described on its website as *"A magical place, it enables visitors to experience life as it was in biblical times. Visitors to Genesis Land are greeted by Eliezer, Abraham's manservant, and by a train of camels which lead you to the reception in Abraham's tent, where you will experience his legendary hospitality. At Genesis Land, the stories of the Bible come to life in the very landscape in which they took place."*

Contact Genesis Land for more information and to schedule your visit.
Phone: 972-2-997-4477 ▪ genesis@genesisland.co.il ▪ www.genesisland.co.il/en

GREATER JERUSALEM

I have posted watchmen on your walls, Jerusalem; they will never be silent day or night. You who call on the Lord, give yourselves no rest and give him no rest till he establishes Jerusalem and makes her the praise of the earth.

ISAIAH 62:6–7

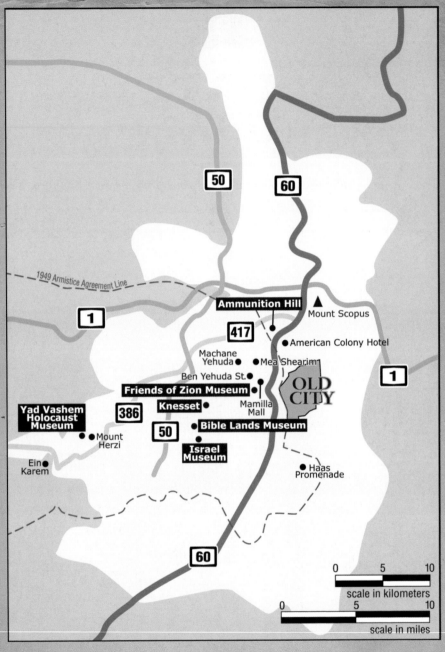

1949 Armistice Agreement Line

Ammunition Hill ▲ Mount Scopus

50 60 417 1 1

● American Colony Hotel

Machane Yehuda ● Mea Shearim

Ben Yehuda St.

Friends of Zion Museum OLD CITY

Knesset Mamilla Mall

Yad Vashem Holocaust Museum 386

50 **Bible Lands Museum**

● Mount Herzl

Israel Museum

Ein Karem ● Haas Promenade

60

0   5   10
scale in kilometers

0   5   10
scale in miles

Please note that two chapters, JUDEA and SAMARIA, also include important and fascinating sites to visit while you are based in Jerusalem.

View additional site info online: Mount Scopus, Mount Herzl, Ammunition Hill, Ein Kerem, Mea She'arim, Rockefeller Museum, American Colony Hotel, Notre Dame, Teddy Park, and Sultan's Pool.

Go to WalkAboutZion.com; click on Inspiration Israel.

But now I have chosen Jerusalem
for my Name to be there...2 CHRONICLES 6:6

LOCATED IN THE JUDEAN MOUNTAINS between the Mediterranean Sea and the Dead Sea, Jerusalem stands at an elevation of 2,600 ft (792 m) above sea level and is Israel's largest city in both population and area. In 2018, Jerusalem was home to roughly 865,000 residents: of which 550,000 are Jews (64%), 300,000 are Muslims (35%), and 15,000 are Christians (1%). *Jeru-salem* means "Provision" or "Payment" of "perfect peace."

During King David's 33-year reign of Jerusalem, Jerusalem became the commanding power for the nation of Israel. After David, all the kings of Judah reigned from Jerusalem. David's son, King Solomon, built the First Temple here—which was later destroyed, rebuilt, and destroyed again. Herod the Great rebuilt the city and reconstructed the temple. The Romans destroyed Jerusalem and Herod's Second Temple in AD 70. Jerusalem has been destroyed completely twice, besieged 23 times, attacked 52 times, captured and recaptured 44 times.

Psalm 76:1-3 conveys that Judah, with Jerusalem as its seat of government, is the place where God's presence has been known and revealed. As such, Jerusalem is the most religiously disputed city in the world and the most contested piece of real estate in all of human history.

Jerusalem is the seat of monotheism—a holy city to the three major religions associated with Abraham: Judaism, Christianity, and Islam. Jewish synagogues worldwide are built with their holy ark facing Jerusalem, and holy arks in synagogues within Jerusalem face the "Holy of Holies" on the Temple Mount. Jerusalem has been sacred to the Jewish people for over 3,000 years, to Christianity since the time of Christ, and to Islam for more than 1,400 years. In the Sunni Islam sect, Jerusalem is their third holiest city.

Both the Jews and the "Palestinians" claim Jerusalem as their capital—contrary to international opinion. As such, international embassies have historically remained in Tel Aviv. However, President Trump formally recognized Jerusalem as the capital of the Jewish state of Israel on December 6, 2017; other countries are following suit. To the delight of most Jews and Christians worldwide, the US embassy made its official move to Jerusalem on the important date of May 14, 2018— Israel's seventieth anniversary!

Unto them will I give in my house and within my walls a memorial and a name [yad vashem]...that shall not be cut off. ISAIAH 56:5, ASV

YAD VASHEM, FOUNDED IN 1953, IS Israel's official memorial to the millions of Jewish Holocaust victims. The center is located on the western slope of Mount Herzl on Jerusalem's Mount of Remembrance.

Yad Vashem is dedicated to a four-fold mission of remembrance: commemoration, documentation, research, and education. This is achieved through the utilization of testimonies, original artifacts, and personal belongings of individual survivors. *Yad Vashem* is Hebrew for a "memorial" and a "name." The center's mission is to preserve both the memory and the names of the 6,000,000 Jewish souls lost in the Holocaust. Since its establishment, Yad Vashem has compiled over 125,000 audio, video, and written survivor testimonies.

The final exhibit in the main museum is the **Hall of Names** (photo to right)—a memorial to every Jew who perished in the Holocaust and a physical place to commemorate them and carry on their name for generations to come. This memorial contains 600 photographs of Holocaust victims and fragments of 2.7 million original "Pages of Testimony" (short personal biographies).

The **Children's Memorial** is a unique tribute to the 1.5 million Jewish children who perished in the Holocaust. Four memorial candles glow brightly and reflect onto 500 mirrors amid darkness, creating the impression of millions of stars shining in the firmament. The names of the children, their ages, and their birthplace are read aloud in the background.

The **Garden of the Righteous Among the Nations** is an outdoor area of Yad Vashem honoring the non-Jews who jeopardized their lives, their freedom, and/or their positions to save Jews during the Holocaust. Two thousand trees are planted in their honor on the Mount of Remembrance. Open rooms are integrated into the forested hills for honoring additional "Righteous Gentiles," and their names are engraved into walls according to their country of origin. In 2018, almost 27,000 names from 51 countries were inscribed; new names are added every year.

"Telling Their Stories: A Race Against Time" is a critical project in light of current world events and the quickly perishing Holocaust Survivors. Yad Vashem's goal is to collect each Survivor's story to educate mankind about the lessons to be learned from the Holocaust. If you are interested in insuring one or more survivors' testimonies will be heard and passed on to future generations, please consider making a donation. Contact christian.friends@yadvashem.org.il.

A minimum of two-three hours in the museum is recommended. Admission is free.
For a fee, your group can tour with an official Yad Vashem guide
and/or visit with a Holocaust Survivor onsite.
They may still offer a special Friday 10:00 A.M. guided tour for a small entrance fee.
Call early for reservations and additional information.
Phone: 972-2-644-3400; Email: webmaster@yadvashem.org.il

DR. JANUSZ KORCZAK, KNOWN affectionately as Mr. Doctor, was not only a doctor, but a writer and educator who oversaw 192 Jewish orphans in the Warsaw Ghetto for many years. On August 6, 1942, he was forced to gather all of his orphans together. He made sure each of the children was dressed in their best clothes, carried a nice blue knapsack, and brought a favorite book or toy. Dr. Korczak refused repeated offers of sanctuary on the "Aryan side" from the Polish underground. He stayed with the children all the way until the end. It is claimed that "Mr. Doctor" led them on their final march with pride and dignity, singing joyfully and waving flags until they arrived at the train that would take them to the Treblinka extermination camp, where they perished together in the gas chambers.

*Your people will rebuild the ancient ruins and will raise up the age-old foundations;
you will be called Repairer of Broken Walls, Restorer of Streets with Dwellings.*
ISAIAH 58:12

THE ISRAEL MUSEUM IS THE LARGEST cultural institution in Israel and one of the world's leading art and archaeology museums. Founded in 1965, the Jerusalem museum houses fine arts and encyclopedic collections, with wings dedicated to Jewish art and life. It also features the most extensive holdings of biblical and Holy Land archaeology in the world.

The impressive **Shrine of the Book** structure (below), houses the entire book of Isaiah, as well as other Dead Sea Scrolls. The enclosure was designed to resemble one of the jars in which the scrolls were discovered. The scrolls are the oldest biblical manuscripts in the world, originally discovered in Qumran by a young Bedouin shepherd in 1947 and purchased by a Hungarian philanthropist as a gift to Israel. Archaeological excavations began in 1949.

Adjacent to the Shrine of the Book is a 50:1 scale Model of Old City Jerusalem (above). The topography and architecture of the model were recreated to provide a realistic visual of Old City Jerusalem during the Second Temple period—prior to its destruction by the Romans in AD 70.

The model, which covers an entire acre, took four years to complete. The reconstruction was based on three main sources of information: 1) *literary works*, especially the books of Josephus, the Mishnah, the Talmud, and the Gospels, 2) *ancient cities* similar to Jerusalem, and 3) *archaeological discoveries* specific to Jerusalem. The model was displayed at a hotel for forty years and then moved to the Israel Museum in 2006.

Contact: Phone: 972-2-670-8811; Email: info@imj.org.il; Address: Derech Ruppin 11

Second Temple model

THE UNIQUE BIBLE LANDS MUSEUM, located across the street from the Israel Museum, is a global center for biblical and historical education. Culture is displayed through an interactive time capsule where the civilizations of the ancient Near East are brought to life and history is traced from the dawn of civilization through the early Christian era.

The museum offers both permanent and temporary exhibits. Permanent exhibits as of this writing include Jerusalem in Babylon: *New Light on the Judean Exiles*, *Gods, Heroes and Mortals in Ancient Greece*, *Dionysus: Wine & Divine*, a *Roman Fresco Room*, and a *Classical Court* room featuring pre-classical Greek and Roman art from in the seventh century BC through the second century AD.

The museum's Main Exhibition Hall is a journey through the ancient lands of the Bible—experienced through a plethora of artifacts and visual presentations in twenty separate galleries. Visitors can learn about various ruling empires, trace Abraham's journeys, explore the importance of Israel and Canaan at the crossroads of history, and study a timeline illustrating major historical events according to region and date. A large, illuminated map displays the lands of the Bible and their boundaries.

Both tours and lectures are available by advance reservation: 972-2-595-5330 or groups@blmj.org. General phone: 972-2-561-1066; Email: contact@blmj.org; Address: Shmuel Stephan Weiz St 21, Jerusalem.

KNESSET TOUR

AROUND THE CORNER FROM THE Israel Museum is Israel's national legislative branch, the Knesset. Visitors are invited to the Knesset, free-of-charge, to gain a greater understanding of how the government work impacts the lives of Israeli citizens. The "Standard" and "Democracy in Action" tours are offered in English on Sundays and Thursdays.

Individual and small groups may join the 60-minute **STANDARD TOUR** which introduces visitors to the nature of Israeli democracy, to the Knesset's roles and responsibilities, and to the works of art displayed throughout the building. The tour visits the Knesset Committees Wing, the Plenary Hall, Chagall Hall, and Israel's Declaration of Independence Exhibit. Current tour times are 8:30 AM, 12:00 PM, and 2:00 PM. Groups of 10 or more (maximum 50) need to contact the Visitors Center Reservations Department to reserve their tour in advance. *Tour times are subject to change. Special tours are also available for visitors with special needs.*

The 90-minute, in-depth **DEMOCRACY IN ACTION TOUR** introduces visitors to all facets of the Knesset's parliamentary roles and responsibilities. It focuses on the election process in Israel, the roles of Knesset members and committees, and the Knesset's direct effect on the daily lives of Israeli citizens. Included in this tour are visits to Knesset Committee rooms, the Plenary Chamber, and Israel's Declaration of Independence Exhibit.

The public is also invited to view the **PLENARY DEBATES** of the Knesset from the Visitors' Gallery on Mondays, Tuesdays, and Wednesdays. Groups of 10 or more must reserve seats in advance.

Bring your **passport** and contact the Visitors Center Reservations Department for additional information and reservations and specifics of the **Knesset Dress Code**: Phone: 972-2-675-3337; Email: Tours@knesset.gov.il. Include your phone number in your inquiry so they can call to confirm the date and time of your visit.

LOCATED IN THE HEART OF JERUSALEM, the Friends of Zion (FOZ) Museum was opened in 2015 with the help of thousands of supporters of Israel worldwide. The museum presents the story of the Jewish peoples' dream of restoration to their historic homeland, alongside the story of the courageous non-Jews who assisted them in the realization of that dream. Supporting this dream throughout history have been Christian Zionists who heroically stood with, nurtured, and, in many cases, sacrificed their lives to protect the Jewish people. The Friends of Zion Museum exists to tell their story.

The story is told magnificently using ground-breaking technology. Visitors embark into a virtual reality where they meet faith-filled biblical figures, scholars, businessmen, and military officials who helped forge lasting bonds between the Jews and Christians. Friends of Zion is part of a non-profit organization that serves as an international platform for fighting Anti-Semitism and the BDS (Boycott, Divestment, and Sanctions) against Israel.

The museum is located at 20 Yosef Rivlin Street in Jerusalem. Tours are offered with a guide only and must be booked in advance. Phone: 972-2-532-9400; Email: reservations@fozhc.com

JERUSALEM PRAYER TOWER

THE JERUSALEM PRAYER TOWER, A ministry of the King of Kings community church, offers individuals and groups an opportunity to pray while overlooking the city of Jerusalem. Their mission is to have a "Messiah-centered sanctuary of Spirit-led worship and prayer, called to reveal the light of Yeshua to Israel and the Nations."

They seek to pray as one new man until Yeshua returns, all Israel is saved, and Jerusalem becomes a praise in all the Earth!

The tower is located on the fourteenth floor of Jerusalem's Clal building, 97 Jaffa Road. Call or email to reserve a time and room to pray. Phone: 972-2-625-1899; Email: reception@jerusalemprayertower.org

TAKE IN A MAGNIFICENT VIEW!

Ten measures of beauty descended on the world; nine were taken by Jerusalem.
TALMUDIC RABBIS

Some Top Picks for Old City Views:

- **Mount of Olives** (viewpoint at top of mountain above Jewish cemetery)
- **Mount Scopus** (north of the Old City)
- **Hass Promenade** (south of the Old City)
- **Austrian Hospice Roof** (northeast corner of the Via Dolorosa and Al-Wad Rd. in the Muslim Quarter)
- **Lutheran Church of the Redeemer:** Climb 177 steps up the bell tower— the highest point in the Old City (directly across the road from the Church of the Holy Sepulchre).
- **Ramparts Walk:** Start near Jaffa Gate or Damascus Gate and take an intimate "walk on the walls of Jerusalem" for ½ to 2½ miles (.8 to 4 km).

GO SHOPPING!

Machane Yehuda Market, or **"The Shuk,"** is a mostly open-air marketplace northwest of Ben Yehuda St. The Shuk is an icon of Jerusalem, appealing to locals and tourists alike and attracting an estimated 200,000 shoppers weekly. The Shuk represents contemporary Jerusalem—an integration of the old and the new. It is a vibrant, bustling marketplace energized by vendors calling out their prices to the shoppers. Many find it especially invigorating to join in the last-minute frenzied shopping before the Friday afternoon trumpet sounds, signifying the closing of the marketplace for Shabbat.

MORE POPULAR SHOPPING DESTINATIONS

Bargaining is expected in the open-air marketplace; in fact, that's half the fun!
The price quoted is never the real price or the final price; it is often two-three times higher.
However, conventional stores generally have fixed prices.

Ben Yehuda Street, known as the *Midrachov*, is located between King George Street and Jaffa Road in downtown Jerusalem—a ten-minute walk from the pedestrian mall, Machane Yehuda. Five blocks of Ben Yehuda Street remain closed to vehicular traffic, but is easily reached by bus or train. This is truly the heart of Jerusalem's tourism and down-

town business, as well as a prime hang-out for both locals and tourists. The street is lined with cafés and shops selling souvenirs, t-shirts, jewelry, and **Judaica** (items pertaining to Jewish life and customs). Enjoy the street musicians, grab a bite to eat, and shop to your heart's content.

The Old City **"Souq"** begins at the final *Stations of the Cross* of the Via Dolorosa. The Souq is a traditional Middle Eastern marketplace that sells foods and souvenirs in

abundance. An excitement in the air compels throngs of visitors to want to stay all day. Most of the shops have passed through multiple generations of family members. Watching vendors from all quarters of the Old City pile their goods into carts and crates, and even on their shoulders and heads, is fascinating! *Tip:* Typically, the farther into the market you venture, the better the deals.

Mamilla Mall, located just outside Jaffa Gate, opened in 2007. The $150 million outdoor mall complex has brought to Jerusalem an unprecedented level of luxury retail, while

forging a bridge between the modern and the ancient. Paved with Jerusalem stone and set in ancient landscapes, a wide selection of fine boutiques and high fashion chain stores with name brands like Rolex, Bebe, and Tommy Hilfiger can be found. The selection of upscale restaurants, cafés, shops, an IMAX theater, as well as its unique street theater, all contribute to render Mamilla Mall a popular destination for both locals and tourists.

Also, check out Genesis Land on p. 140 and the Caliber 3 Shooting Adventure on p. 208.

TEMPLE MOUNT SIFTING PROJECT

A highlight for many pilgrims, the **Temple Mount Sifting Project** is located at the foot of Mt. Scopus within the Emek Tzurim Park on Hadasa Lempel Street—just minutes from the foot of the Mount of Olives. Tour groups are given an introduction to local archaeology followed by an opportunity to participate in "wet-sifting," one of the phases of archaeology. Participants look through debris removed from the Temple Mount, searching for as many artifacts as possible. Common finds include pottery, glass shards, bones, metals, mosaic stones, coins, and jewelry. Most of the finds can be identified and dated, and gener-ally each group has a significant number of finds. *Please note, as of this writing, the Sifting Project is presently closed to individuals. If you are with a tour group, ask your tour operator if they can book your group.*

SHABBAT OF A LIFETIME

Experience an authentic Shabbat dinner in a private home in the heart of Jerusalem!

Shabbat is the Jewish Sabbath that begins Friday at sundown and continues until sundown on Saturday. "Shabbat of a Lifetime" was created by a team of Jewish educators with the goal of developing a Shabbat evening program for diverse tourists to experience a typical Friday night of practicing Jews in Jerusalem. Over 100 local host families and 60,000 guests have joined Shabbat of a Lifetime. Dinners generally include 12 to 16 guests.

Host families come from a variety of backgrounds, each bringing their own unique touch. It is recommended that Christians opt for Orthodox or Conservative host families; those that practice Kaballah would be inconsistent with biblical values and beliefs.

You are encouraged to visit the Western Wall before the Shabbat meal that begins after sunset. All host homes are located in central Jerusalem neighborhoods and are accessible either by foot or by a short cab ride from many of the central hotels.

The program generally lasts a minimum of 2 ½ hours and consists of:

- Meeting your host family
- Learning about and participating in the traditions of the Shabbat meal
- Feasting on a kosher, five-course meal with a variety of traditional Shabbat cuisine from nine Jewish communities around the world
- An opportunity to ask questions about traditions, Jewish lifestyle, etc.
- Provision of *Shabbat of a Lifetime Table Companion* books which are beautiful, informative books that include a history of the Western Wall, Shabbat prayers, blessings and rituals, Shabbat songs, and traditional Shabbat recipes

More information and pricing: www.shabbatofalifetime.com. Phone: 972-52-595-3997; E-mail: david@shabbatofalifetime.com

ISRAEL SCAVENTURES EXISTS TO EDU-
cate, to engage, and to inspire its participants
to discover Israel, while having fun at the same
time! You can choose one of their existing
scavenger hunts or create a custom tailor-made
activity for your group.

They offer several options for games that
are a cross between a scavenger hunt and an
adventure of discovery within the city of
Jerusalem. With maps and mission packs in
hand, your group navigates its way through
streets, alleys and markets, while connecting
to the history of Israel and its people.

Each ScaVenture lasts about two hours
and is geared toward groups of all sizes,
ages six through adults. Some ScaVentures
are competitive, while others are not. Older
children will naturally get more out of the
educational content, but younger children
enjoy the excitement!

Prices vary according to group size. Visit
www.israelscaventures.com for more information. Phone: 972-52-835-8072; Email:
info@israelscaventures.com

Four Jerusalem ScaVentures are offered at the
time of this writing:

- **Old City Christian ScaVenture:**
  Travel through modern Mount Zion
  and the Jewish Quarter using Scripture,
  while bearing witness to fulfillment of
  ancient prophecy.

- **Jewish Quarter Old City ScaVenture:**
  Discover the secrets of the Jewish Quarter
  as tales of inspiring people, ancient places,
  and significant events come to life.

- **Machne Yehuda ScaVenture:** Teams
  make their way through the hustle and
  the bustle of Machne Yehuda marketplace completing their assignments such
  as selling fruit, posing with a fish, or
  finding someone from Greece!

- **Windmill ScaVenture:** Beginning at the
  Montefiore Windmill, stroll through the
  winding alleys of a beautiful, frontier
  neighborhood to discover the fascinating
  story of the expansion of Jerusalem
  beyond the Old City.

NIGHT SPECTACULAR

THE ANCIENT STONE WALLS AND
towers of the **Tower of David** (known as
the **Citadel**) serve as a backdrop for two
magnificent outdoor productions with
breathtaking virtual reality images projected
onto walls, archeological ruins, and hidden
pathways. These 45-minute celebrations of
light and sound are accompanied by original,
magnificent soundtracks. *Night Spectacular*
relates the history of Jerusalem. *King David*
tells the timeless story of David from shepherd
boy-to-king with a simulated background of
great works of art by Chagall, Matisse,
Michelangelo, and several others who have
immortalized the legendary King David.

Performances on Monday, Wednesday,
Thursday, and Saturday nights. For more
information and reservations (required),
visit www.tod.org.il/en and click on "Night
Experiences," or call 972-2-626-5333.

THE OLD CITY

*For Zion's sake I will not hold my peace, and for Jerusalem's sake I will
not rest, until her righteousness goes forth as brightness, and her salvation as
a lamp that burns. The Gentiles shall see your righteousness, and all kings
your glory. You shall be called by a new name, which the mouth of the
Lord will name. You shall also be a crown of glory in the hand of the Lord,
and a royal diadem in the hand of your God.*

ISAIAH 62:1–3, NKJ

THE OLD CITY

Walk about Zion, go around her, count her towers, consider well her ramparts,
view her citadels, that you may tell of them to the next generation.
For this is our God for ever and ever… PSALMS 48:12-14

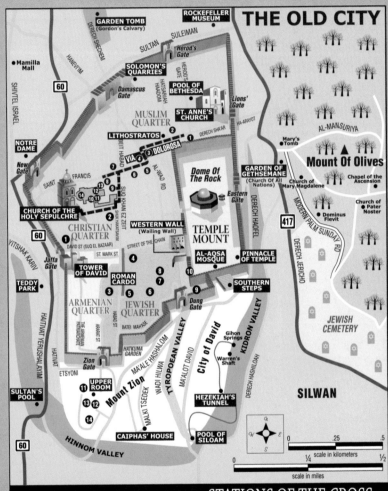

POINTS OF INTEREST

1. Ramparts Walk (start)
2. Church of the Redeemer
3. Old Yishuv Court Museum
   (Pre-1948 Jewish Quarter)
4. Broad Wall
5. Hurva Synagogue
6. Herodian Mansions
   (Wohl Archaeological Museum)
7. Burnt House
8. Temple Institute
9. Davidson Center
   (Jerusalem Archaeological Park)
10. Robinson's Arch
11. Chamber of the Holocaust
12. King David's Tomb
13. Dormition Abbey
14. Pauline Rose Home
    (Jerusalem Intercultural Center)

STATIONS OF THE CROSS
VIA DOLOROSA (WAY OF THE CROSS)

Stations not found in Bible are in black text.

1. Jesus is condemned to death.
2. Jesus takes up the cross.
3. Jesus falls under weight of the cross.
4. Jesus meets his mother.
5. Simon of Cyrene helps Jesus carry the cross.
6. Veronica wipes the face of Jesus.
7. Jesus falls the second time.
8. Jesus consoles the women of Jerusalem.
9. Jesus falls the third time.
10. CHS: Jesus is stripped of his garments.
11. CHS: Jesus is nailed to the cross.
12. CHS: Jesus died on the cross.
13. CHS: Jesus' body is taken from the cross.
14. CHS: Jesus is laid in the tomb.

CHS – CHURCH OF THE HOLY SEPULCHRE

THE RAMPARTS WALK IS AN EXCEL-lent way to begin your tour of the Old City. You can climb the ramparts and circle around the city from above for a stunning 360° view of the areas inside and outside the walls. From this elevated platform, unparalleled views into life in the Old City can be experienced: the cloistered Armenian Quarter, the courtyards of Muslim homes, the Christian Quarter, and the bustle of the Arab market.

Suleiman the Magnificent restored the ancient city walls, built on the foundations of medieval ramparts, in 1536. Since then, they have functioned as military fortifications and a path for guards to patrol the city, protecting it from thieves and predators. From 1948 to 1967, Jordanian snipers used the ramparts as a vantage point from which to shoot at Israelis living outside the walls.

The walls, which are roughly 2 ½ miles (4 km) long, more or less follow the outline of the ramparts surrounding ancient Jerusalem. They can be accessed at either the Damascus Gate or across from Jaffa Gate, behind David's Citadel. The Damascus Gate portion ends at the Lions' Gate. The Jaffa Gate segment ends near the Dung Gate, opposite the Jewish Quarter. The wall surrounding the Temple Mount is off limits to tourists.

Comfortable walking shoes are recommended, as the Ramparts Walk is made of ancient Jerusalem stone.

As Jesus was leaving the temple, one of his disciples said to him, "Look, Teacher! What massive stones! What magnificent buildings!" "Do you see all these great buildings?" replied Jesus. "Not one stone here will be left on another; every one will be thrown down."
MARK 13:1-2

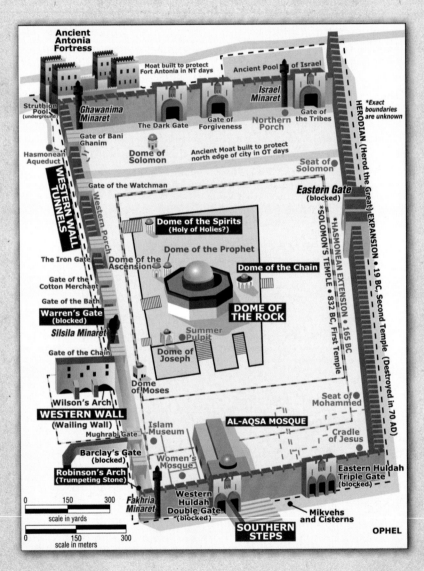

What agreement is there between the temple of God and idols? For we are the temple of the living God. As God has said: "I will live with them and walk among them, and I will be their God, and they will be my people." 2 CORINTHIANS 6:16

Temple Mount

THE TEMPLE MOUNT, ENCOMPASSING one-sixth of today's Old City, is the most contested and significant religious site in the world—as well as the epicenter of world history. Most biblical scholars believe the Temple Mount was Mt. Moriah, the site of the binding of Isaac. Judaism regards the Temple Mount as the place where God chose His Divine Presence to rest. This revered site has been used by the Canaanites, the Jews, Roman pagans, Christians, and Muslims.

The First Temple, built by King Solomon on King David's threshing floor almost 3,000 years ago, was almost totally destroyed by the Babylonians in 586 BC. However, in 165 BC the Hasmoneans built an extension to what remained of its southern portion. In 19 BC, King Herod began a massive expansion of the site and it was refashioned into the magnificent Second Temple, only to be destroyed once again by the Romans in AD 70 under the rule of Titus.

Today, the Islamic Waqf controls the Temple Mount. They require men and women to enter through separate gates and they do not allow religious materials, prayer, or singing on the mount, except those connected with the Muslim faith; any breach is against the law and warrants an arrest.

DOME OF THE ROCK

The Dome of the Rock is the highest point on the Temple Mount. Its Byzantine, octagonal design and rotunda were completed in AD 691 by Muslim ruler Abd el-Malik (who also built Al-Aqsa mosque several years later). The outside of the structure is made of marble, mosaics, and stained glass. Due to rust, the dome received a new gold coating in 1993. Muslims traditionally believe the Dome of the Rock protects the spot from which Muhammad is said to have risen to heaven, accompanied by the angel Gabriel. Hence, it is not really a mosque, but a shrine.

Dome of the Rock and Dome of the Chain

AL-AQSA MOSQUE

Al-Aqsa Mosque, dating back to AD 705, was destroyed in two earthquakes and rebuilt in AD 1035. Its original dome was reconstructed and covered with anodized aluminum in 1969.

According to the Quran, Al-Aqsa Mosque is the place from which Muhammad ascended on a night journey to Mecca. It is considered the third holiest site in Sunni Islam, following Mecca and Medina in Saudi Arabia. Abu al-Dardaa of Medina, companion to Prophet Muhammad, is quoted as saying, *"the Prophet of God, Muhammad, said a prayer in the Sacred Mosque (of Mecca) is worth 100,000 prayers; a prayer in my mosque (Medina) is worth 10,000 prayers; and a prayer in Al-Aqsa Mosque is worth 1,000 prayers"*

(more than in any other mosque). Al-Aqsa, which can hold up to 5,000 people, overflows every Friday with thousands of worshippers.

DOME OF THE SPIRITS

The Dome of the Spirits, also known as the *Dome of the Tablets*, stands to the north of the Dome of the Rock. Islam connects this dome with the Holy of Holies of the Jewish temple. Some believe this is the location of the Foundation Stone of the Holy of Holies which at one time held the Ark of the Covenant. Others believe it is either under, or to the south of, the Dome of the Rock.

DOME OF THE CHAIN

The Dome of the Chain is located to the east of the Dome of the Rock. The structure was built in AD 691; its exact purpose is unknown. Since it is built similarly to the Dome of the Rock in design with standing pillars and columns in both of their inner and outer circles, it may have been a prototype for the Dome of the Rock (see photo on previous page). The Dome of the Chain is one of three important structures built in the early Islamic period of Israel; the other two are the Dome of the Rock and the Al-Aqsa Mosque.

JAFFA GATE

Jaffa Gate is one of the Old City's busiest gates. In ancient days, if you were a pilgrim at the Port of Jaffa and walked east for three days along the Jaffa road, you would eventually reach this gate. Today, Jaffa Gate is the main exit into West Jerusalem.

DAMASCUS GATE

The Damascus Gate, located on the northwest side of the Old City, leads straight into the hub of the Old City marketplace. On Fridays and Saturdays, this is the busiest gate. In ancient times, Damascus Gate led first to the city of Nablus, and finally concluded in Damascus, Syria's capital.

LIONS' GATE
(ST. STEPHEN'S GATE; SHEEP GATE)

Four lions (or possibly leopards or panthers) are carved into the wall near the top of Lions' Gate. Legend has it that Sultan Suleiman the Magnificent ordered this construction because he had a dream—if he didn't build a wall around Jerusalem, he would be killed by lions.

During the Six-Day War, Israeli paratroopers charged through Lions' Gate and unfurled the Israeli flag high above the Temple Mount.

DUNG GATE

Dung gate is the gate closest in proximity to the Temple Mount and the only gate leading directly into the Jewish Quarter and the Western Wall. Since the second century AD, all the trash of the city was removed through this gate. It was then taken to the Hinnom Valley to be burned — hence the name.

The Old City gates never close. Its walls are 2 1/2 miles (4 km) lon

NEW GATE

The Turkish Sultan opened the Old City's "newest" gate in 1887 after powerful petitioning by Christians living outside the walled city; they insisted upon this gate in order to have direct access to Church of the the Holy Sepulchre. New Gate leads straight into the Christian Quarter.

HEROD'S GATE (FLOWERS GATE)

Herod's Gate, named after Herod the Great, serves as the northern entrance into the Muslim Quarter. It is the only major landmark in all of Jerusalem that bears Herod's name, and it was built 1,600 years after his reign.

EASTERN GATE (GATE OF MERCIES)

Based upon Ezekiel 44, Jews believe the Messiah will enter Jerusalem through the Eastern Gate. To prevent this, the Muslims sealed the gate. However, the Messiah has ALREADY come through the gate:

"Then He brought me back to the outer gate of the sanctuary which faces toward the east, but it was shut. And the Lord said to me, 'This gate shall be shut; it shall not be opened, and no man shall enter by it, because the Lord God of Israel has entered by it; therefore it shall be shut.'" (Ezekiel 44:1–2, NKJ)

ZION GATE

Zion Gate faces Mount Zion and also leads to the Jewish and Armenian Quarters. The stones surrounding the gate are riddled with bullet holes, a reminder of the fierce combat of the 1948 war. In 1967, the IDF entered and captured the Old City through Zion Gate.

n average of 40 ft (12 m) high and almost 9 ft (3m) thick.

THE MUSLIM QUARTER

The Muslim Quarter is by far the largest and most populous of the four quarters, encompassing more than half of the Old City's area. Its population of roughly 22,000 is predominately Muslim, along with about 60 Jewish families and 1,000 Arab Christians. The quarter has four gates, including the closed-off Eastern Gate. The Muslim Quarter can be accessed through the other three gates: Lions' Gate, Herod's Gate, and the popular Damascus Gate. Al-Aqsa Mosque is the Muslim Quarter's southern border.

The vibrant outdoor marketplace, known as the *Shuk*, is the heartbeat of the Muslim Quarter. Other places of interest include the Western Wall Tunnels, the first seven "Stations of the Cross" of the Via Dolorosa, the Church of St. Anne, the Pool of Bethesda, and Solomon's Quarries, as well as many Roman and Crusader sites. Good food and lodging abound in the Muslim Quarter.

THE CHRISTIAN QUARTER

The Christian Quarter, the northwestern portion of the Old City, is the second largest of the quarters covering close to one-fourth of the entire Old City. Most of its residents are religious Arab Christians such as monks, nuns, and priests of the Latin and Greek Patriarchates of Jerusalem. They reside in several houses in the southeastern part of the quarter; however, their numbers are dwindling.

The Christian Quarter has two access gates: New Gate on the north and Jaffa Gate (the traditional entrance to the Old City for Christians) to the west. Just inside the Jaffa Gate is a Christian Information Center which provides maps and information regarding Christian services and sites of the Old City.

The central feature of the Christian Quarter is the most holy site to the Catholic church, the Church of the Holy Sepulchre. Additionally, there are about forty Christian holy places in the quarter, including two monasteries and the other two most prominent churches after the Holy Sepulchre, the Lutheran Church of the Redeemer and the Church of John the Baptist. The Christian Quarter is also home to the prominent Tower of David, two mosques, and restaurants and hotels in abundance. A multitude of shops are concentrated in the Christian Quarter *Shuk*, mostly on David Street. The countless shops and vendors render it virtually impossible to know where the Christian Quarter ends and the Muslim Quarter begins!

THE ARMENIAN QUARTER

The Armenian Quarter, the smallest of the four quarters, began as a self-sustaining community in the fourth century AD. It was started by a small group of monks and pilgrims desiring to settle near Mount Zion's *Upper Room*, the traditional gathering place of early Christians. Some Christian historians believe the Armenian Quarter was the biblical Mount Zion.

During the 1948 Arab/Israeli war, when the quarter had about 16,000 residents, a segment of them took refuge at St. James Cathedral; however, many fled from Israel to safety abroad. The Armenian Quarter was caught in the middle of the 1967 Six-Day War, and what was left of it suffered extensive damage from bombing. The ornate St. James Cathedral is believed to be the burial site of the actual head of the apostle James who was beheaded (Acts 12:1-2). The cathedral is part of the larger compound of the St James Convent with residences for more than 1,000 families. The future of Israeli Armenian Christians in the Armenian Quarter is uncertain. Only about 1,000 Armenians live there today which represents half of Israel's total Armenian population; much of the quarter is closed off to tourists.

THE JEWISH QUARTER

The Jewish Quarter is home to an estimated 2,000 residents who hold long-term leases from the Israel Lands Administration. The quarter also encompasses many synagogues and yeshivas (Jewish places of study). Some of the Jewish Quarter is higher in elevation than the Temple Mount, requiring a significant climb to reach several sites.

The present Jewish Quarter was established in AD 1267, following the Crusader conquest of Israel. It began as a small group of Jews and has remained the center of the Old City Jewish community ever since.

At the time of the 1948 Arab-Israeli War (War of Independence), about 2,000 Jews were living in the Jewish Quarter. However, they were ultimately conquered by the Jordanian Arab Legion; many were slaughtered and the rest were forced to evacuate. The Jewish community surrendered to Jordan on May 28, 1948—just two weeks after Israel had become an official state. The quarter remained under Jordanian control until the 1967 Six-Day War, when Israel recaptured the Old City. Sadly, during those nineteen years, the community had been systematically demolished. A third of their buildings were destroyed and only one

out of thirty-five Jewish houses of worship remained standing. Since 1967, the quarter has been rebuilt and rejuvenated.

Hurva Square is the heart and social center of the Jewish Quarter. The open square offers cafés and snack bars, souvenir shops, Judaica, jewelry, and ample outdoor seating for the weary. On its west side is the **Hurva Synagogue**. *Hurva* means "ruins" and sadly, it has lived up to its name. The synagogue was originally built in 1701, but the project proved to be considerably more costly than anticipated. The Ashkenazi Jewish community was forced to take loans from local Arabs, which they unfortunately were not able to pay back in a timely manner; in 1720, their creditors burned Hurva to the ground. Hurva was rebuilt in 1864 and became Israel's most important Ashkenazi synagogue until it was destroyed once more, this time by Jordan in the 1948 War of Independence. In 2006, construction of the site began once again; it was completed in 2010. The new Hurva Synagogue, in its original Byzantine Revival architectural style, was rededicated in 2010. Tours are available but must be booked in advance. Phone: 972-02-626-5906

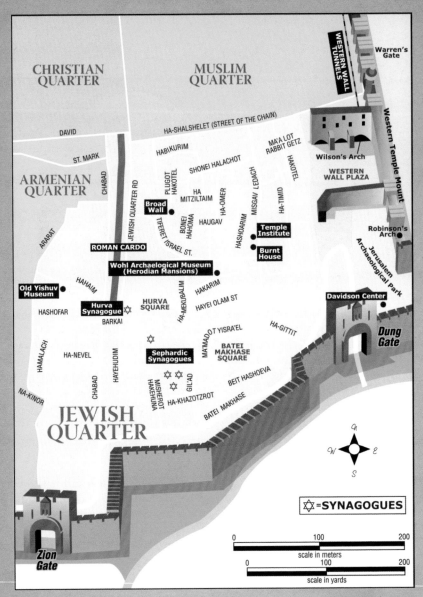

The Jewish Quarter, with its cobblestone streets and hidden alleyways, stands as a memorial to the heroic Jewish people who sacrificially persevered to keep their God-given home. Here lies the heart of their poignant community and their priceless spiritual heritage. Beautiful artisan shops in the Cardo stand on the same stones as in Roman times. Remains of the ancient city walls and demolished holy buildings make their painful past and hopeful future resonate within our souls. The Jewish Quarter is the place to connect with Jerusalem's rich history, its vibrant present, and its prophesied ultimate victory.

FOUR SEPHARDIC SYNAGOGUES

Just a one-minute walk through a short tunnel south of Hurva Square will bring you to a courtyard and synagogue which commence a complex of four adjoining *Sephardic* synagogues. Sephardic Jews are descendants of Spain who were expelled by royal edict in 1492. The four synagogues were built at different periods to meet diverse needs and practices of the Sephardic community. All four were seriously damaged and gutted during the 1948 Arab-Israeli War, but were beautifully refurbished and restored, preserving their original stonework, after the 1967 Six-Day War.

The **Eliahu Hanavi Synagogue**, also known as the **Elijah Synagogue**, is the oldest of the four synagogues; it was established in the sixteenth century for the purpose of Torah study. Its name is derived from a legend of a mysterious man who showed up for fasting and prayer on Yom Kippur, then mysteriously disappeared after the concluding prayer. He was believed to have been the prophet Elijah.

The **Yochanan ben Zakai Synagogue**, constructed below street level at the beginning of the seventeenth century, is believed to stand on the very spot where the Torah was read by rabbinic sage Yochanan ben Zakai, founder of the first century AD Sanhedrin, following the destruction of the Second Temple.

The largest synagogue is the **Istanbuli Synagogue**. As the name implies, it was originally built for immigrants from Istanbul, beginning in 1764. Today it is used by a Spanish and Portuguese congregation as well as serving as an "overflow" facility for important religious holidays, and the site for the inauguration of the chief Sephardic rabbi of Israel.

The last to be built was the small **Emtsai Synagogue**, known also as the Middle Synagogue due to its position in the "middle" of the other three synagogues. It was most likely used as a courtyard for the women of the Yochanan ben Zakai Synagogue, which was later roofed in the middle eighteenth century.

Visitors are welcome; Modest dress is requested and men must cover their heads. The ticket desk is at the back of the Yochanan ben Zakai Synagogue. Address: 2 Mishmeot Hakehuna St.; Phone: 972-2-628-0592

OLD YISHUV COURT MUSEUM

The Old Yishuv Court Museum displays the décor, original artifacts, and crafts typical of daily life in the Ashkenazi and Sephardic communities of the Jewish Quarter from the middle of the nineteen century to the end of the Ottoman rule in 1917. *Old Yishuv* is the name for this community before 1917, prior to its

move outside of the walls of the Old City to new neighborhoods within greater Jerusalem.

The museum is a hub for both storytellers and story enthusiasts. Old Yishuv community members come to life through original artifacts and engaging personal accounts of their struggles, their family life, their joys and sorrows, and their faith in God.

The museum offers guided tours that are both thematic and dramatized for organized groups and the general public. Check for current hours and fees. Address: 6 Or Hayim St., Jewish Quarter; Phone: 972-2-628-4636

The Davidson Center is the entry point to the Jerusalem Archaeological Park. Visitors can catch a realistic glimpse of Jerusalem in the late Second Temple period through a "virtual reality" reconstruction of the Temple Mount just prior to its destruction—achieved using illustrations, films, and computerized media. The Center encompasses many informative exhibitions highlighting the Southern Temple Mount (or *Ophel*) excavations. *Ophel* means "high place" in the Bible.

JERUSALEM ARCHAEOLOGICAL PARK

The **Jerusalem Archaeological Park** maintains the Southern Temple Mount Excavations. A plethora of archaeological finds span some 5,000 years, beginning with the Canaanite (Bronze) Age and continuing through the First and Second Temple periods. Finds include a staircase leading up to the temple, several **gates that led into the temple**, **residential houses**, **fortifications**, dozens of **cisterns**, and at least forty **mikvahs** or "ritual baths." The mikvahs would have been positioned around the entrance to the temple so visitors could cleanse themselves prior to entering. Other significant remains include a first century **Herodian Street** (likely the busiest street in Jerusalem at the time) and various ruins from the Byzantine and early Arab periods. Adjacent to the Western Wall is a large pile of huge **Herodian stones** in the exact same place where they fell nearly 2,000 years ago, at the destruction of the Second Temple in AD 70. Jesus had prophesied this event in Mark 13:2, *"'Do you see all these great buildings?' replied Jesus. 'Not one stone here will be left on another; every one will be thrown down.'"*

ROBINSON'S ARCH

At the southwestern Temple Mount, just around the corner from Al-Aqsa Mosque is **Robinson's Arch** (above), discovered by American Edward Robinson in 1838. The arch was incorporated into King Herod's Temple Mount expansion as part of its western retaining wall; it supported a massive stairway leading up to the Temple Mount plaza. At its base is the **"Trumpeting Stone"** (circled in photo above) protruding from the Temple Mount wall. The stone was found bearing a Hebrew inscription: *"to the place of trumpeting to."* This was likely the place where the trumpeter announced the commencement of the new moon, the beginning and close of the Sabbath, as well as the feasts of the Lord.

SOUTHERN STEPS

Just to the right of Al-Aqsa is a monumental staircase, the renowned "Southern Steps." Jesus would have climbed these steps often to reach the temple entrance. They are also sometimes referred to as the "Teaching Steps" because Jesus (and other rabbis) would have taught from the top of these steps, directly in front of the Temple gates.

GROUP ACTIVITY: read the first verse of each of the Psalms of Ascents (120–134) as you successively climb the fifteen wide steps until you reach the top of the staircase.

HULDAH GATES

The Southern Steps led to the Huldah Gates—the main gates through which visitors passed to reach the Temple Mount in the time of Christ. Jews would enter the gates, proceed up a tunnel, and then arrive at the Temple Mount plaza.

There are two sets of Huldah Gates: a **Double Gate** and a **Triple Gate**, both sealed shut by the Muslims who built Al-Aqsa Mosque on top of them. The Double Huldah Gate is ¾ covered; only its eastern right quarter is visible.

Triple Huldah Gate

Double Huldah Gate

The Davidson Center and the Jerusalem Archaeological Park are located just inside Dung Gate, adjoining the southern wall of the Western Wall Plaza. For more information, visit their website at www.archpark.org.il. Phone: 972-2-627-7550

WESTERN WALL PLAZA

WESTERN WALL ENTRANCE SIGNAGE:

"The present Western Wall before you is a remnant of the western Temple Mount retaining walls. Jews have prayed in its shadows for hundreds of years, an expression of their faith in the rebuilding of the Temple. The Sages said about it: 'The Divine Presence never moves from the Western Wall.' The Temple Mount continues to be the focus of prayer for Jews from all over the world."

THE **"WESTERN WALL,"** KNOWN AS THE *Kotel* in Hebrew, stands tall at 50 ft (15 m) high. In the nineteenth century, Jews would gather here to mourn their fallen state and the wall became known as the "Wailing Wall." Since the Talmud teaches that all prayers ascend to God in heaven from Jerusalem, and the Western Wall is the most holy place on the Temple Mount accessible to the Jewish people, the wall has been the foremost site for prayer and pilgrimage of Jewish people for centuries. However, from 1948–1967 (when the Old City was under Arab control), Jews were forbidden access. Today, Jews world-wide place more than a million written prayers in the cracks of the Wall each year.

At the lower northeast corner of the Western Wall plaza is **Wilson's Arch**, the present-day name for the 25 ft (7.6 m) high remains of an ancient stone arch. At one time, Wil-son's Arch was 75 ft (23 m) high and 42 feet (13 m) long; only the top of the arch is visible today. According to Josephus, the arch was a segment of a bridge adjoining the Temple Mount to the Upper City. It also serviced an aqueduct that transported water from Solomon's Pools, south of Bethlehem, all the way to the Temple Mount. **Warren's Shaft** is directly below Wilson's Arch (p. 191).

If you're visiting the wall on a Monday or Thursday between 7:00 AM and 3:00 PM, you have a good chance of viewing a joyous **Bar Mitzvah** celebration. As dusk approaches on Friday evenings, you can join thousands of Jews to welcome in the **Shabbat at the Western Wall** with singing and dancing: soldiers in uniform with rifles on their backs, men in long back coats, teenagers with backpacks, and Jews from all over the world!

WESTERN WALL TUNNELS

The fascinating Western Wall underground tunnels link the Western Wall plaza to the northwest side of the Temple Mount. The tunnels run adjacent to the western side of the Temple Mount, underneath current housing of the Muslim Quarter of the Old City, and ultimately exit at the Via Dolorosa. Approximately 200 ft (60 m) is visible today. However, 1,591 ft (485 m) of the Western Wall remains concealed underground.

Remarkably, there is no cement or bonding agent between the massive base stones of the tunnel; their sheer weight and seamless fit alone have held the wall firmly intact, allowing it to survive immense pressure over two millennia. The Western Stone is the largest stone in the Western Wall, as well as one of the largest stones in the world to be used in construction. The stone measures 46 ft (14m) wide, 13 ft (4m) high, 15 ft (4.6 m) deep, and weighs over 500 tons!

Warren's Gate, about 150 ft (46 m) into the Western Wall Tunnels, was once one of the major entrances to the Temple Mount, as well as a synagogue, during the early Muslim rule of Jerusalem. Today, it is a sealed-off gate known as "The Cave" believed to be located just opposite of the foundation stone. Warren's Gate is the closest spot to the Holy of Holies where Jews can pray.

A tour of the Western Wall Tunnels is a must! Toward the end of the tour is an ancient water reservoir called the Struthion Pool, located in the basement of the Sisters of Zion Convent, next to the third "Station of the Cross" of the Via Dolorosa. This large cistern, once utilized as a moat for the Antonia Fortress, continues to collect winter rain water from rooftops today.

It is wise to book your tour several days prior to your visit. Book a tour online or call: 972-2-627-1333.

ROMAN CARDO

The Cardo, also known as "Street of the Pillars," is today's main street of the Old City, as it was for ancient Byzantine Jerusalem—spanning from Damascus Gate down to Zion Gate. A life-sized mural (above) depicts the everyday life of Jerusalem during this time period.

Only a small part of the Cardo has been excavated; the remainder is buried under the buildings of the city. In the 1970s, several large churches and columns lining both sides of a 40 ft (12 m) wide main street were uncovered. Some of the columns have been restored.

One segment of the Cardo has been rebuilt as a modern shopping mall. While the mall is constructed with contemporary building materials, it still preserves the style of an ancient Roman street, incorporating a second century BC Hasmonean wall. Jewish shop owners carry upscale Judaica and souvenirs. Local artists sell quality art work, antiquity replicas, and sterling silver jewelry.

BROAD WALL

Located on Jewish Quarter Street are the remains of the "Broad Wall," an impressive wall measuring almost 23 ft (8m) both high and wide. Unearthed in the 1970's and visible today is a section running roughly 147 ft (45 m) of its total 213 ft (65 m) length. The section that is not visible runs beneath new homes of the Jewish Quarter.

The Broad Wall is a section of the First Temple wall built as a defensive wall. Most archaeologists believe this to be the wall King Hezekiah built in the late eighth century BC to protect Jerusalem against the Assyrians. Although, its name "Broad Wall" was used *later* in history when Nehemiah returned from the Babylonian exile and rebuilt the city to a smaller scale: *"They restored Jerusalem as far as the Broad Wall."* (Nehemiah 3:8; 12:27–38).

Isaiah 22:10 states they *"tore down houses to strengthen the wall."* Interestingly, the western part of the Broad Wall cuts through the remains of a house, apparently one of a group of original houses built outside the first walls of the city. It is believed the house was under royal orders to be evacuated for the Broad Wall to be built.

TEMPLE INSTITUTE

The Temple Institute has spent millions of dollars in preparations to build the Third Temple on the present Temple Mount site—which must first be cleared of the Dome of the Rock and surrounding Muslim structures.

These preparations are well on their way. Over the past decade, skillful Temple Institute craftsmen have produced exact replicas of the sacred temple vessels and priestly garments as specified in Scripture.

One essential mission of the Institute has been to find a red heifer that follows the strict requirements laid out in both Numbers 19:1–22 and the Mishnah. On August 28, 2018, a red heifer without blemish was born in the land of Israel for the first time in 2,000 years. It is believed the heifer is the result of an implantation of a frozen embryo of a United States Red Angus cow into an Israeli domestic cow. The red heifer candidate is being raised and specially cared for under the support of the Temple Institute. It must be periodically re-examined to determine if it is still a viable candidate for the biblical red heifer.

In early August of 2016, the Institute announced the establishment of the *Nezer HaKodesh Institute for Kohanic Studies*, the world's first institute for training *Kohanim* (Hebrew for "priest" in reference to the Aaronic priesthood).

The Institute is dedicated to teaching both Jews and Gentiles the traditions of the Holy Temple because Isaiah 56:7 refers to the Temple as "a house of prayer for all nations." The third Temple will be a "house of prayer for all monotheistic religions," e.g., Jews, Christians, and Muslims. Many Christians believe this Temple will be the stage of the Antichrist, as specified in 2 Thessalonians 2:1–4.

HERODIAN MANSIONS

The **Wohl Museum of Archaeology** encompasses six aristocratic homes from the time of Herod (and Jesus); these homes are known as the Herodian Mansions. The houses were built on a slope, one on top of another, enabling unobstructed views of the temple. Scorched remains are indicative of the Roman torching of the neighborhood in AD 70.

The exhibit focuses on three Hellenistic/Roman style homes, a popular style during this time period. The homes likely belonged to temple priests and their families. The quality utensils and artifacts, the mosaic flooring, vibrant wall frescoes, as well as other luxuries attest to the wealth of the residents. The largest of the mansions measured nearly 6,000 sq ft (2,000 sq m).

BURNT HOUSE

The Burnt House is a Second Temple period home that was located in the wealthy Herodian Quarter. An inscription on a stone weight found during excavation, "[of] Bar-Katros," indicates this house belonged to a family of temple priests cited in the Talmud.

The virtually-intact basement revealed a home with a small courtyard, four rooms, a kitchen and a mikvah. A twelve-minute audio-visual presentation re-enacts nearly 2000-year-old events: family members debating politics, reactions to the disturbing news of the imminent approach of the Roman Legion, the destruction of the Temple, the raid on the city, and finally the torching of the house—evidenced by the layers of ash and soot.

Jewish Quarter

SOLOMON'S QUARRIES

SOLOMON'S QUARRIES, LOCATED IN the Muslim Quarter, is also known as **Zedekiah's Cave,** even though there is no clear biblical connection of Zedekiah to a cave. The entrance to the quarry is located on the Old City wall about 500 ft (152 m) east of the Damascus Gate, under the Temple Mount.

Most archaeologists believe that King Solomon utilized this quarry in building the First Temple around 970 BC (1 Kings 6:1). 1 Kings 5:15-18 relates that he employed over 150,000 men for the project. It is likely that King Herod also would have used this as his primary quarry for building the retaining walls for the Second Temple renovation, which would have included the Western Wall.

Inside, the manmade cave slopes down into a vast 300-foot-long open chamber. The part of the quarry visible today is about 330 ft (100 m) wide, 650 ft (250 m) long, and up to 49 ft (15 m) high. There are several galleries in the quarry with diverse patterns, formations, and random chisel marks, as well as several large signs on the cave walls expounding various legends of the cave. There is also an underground spring near the lowest point of the cave, from the same water source as the City of David's Gihon Spring.

The cave runs below the street level of the Muslim Quarter, includes several lower levels, and leads to numerous tunnels under the Old City, many of which are blocked. Interestingly, there are a significant number of ancient accounts claiming the cave system extended for miles.

Historical timeline of Solomon's Quarries:

- The quarries were referred to as the "**Royal Caverns**" by Josephus Flavius (War 5:147).
- In the tenth century AD, the present Damascus Gate of the Old City was called "the Gate of the Grotto."
- The cave was used for textile storage in the fifteenth century AD and known as the "**Cotton Grotto.**"
- The entrance to the quarry was built by **Suleiman the Magnificent** in AD 1535, which he subsequently mined; Suleiman closed it off in AD 1540 for security reasons.
- In 1851, **Dr. James Barclay** was sent to Jerusalem as a medical missionary. While there, he heard rumors of an underground cave near the Damascus Gate. In 1854, while Dr. Barclay and his son were walking their dog, she started digging for bones and dug up the entrance to the cave. Dr. Barclay and his two sons secretly returned that night to the cave through the hole the dog had started digging. Once inside, they discovered ancient Hebrew and Arabic inscriptions, crosses carved into walls, and massive piles of blocks and chippings. They had discovered King Solomon's temple quarries!
- **Freemasons** revere Solomon's Quarries because they believe King Solomon was their first Grand Master. In 1868, they held their first ceremony in the cave and have continued to do so ever since; the Freemasons of Israel hold their annual ceremony at Solomon's Quarries.
- In 1969, an archeologist discovered cherub graffiti dating back to the time of Solomon.
- In the late twentieth century, the Jerusalem Foundation carried out major restorations to the cave to make it accessible to tourists.
- From 2000 to 2002, the first excavations began. Archeologists determined that many of the relics were from the Roman and Byzantine periods.

POOL OF BETHESDA

Now there is in Jerusalem near the Sheep Gate a pool, which in Aramaic is called Bethesda and which is surrounded by five covered colonnades. Here a great number of disabled people used to lie — the blind, the lame, the paralyzed. One who was there had been an invalid for thirty-eight years... Then Jesus said to him, "Get up! Pick up your mat and walk." At once the man was cured; he picked up his mat and walked. JOHN 5:2–9

The excavated pool, believed to be the authentic Pool of Bethesda, is located near the Lions' Gate in the Muslim Quarter of the Old City, close to the beginning of the Via Dolorosa. It is also believed to be the "Upper Pool" alluded to in 2 Kings 18:17 and Isaiah 7:3. When the site was excavated, it revealed a rectangular pool with two basins separated by a wall—in essence a five-sided pool with a tall colonnade on each side, identical to the pool described above in John 5:2. In Hebrew, *Bethesda* means "house of mercy" or "house of grace," portraying divine mercy and compassion. In the time of Jesus, multitudes who were ill sought the pool's alleged healing powers. As soon as the water would become stirred up, the first person to enter the pool would purportedly be cured of his or her infirmity.

CHURCH OF ST. ANNE

Located just north of the Temple Mount, on the same grounds as the Pool of Bethesda, stands the Church of St. Anne. This majestic, fortress-like structure is deemed the best-preserved Crusader church in Jerusalem. Completed in AD 1138, St. Anne's was constructed to replace a much older Byzantine church built by Emperor Hadrian in the second century AD. It was built over the remnants of a pagan shrine to a god of healing (possibly related to the Pool of Bethesda).

According to tradition, the Church of St. Anne stands over the site of a grotto, which was originally the home of Joachim and Anne, parents of the virgin Mary. Additionally, many believe this to be the birthplace of Mary. A flight of steps leads down to a crypt in the grotto, where an altar was erected in her honor.

Today, the Church of St. Anne is renowned for its extraordinary acoustics and resounding echoes which make even the smallest vocal group sound like a large assembly in an immense church!

VIA DOLOROSA

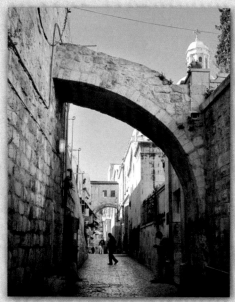

ECCE HOMO ARCH

The Ecce Homo Church is part of the Sisters of Zion Convent which encompasses a segment of the *Ecce Homo Arch* (left), Latin for "Behold the Man." The central opening of the arch can be seen between Stations #2 and #3 on the Via Dolorosa. According to popular tradition, this marks the site where Pilate presented Jesus to the masses.

LITHOSTRATOS

The location of the *Praetorium*, or "Hall of Judgment," is uncertain. One possible location is below current street level on the Via Dolorosa, beneath the Sisters of Zion Convent. Here, a large area of second-century Roman flagstones was discovered (below). In Scripture, the flagstone floor was referred to as *Lithostratos* or the "Stone Pavement" (John 19:13). Etchings in the pavement indicate a dice game known as the "King's Game," with the objective of executing a mock king.

Commencing at the Lion's Gate in the Muslim Quarter is the *Via Dolorosa*, also known as the "Way of the Cross" or the "Way of Grief" in Latin. The Via Dolorosa commemorates the path Jesus walked under the weight of the cross, beginning at the *Praetorium* (the place of judgment) and ending at Calvary.

Over the centuries, the route has changed several times; the current Via Dolorosa is most likely from the Crusader era. It is marked with fourteen "stations of the cross," each commemorating an event believed to have taken place along the way to Calvary—nine of which are found in Scripture. The last five stations of the cross are in the Christian Quarter.

Although the exact places of the events are unknown, the *Way of the Cross* was undoubtedly a tremendously sorrowful journey for our Saviour. The physical pain He endured was mild compared to the tormenting pain caused by our sin.

Every Friday, a Roman Catholic procession led by Franciscan priests walks the Via Dolorosa path. Re-enactments are also common.

CHURCH OF THE HOLY SEPULCHRE

The ornate Church of the Holy Sepulchre, initially constructed by the Crusaders in the twelfth century AD, is the most holy site for the Greek Orthodox and Catholics.

Station #13

The church is believed by many to be the location of the crucifixion, burial, and resurrection of Jesus. Its location was both outside the city and close to one of the city gates, rendering it an appropriate site for a crucifixion. The last five Stations of the Cross are located on the church grounds.

Station #13 represents Jesus' body being taken down from the cross and laid on top of a stone. Multitudes of visitors kneel, pray, and kiss the stone, known as the "stone of anointing."

Station #14 represents Jesus' body laid in the tomb. A large rotunda encloses this final station. This is believed to be the tomb of Jesus.

The church is managed jointly by six different denominations.

Station #14

One of the Old City's oldest Muslim families holds the key to the building.

LUTHERAN CHURCH OF THE REDEEMER

The Lutheran Church of the Redeemer, located right across from the Church of the Holy Sepulchre, is Israel's headquarters for the Lutheran Church. It is one of only two Protestant churches in the Old City, along with Christ Church Guesthouse. Lutheran Church of the Redeemer is also the newest church in the Old City, dedicated on Reformation Day, 1898.

Today, diverse congregations worship at the church; services are held in Arabic, German, Danish, and English. In 2012, an excavated area beneath the church was opened to the public, revealing remains from the pre-Christian era.

It is worth the 178-stair hike up the church's circular staircase to reach its bell tower at over 130 ft (40 m) high. Here you will find one of Jerusalem's best views. The bell tower offers panoramic views of both old and new Jerusalem.

CHRIST CHURCH

Christ Church, founded in 1849, is located just within the Jaffa Gate. The church describes itself as *"a center of prayer for all nations with worship reflecting the Jewish context of the gospel."* Christ Church is the first Protestant church in the Middle East as well as the only church in the Old City to focus on its Jewish roots in its liturgy, symbols, and architecture. The church was conceived from the founders' shared love and concern for the Jewish people. They wanted the Jewish people to know the Good News of their Jewish Messiah and they desired to be a part of the prophesied global return of the Jews to the land of Israel.

Church meetings in English are currently held on Sundays and Wednesdays, with a convenient Sunday evening worship time (after a day of touring) at 7:00 PM.

This beautiful, peaceful property also encompasses **Christ Church Guesthouse** a Christian guesthouse, courtyard, and prayer garden. Christian staff members and volunteers from around the world serve and minister to the guests. Christ Church Guesthouse is a prime accommodation for touring all parts of the Old City at whim! The marketplace, the Church of the Holy Sepulchre, the Via Dolorosa, the Western Wall, the Temple Mount, and much more are all within a short walking distance.

Locals and savvy tourists know they can procure healthy and delicious refreshments, salads, and full meals at the **Christ Church Coffee Shop** located directly on their grounds. Christian tourists can also join a **traditional Shabbat meal** in the Christ Church Guesthouse dining room on Friday evenings.

Reservations are required for both the guesthouse and the Friday Shabbat dinner. Contact the guesthouse for information and current rates. Phone: 972-2-627-7727; Email: christch@netvision.net.il

HEZEKIAH'S POOL

Few visitors to the Old City know about Hezekiah's pool, an impressive water supply system utilized for Jerusalem and the Temple Mount. The pool dates back to the Second Temple period. Hezekiah's Pool is in the Christian Quarter, but hidden to the public eye, as it is surrounded by many buildings crammed into small spaces. The southern side of the pool adjoins David Street and its eastern border is Christian Quarter Road, where most of the shops on the western side overlook the pool. The best place to view the pool is on the roof of the New Imperial Hotel, right across from the Tower of David. Simply inquire at their reception desk as to the location of the steps leading to the rooftop.

TOWER OF DAVID

"Your neck is like the tower of David, built with courses of stone;
on it hang a thousand shields, all of them shields of warriors."
Song of Songs 4:4

The Tower of David, also known as "**The Citadel**," has been one of Jerusalem's most significant landmarks since ancient times. However, there is no connection to the biblical King David; its foundations were first laid nearly 1,000 years after his death. The tower is located just south of the Jaffa Gate at the highest point of southwest Jerusalem.

The Tower of David is a medieval fortress with a series of fortifications spanning more than twenty centuries. Its elevation and fortifications, beginning with King Hezekiah, have made it a strategic stronghold to many civilizations. Today it incorporates the remains of several earlier citadels. Its courtyard displays 2,700-year-old archeological ruins and a quarry dated to the First Temple period.

During the Second Temple period, **King Herod** added three massive towers: the **Phasael Tower** (named after his brother), the **Hippicus Tower** (named after his friend), and the **Mariamne Tower** (named after his favorite Hasmonean Jewish wife, whom he

later murdered). **Of the three towers, only the base of one remains today**—disputed to be either the **Phasael** or the Hippicus Tower.

The fascinating **Tower of David Museum** opened in 1989. It encompasses a series of chambers (medieval guardrooms) in the original citadel; each exhibit room depicts Jerusalem under a different ruler. Tours present 4,000 years of Jerusalem's history chronologically, utilizing state-of-the-art technology: multi-media presentations, holograms, laser projections, animation, maps, drawings, models, dioramas, and even games and apps for children. A highlight is the 1:100 scale model of the Tower of David, which can be viewed while simultaneously listening to an audio guide and viewing the structure itself. For more information, visit www.tod.org.il. Email: education@tod.org.il

If at all possible, attend one of their magnificent evening sound and light shows, either the **Night Spectacular** or the **King David Show!** For more information, see p. 152.

OUTSIDE THE CITY WALLS

*"The days are coming," declares the Lord, "when this city will be rebuilt for
me from the Tower of Hananel to the Corner Gate. The measuring line will
stretch from there straight to the hill of Gareb and then turn to Goah.
The whole valley where dead bodies and ashes are thrown, and all the terraces
out to the Kidron Valley on the east as far as the corner of the Horse Gate, will
be holy to the Lord. The city will never again be uprooted or demolished."*

JEREMIAH 31:38–40

View of the Old City from Dominus Flevit

JERUSALEM HAS THREE SIGNIFICANT valleys that provide a natural, geographical defense for the city. The Tyropoean Valley runs directly down the center of the Old City with the Hinnom Valley to its west (located to the south and west of the Old City) and the Kidron Valley to its east. Viewed from above, the valleys look remarkably like the Hebrew letter *shin*, which denotes the word *Shaddai*, a name meaning "God Almighty." Perhaps it is a coincidence, or perhaps our Lord created the geography of Jerusalem to fulfill 2 Chronicles 6:6 both physically as well as spiritually: "But now I have chosen Jerusalem for my Name to be there…" If He did this purposefully, it's interesting to note that Mount Moriah (today's Temple Mount) is positioned at the top of the name of God.

TYROPOEAN VALLEY

The Tyropoean Valley is also known as the *Central Valley* and the *Valley of the Cheesemakers* (as named by Josephus Flavius). In ancient times, this valley was a rugged ravine separating the eastern hill of Mount Moriah from the western hill of Mount Zion. It commenced in the upper part of the city and passed the Western Wall of the temple on its west side prior to merging with the other two main valleys at its southern end point—the Hinnom Valley to its west and the Kidron Valley to its east. *See Old City map on p. 154.*

During the days of Hezekiah, the valley was leveled off for building purposes. Over the centuries, mounds of both rubble and remains from the frequent destruction and rebuilding of Jerusalem have largely filled the valley, leaving it level today.

In Jesus' time, the Tyropoean Valley functioned as a main street lined with shops and markets. The Western Wall rose from the bottom of the Tyropoean Valley to its top. At this point, it was level and provided access to the main thoroughfare and southwestern corner of the Second Temple where Robinson's Arch can be viewed today. There were several bridges above the valley, the most well-known being the Zion Bridge that connected Mount Moriah's temple to Mount Zion's royal palace.

Today, Tyropoean is more of a plain (filled with debris) than a valley. It runs southward under the Damascus Gate, then southeast through the middle of the Old City, to the Pool of Siloam, until it finally meets the Hinnom and Kidron valleys, just south of the City of David. The paved Herodian street that can be seen in the Southern Wall excavations, running along the Western Wall under Robinson's Arch, follows its original course.

KIDRON VALLEY

Then David said to all his officials who were with him in Jerusalem, "Come! We must flee, or none of us will escape from Absalom…"…The king also crossed the Kidron Valley,…
2 SAMUEL 15:14, 23

The Kidron Valley borders the Arab village of Silwan on the eastern side of the Old City, separating the Temple Mount and the City of David from the Mount of Olives. The 20 mile (34 km) long valley continues east en route to the Dead Sea, where its elevation drops 4,000 ft (1.2 km).

The Kidron Valley was known as the "King's Valley" when Old Testament kings actually owned its land, cultivated the land, then benefitted from its revenues. The valley was also one of the primary burial grounds for the elite, wealthy families of Jerusalem in the Second Temple period. Today, hundreds of olive trees have been planted to restore the once-fertile, ancient landscape.

Many scholars believe the Kidron Valley is the valley the Bible refers to as the "Valley of Jehoshaphat" or "the valley where God will judge" (Joel 3:1–3). **King David** fled from his son, **Absalom,** in this valley (2 Samuel 15); **King Asa** burned his grandmother's idolatrous image of Asherah in the Kidron Valley (1 Kings 15:13); Judah's wicked **Queen Athaliah** was probably executed in the Kidron Valley

(2 Kings 11:13–16); and **Jesus** often crossed the Kidron Valley while traveling between Jerusalem and Bethany.

Three renowned rock-hewn tombs are found on the eastern side of the Kidron Valley. The predominant tomb is known as "Absalom's Pillar" from 2 Samuel 18:18 (photo below). Two other tombs are close by. The first of these is associated with the temple priest **Zechariah** (first century BC) and the second with the **"sons of Hezir"** (a Second Temple-era priestly family). However, the tombs date back to only the Second Temple period, not to the time of King David.

HINNOM VALLEY

With the reward he got for his wickedness, Judas bought a field; there he fell headlong, his body burst open and all his intestines spilled out. Everyone in Jerusalem heard about this, so they called that field in their language Akeldama, that is, Field of Blood.
ACTS 1:18-19

The Hinnom Valley (also known as *Gehenna*) marked the tribal border between Benjamin and Judah (Joshua 15:8, 18:16). This deep, narrow ravine runs south from the Jaffa Gate on the west side of the Old City, then continues eastward along the south side of Mt. Zion until it meets the Kidron Valley. The lowest point of the Hinnom Valley is also the lowest point in Jerusalem, illustrative of the valley's reputation.

The Hebrew name *Hinnom* or *Gehenna* in Greek is associated with eternal torment and is translated "hell" in Matthew 5:22;29. In Judaism, Christianity, and Islam, Gehenna is the destination of the wicked, the place of eternal fire, judgment, hell, and *"the worm that never dies."* It is the place where both body and soul will be destroyed in *"unquenchable fire."* Hinnom Valley is the *Gehenna* of the New Testament (Mark 9:44-48).

The Valley of Hinnom demonstrates an atrocious history of curses and evil over a period of many years. One portion of the valley was named *Tophet*, meaning "fire-stove." This was where apostate Israelites and followers of the pagan gods, *Baal* and *Molech* (which included King Ahaz and his grandson Manasseh), sacrificed their children by fire to Molech (2 Chronicles 28:3, 33:6). Jeremiah wrote that the worshippers of Baal had *"filled this place with the blood of innocent children,"* and he warned that they would pay with the destruction of their sacred temple and exile (Jeremiah 11:13). The only good act recorded in Scripture, concerning the Valley of Hinnom, was the account of King Josiah's destroying the shrine of Molech, preventing further child sacrifice at the site (2 Kings 23:10).

In Roman times (AD 70), the Hinnom Valley was utilized both as a burial site and the city dump. Garbage, as well as anything deemed to be unclean, was incinerated in this valley, including executed criminals and animal carcasses—for which a fire was kept continually burning. The constant filth and thick smoke kept the Valley of Hinnom a very dark and gloomy place. It was in the Hinnom Valley where Judas received his just reward. Jeremiah 19 prophesies that Gehenna will become a valley of slaughter, flames, and punishment for the wicked in the end times.

You can get a good view of Hinnom Valley from the Mt. Zion Hotel or by standing in the southwest corner of the parking lot of the Church of St. Peter in Gallicantu (location of Caiaphas' House).

Beautiful in elevation, the joy of the whole earth, is Mount Zion in the far north, the city of the great King. PSALMS 48:2, NASB

IN THE ERA OF THE OLD TESTAMENT, Har Tzion (Mount Tzion) was the "stronghold of Zion," the eastern fortress that King David captured from the Jebusites and named the City of David (2 Samuel 5:6–9). After the construction of King Solomon's temple, Mount Zion referred to the Temple Mount. The word "Zion" became synonymous with the Jewish yearning for their homeland, and from it came the term "Zionism."

In the time of Christ, Mount Zion was an affluent neighborhood at the highest point in Jerusalem. The neighborhood was inside the city walls unlike Mount Zion is today. During the Byzantine era, pilgrims thought that the larger, flatter western hill south of the Old City must be the original City of David (Mount Zion). Hence, the present location came to be known as Mount Zion and has remained so ever since.

Today, there are several sites of interest on Mount Zion: Dormition Abbey, King David's "alleged" tomb, the Upper Room, Church of St. Peter in Gallicantu, Chamber of the Holocaust, and both a Protestant and Catholic cemetery (where Oskar Schindler is buried).

DORMITION ABBEY

The picturesque Dormition Abbey, resembling a stately medieval castle, towers over the summit of Mount Zion. This is the site where the virgin Mary is said to have died (or fallen into "eternal sleep"). "Dormition Abbey" in Latin is *Dormition Sanctae Mariae*, literally "sleep of St. Mary." The Scriptures, however, are silent regarding the location of Mary's death.

The Latin Patriarch of Jerusalem completed the Abbey's construction in 1910. It was built over the site of a much older Byzantine church from a previous era; the relics of the Byzantine mosaic floor can still be viewed through protective glass in the courtyard.

Today Dormition Abbey is a regal, circular structure with several niches accommo-

dating various altars. Two spiral staircases lead down to a crypt that surrounds a reclining sculpture of the virgin Mary, depicting her state of death. Mosaics decorate the interior of the Abbey, including a mosaic depicting "Madonna and Child" and a zodiac mosaic embellishing the Abbey's rotunda—highly unusual for a Christian church.

KING DAVID'S TOMB

Then David rested with his ancestors and was buried in the City of David.
He had reigned forty years over Israel—seven years in Hebron and thirty-three in Jerusalem.
1 KINGS 2:10–11

Most historians and archeologists do not consider "King David's Tomb" the authentic burial site of King David. 1 Kings 2:10 records that King David was buried in the City of David, which at that time was the original Mount Zion, not this new location. Still others believe the original Mount Zion was Bethle-

hem. It was the Christian Crusaders who, over a thousand years ago, built the present memorial and named it King David's Tomb. Over time, the site has come to be regarded as such, first by the Jews and later by the Muslims. Interestingly, the Talmud teaches King David's death occurred during the feast of Shavuot (Pentecost).

UPPER ROOM

When they arrived, they went upstairs to the room where they were staying. Those present were Peter, John, James and Andrew; Philip and Thomas, Bartholomew and Matthew; James son of Alphaeus and Simon the Zealot, and Judas son of James. ACTS 1:13

Upstairs from King David's Tomb is the room known as the "Upper Room," the "Room of the Last Supper," and the *Coenaculum* (in Latin). The Crusader-style architecture indicates this structure was probably built under Crusader rule—sometime between AD 1095–1291.

The "Upper Room" commemorates the Last Supper of Jesus and His disciples prior to His death (Matthew 26:17–30). It was here that Matthias was chosen to replace Judas (Acts 1:12–23) and the Holy Spirit mightily came upon the disciples (Acts 2).

CHAMBER OF THE HOLOCAUST MUSEUM

South of Zion Gate and across the street from King David's Tomb is the Chamber of the Holocaust Museum, literally the "Cellar of the Catastrophe." Founded in 1948, it was Israel's first memorial to the Holocaust.

A staircase leads down to an underground Crusader dungeon. Ten somber and dimly-lit rooms resembling caves create a cemetery-like atmosphere of mourning. The walls of the rooms and an adjoining courtyard are flanked with tombstone-like tablets and plaques, inscribed in Hebrew, Yiddish, and English. Each commemorates one of the more than 1,000 Jewish towns and communities destroyed in the Holocaust. A large structure resembling a grave represents those lost in the Holocaust who were never found.

Ashes of Holocaust victims found at concentration camps were sent to Jerusalem; some are buried at Yad Vashem Holocaust Museum, but most are buried in the Chamber of the Holocaust. For years, Holocaust survivors and descendants of Holocaust victims came here to light memorial candles, recite the *Kaddish* (the Jewish mourners' prayer) and mourn. From 1948 to 1967, when the Western Wall was not accessible to the Jewish people, this chamber served as a substitute holy place for many.

The museum displays dozens of memorials and monuments, as well as salvaged artifacts donated by survivors and victims' families.

Each one offers insight into the Holocaust and Judaism; each one tells a different story. Some of the intriguing (yet gruesome) artifacts include: an old book found near Auschwitz that was used to record births, deaths, and illnesses of many at the camp, a concentration camp uniform, reproductions of the ovens used to cremate remains in the camps, a container of *Zyklon B* the pesticide used in the gas chambers, a bloodstained Torah scroll that was used to wrap a rabbi who was stabbed to death, and even several bars of soap believed to be made from human remains.

One display case contains hats, boots, bags, and other items made by Nazis from the very pages of Torah; the purpose was to "dehumanize" and "desecrate" the Jewish people. One Nazi soldier, desiring to mock the Jews, commissioned a Jewish tailor to sew him a jacket out of Torah pages. The tailor used pages containing the 98 curses found in the *Ki Tavo* portion of the Torah (Deuteronomy. 26:1–29:8, *"When you enter the land…"*). Perhaps the soldier cursed himself!

The museum has undergone extensive renovations in recent years. Admission is free, but donations are greatly appreciated. Ilan Goodman, curator of the Chamber of the Holocaust, states,

"This isn't just a story about the Holocaust; it's part of the story itself."

PAULINE ROSE HOME
The "Lady of Mount Zion"

A one-minute walk south from the Chamber of the Holocaust is the **Jerusalem Intercultural Center**, the previous home of Mrs. Pauline Rose (1898-1973). Born in South Africa, Pauline Rose became known as the "Lady of Mount Zion." She could also be considered the first lady of twentieth-century Messianic Judaism; Mrs. Rose founded the first modern-day Messianic Jewish congregation in Jerusalem.

In 1946, Pauline and her husband Albert came to Jerusalem to "kindle the Sabbath Light of Messiah." Two years later, at the end of the 1948 Arab-Israeli War, Old City Jerusalem was under Jordanian control and the Jews had been banished from the city. Destruction of the Jews' beloved Jerusalem was widespread. The homes of those who had lived on Mount Zion were left dilapidated, some reduced to rubble. This spurred Pauline Rose to her ultimate vision of living and planting a garden on Mount Zion. She wanted to make the deserted, war-torn hill bloom again in anticipation of the fulfillment of biblical prophecy, and she desired to be part of that restoration. Mrs. Rose wanted her home to be a place of hospitality wholly dedicated to peace, brotherly love, and the messianic hope.

Since residents on Mount Zion had been forced to move, all the homes were abandoned. Due to the hill's precarious position directly on the border and opposite the Jordanian positions, Mount Zion had become a militarized zone. Only the Israeli army occupied the hill; it was deemed too dangerous and isolated for civilians.

In 1963, after a lengthy process and many setbacks, Pauline Rose and her husband Albert miraculously received permission to live on Mount Zion. They soon found their house close to Zion Gate—a house that seemed to "guard" Mount Zion with views to the east, west, and south. Pauline and Albert lovingly restored the house and planted their garden. During the build-up to the 1967 Six-Day War, their home became a center of hospitality for visitors to Mount Zion. Soldiers, Jews, Christians, Arabs, pilgrims of all faith, artists, poets, thinkers, philosophers, and statesmen were all welcomed into the Rose home. Through her "window on Mount Zion," Pauline Rose witnessed the dramatic Six-Day War unfold, ultimately resulting in the triumphant reunification of Jerusalem.

Today, visitors can walk through her home, now the Jerusalem Intercultural Center, which was founded in 1999. It is quite fitting that her home became a center dedicated to building an infrastructure for dialogue among Jerusalem's many cultural, religious, and ethnic groups. The center's goal is to assist the city's diverse residents in becoming responsible, active partners in shaping their communities and Jerusalem's future.

The stories of Pauline Rose are fascinating! She has written two highly-recommended books of her memoires which have been published by the **First Fruits of Zion** (FFOZ) ministry: *Window on Mount Zion* and *The Siege of Jerusalem*. You can easily find them online by typing the name of the book into your search engine. They can be purchased on the FFOZ website, www.ffoz.com.

CAIAPHAS' HOUSE

I am counted among those who go down to the pit; I am like one without strength.
I am set apart with the dead, like the slain who lie in the grave, whom you remember
no more, who are cut off from your care. You have put me in the lowest pit,
in the darkest depths. PSALM 88:4–6

The modern Church of St. Peter in Galli-cantu, built into the eastern slope of Mount Zion in 1931, encompasses the remains of **"Caiaphas' House."** *Galli-cantu* is Latin for "cock-crow." This is widely believed to be the authentic site of the palace of Caiaphas the high priest, where Jesus was incarcerated after His arrest.

The lower level of the church has Second Temple era caves that were cut into the rock under the ancient houses—revealing a realistic setting of the arrest, trial and suffering of Jesus. There appears to have been a prisoner's cell or dungeon (actually a pit known as the "Sacred Pit") in the caves. Another room, known as "the guardroom," has holes in the stone walls that were used to secure a prisoner's hands and feet while he was being flogged.

On the church's north side is an ancient staircase leading toward the Kidron Valley. This was likely the path descending from the Upper City during the First Temple period, the path that Jesus would have followed from Gethsemane on the night of His arrest.

A statue of Peter's denial stands in the church courtyard as a visual remembrance of the three-fold denial of Peter. The statue includes Peter, the two maids, the Roman soldier, and the rooster (seen on top). The inscription at the base, *Non novi illum*, is Latin for "I do not know him."

Nevertheless, David took the stronghold of Zion, that is, the City of David.
2 SAMUEL 5:7

THE ORIGINAL INHABITANTS OF Jerusalem did not live on the site of today's Old City; they lived on a narrow ridge, just twelve acres (five hectares) in area, descending south from the present Temple Mount. This was the "City of David," purposefully built around the Gihon Springs, the area's primary source of plenteous water.

Today, the City of David National Park is located just south of the Old City walls in the predominantly Arab village of Silwan. Since 2007, the Hebrew University and the Israel Antiquities Authority have been conducting extensive excavations in the former Givati parking lot, west of the entrance to the City of David. Most biblical archaeologists believe this to be the actual hilltop where King David dedicated Jerusalem as his capital nearly three millennia ago. If so, the exclusive hilltop would have been inhabited by many kings and prophets of old—

including kings Solomon, Hezekiah, and Josiah and prophets Isaiah and Jeremiah.

Elegant homes designed especially for Jerusalem's elite have been uncovered in the City of David. The artifacts, cosmetics, and imported Syrian furniture all attest to the affluence of its residents. Likewise, the devastating destruction of the Roman conquest is also evident in the relics strewn across the basement level.

The excavated "House of Ahi'el" was a typical four-room home with an outside stairway that likely had led to either a second story or a flat roof. A limestone toilet seat (one of four found on site), with a cesspit beneath, was embedded in the plaster floor in one of the rooms. The House of Ahie'el was found below the large "Stepped-Stone Structure" that likely supported a royal building such as the king's palace.

HEZEKIAH'S TUNNEL

It was Hezekiah who blocked the upper outlet of the Gihon Spring and channeled the water down to the west side of the City of David. He succeeded in everything he undertook.
2 CHRONICLES 32:30

The City of David provides an awesome opportunity to trek through the tunnels through which the city was conquered and its residents fled, while viewing the hidden spring where kings of old were coronated. *Check out various tunnels on p. 193.*

Hezekiah's Tunnel is considered one of the greatest technological achievements of water engineering from the pre-Classical period. In 701 BC, King Hezekiah directed the challenging construction of a tunnel that was to be used as an aqueduct. The aqueduct would provide water for Jerusalem in preparation for the imminent Assyrian siege (2 Chronicles 32:2–4). Hezekiah's Tunnel, 1,750 ft (530 m) in length, was excavated through solid bedrock.

In 1880, Jacob Spafford (adopted son of Horatio Spafford) was wading in the tunnel near the Siloam Pool when he discovered the **"Shiloah Inscription"** carved into a rock approximately 19 ft (5.8 m) into the tunnel. The inscription dates to 701 BC and records the account of the meeting of the two groups of quarriers digging Hezekiah's tunnel from opposite sides and how they met—one group above the other group. The inscription was cut out of the wall of the tunnel in 1891.

The **Gihon Spring** was, and still is, the only spring in Jerusalem. *Gihon*, meaning "gushing," is linked to the Gihon River, the second of four headwaters emerging from the same

Warren's Shaft

river that watered the Garden of Eden (Genesis 2:10–14). The Gihon Spring became the main source of both drinking water and irrigation water for ancient Jerusalem, as it is today. The tunnel takes water from the Gihon Spring and empties it into the **Pool of Siloam**, providing the city of Jerusalem its only reliable supply of fresh water. Solomon was anointed King of Israel at the Gihon Spring while his scheming brother Adonijah, attempted to take the throne (1 Kings 1:38, 39).

In 1867, British explorer Charles Warren entered the Gihon Spring, crawled through Hezekiah's Tunnel, and scaled up a vertical shaft landing in a large upper tunnel. This became the official discovery of the 38 ft (11 m) long **Warren's Shaft** (photo left) which functioned like a well; a person at the top could lower a bucket on a rope to the bottom of the shaft and draw fresh water from the reservoir below. Warren's Shaft was most likely the opening through which Joab ascended in response to King David's challenge (2 Samuel 5:8; 1 Chronicles 11:6), resulting in the demise of the Jebusites, King David's unsuspecting enemies.

POOL OF SILOAM
(SHILOAH)

As he went along, he saw a man blind from birth. His disciples asked him, "Rabbi, who sinned, this man or his parents, that he was born blind?" "Neither this man nor his parents sinned," said Jesus, "but this happened so that the works of God might be displayed in him. As long as it is day, we must do the works of him who sent me. Night is coming, when no one can work. While I am in the world, I am the light of the world." After saying this, he spit on the ground, made some mud with the saliva, and put it on the man's eyes. "Go," he told him, "wash in the Pool of Siloam." So the man went and washed, and came home seeing.
JOHN 9:1–7

Siloam is the Greek translation of the Hebrew term, *Shiloah*, meaning "to send" or "sent out." The Pool of Siloam is where Jesus "sent" the man blind from birth to wash mud off his eyes and receive his sight. Pottery indicates that the Pool of Siloam was in use during the first century.

Prior to 2004, a Byzantine structure was considered the original Pool of Siloam. However, a new city sewer system, installed in 2004, resulted in the discovery of what is believed to be the actual Pool of Siloam in the City of David.

The water from the Gihon Spring and Hezekiah's Tunnel that came to the ancient Pool of Siloam continues to flow today. However, it now flows out across the street into a drain.

Sign at Pool of Siloam:

Remains from the pool that King Hezekiah built in the First Temple period have yet to be found. However, in the summer of 2004, remains of a very large pool (covering three-quarters of an acre) from the Second Temple period was revealed. Nearby, archaeologists uncovered the remains of a stepped street, the path taken by pilgrims ascending from the pool to the Temple Mount. Beneath the paving stones of the street, they found a drainage channel that apparently served as a hiding place for the last of the Jewish rebels against the Romans in the year 70 AD. The pool ceased to function after the destruction of Jerusalem and, over time, it became filled with earth and disappeared from sight.

CITY OF DAVID ACTIVITIES

City of David offerings change on a regular basis; the four offerings below are current as of early 2019. Check current options, prices, and hours, and purchase tickets on their website; type "City of David Jerusalem" into your search bar. Phone: 972-2-626-8700

BIBLICAL CITY OF DAVID TOUR
(two hours)

If you're in an organized group, it's likely that your tour guide will take you on a biblical tour through the City of David. Full tours include a 3D movie about the history of the City of David, a panoramic view from its walls, palace excavations from the period of the Judean kings, remnants of remarkable homes from biblical times, and a walk (with a fair number of steps) through one of two underground water system tunnels from the time of Abraham, ending up at the Pool of Siloam. There is a choice of the "dry" Canaanite tunnel or the "wet" Hezekiah's Tunnel (bring water shoes and a flashlight). Depending on the time of year, the water may rise as high as 28 inches (70 m). You can sing hymns and praise songs while enjoying the refreshing hike!

THE TEMPLE MOUNT ASCENT TOUR
(90 minutes)

Walk the streets of Second Temple Jerusalem! This is a fascinating walking tour of recently excavated sites in the Central (Tyropoean) Valley. You begin at the City of David and walk through a tunnel, which is actually a section of the Second Temple period drainage channel. When you exit the tunnel, you arrive at the foundation stones of the Western Wall at the foot of the Temple Mount!

From there, you climb until you reach the ancient road where Jewish pilgrims walked 2,000 years ago.

"HALLELUJAH!"
(75 minutes)

"Hallelujah" (photo above) is a unique and moving musical production presented in the open air under the evening stars at the City of David. The musical tells the riveting story of the Jews' epic return to Jerusalem and the rebirth of the ancient city over 2,500 years. The story is presented through innovative and cutting-edge video mapping technology projected onto the ruins of the City of David—the actual site where the story unfolded. Please note that substantial walking on uneven surfaces is required. Unfortunately, due to the limitations of the archeological site, "Hallelujah!" is not wheelchair accessible.

CITY OF DAVID GIFT SHOP

The City of David gift shop offers unique gifts such as replicas of artifacts found at the City of David and diverse artwork of some of Israel's most talented artists. Visitors can also purchase publications from the *Megalim Institute*, a learning and research center dedicated to ancient Jerusalem featuring the latest archaeological information available about Jerusalem from leading archaeologists and scholars.

On that day his feet will stand on the Mount of Olives, east of Jerusalem, and the Mount of Olives will be split in two from east to west, forming a great valley, with half of the mountain moving north and half moving south...Then the Lord my God will come, and all the holy ones with him. ZECHARIAH 14:4–5

THE MOUNT OF OLIVES, facing the Old City to the east, acquired its name from the many groves of olive trees that covered its slopes in ancient times. Today, there are six Christian sites strewn across the mountain: **Chapel of the Ascension, Church of Pater Noster, Dominus Flevit, Mary's Tomb, Church of Mary Magdalene**, and **Church of all Nations** (encompassing Gethsemane).

The Mount of Olives is referred to eleven times in the Bible. **King David** fled from the Kidron Valley to the Mount of Olives to take refuge from his son, **Absalom**. After **King Solomon** turned away from the Lord, he built pagan temples here for the gods of his foreign wives. **Ezekiel** had a vision of "the glory of the Lord" ascending from Jerusalem and resting on the Mount of Olives. **Jesus** travelled often to the Mount of Olives to teach, to pray, and to rest. It was here that He prayed with His disciples the night before His arrest, it was here where He ascended into heaven, and it is this very same place where He will return at His Second Coming.

JEWISH CEMETERY

The vast 3,000-year-old Jewish cemetery on the Mount of Olives holds roughly 150,000 graves and is still in use today. For centuries, Jews have fervently sought to be buried here because of their belief that the Mount of Olives is associated with the resurrection and the coming of the Messiah.

Instead of leaving flowers, which Orthodox Jews view as a pagan tradition, Jews leave a more lasting tribute: a small "visitation stone" at the gravesite monument of a loved one. This custom is part of the Jews' act of remembrance. Stones are also connected to Genesis 3:19, "...for dust you are and to dust you will return."

Visitation Stones

CHAPEL OF THE ASCENSION

While he was blessing them, he left them and was taken up into heaven. LUKE 24:51

The Chapel of the Ascension, located at the top of the Mount of Olives, is traditionally believed to be the site where Jesus ascended into Heaven forty days following His resurrection. The dome surrounding the "Ascension Rock" allegedly contains an impression of

the right footprint of Jesus that was left as He ascended into Heaven. (Apparently, the section holding the left footprint was transported to Al-Aqsa Mosque during the Middle Ages).

Near the chapel is a burial crypt revered by all three primary monotheistic religions, each convinced of a different occupant. Jews believe it is the seventh-century BC prophetess Huldah, Catholics believe it to be the fifth-century AD Saint Pelagia, and Muslims maintain the crypt holds the remains of Rabi'a al-Adawiya, a holy woman from the eighth-century AD.

CHURCH OF PATER NOSTER

...Our Father which art in heaven, Hallowed be thy name.
Thy kingdom come, Thy will be done in earth,
as it is in heaven. MATTHEW 6:9–10

The Church of Pater Noster (Latin for "Our Father") stands on the traditional site where Jesus taught His disciples how to pray. Writings of twelfth-century pilgrims were found at the church, describing marble plaques with the Lord's Prayer inscribed in three languages—Hebrew, Greek, and Latin. Today, the Lord's Prayer is inscribed on plaques throughout the church in well over 100 languages.

PALM SUNDAY ROAD

*...Hosanna! Blessed is he who
comes in the name of the Lord!*
MARK 11:9

The first event in "Passion Week" was the
"Triumphant Entry" of Jesus on Palm Sunday
Road. As Jesus rode a donkey down the
Mount of Olives towards the Eastern Gate,
the crowds rejoiced and shouted, *"Hosanna!
Blessed is he who comes in the name of
the Lord!"* This fulfilled two prophecies:
Zechariah 9:9 and Psalm 118:26.

Although the street was not paved at that
time, the current Palm Sunday Road is
believed by many to be the road Jesus would
have taken to the temple. Others believe Jewish tradition would have precluded this road
because of its proximity to a graveyard.

DOMINUS FLEVIT

As he approached Jerusalem and saw the city, he wept over it. LUKE 19:41

Dominus Flevit (Latin for "The Lord wept") is a small
Franciscan church built over several Canaanite burial caves.
Located close to the top of the Mount of Olives, it provides
beautiful, panoramic views. The church was designed in the
shape of a teardrop to represent the tears of Christ as He
rode down Palm Sunday Road, then stopped and wept
openly, grieving the future destruction of the city. Dominus
Flevit commemorates this event.

MARY'S TOMB

Mary's Tomb is believed by some Christian denominations to be the burial place of Mary, mother of Jesus. There is also a traditional belief that Mary was "assumed" into heaven, foregoing physical death, leaving behind an empty tomb.

However, Biblical accounts provide no information about the end of Mary's life or the place of her burial.

A lavishly-decorated church with religious icons and hanging lanterns is accessed through a series of descending flights of stairs. A small square chapel inside the structure accommodates Mary's tomb and halfway down the stairs are several niches believed to hold the remains of Mary's husband Joseph, as well as her parents Joachim and Anne.

This site is also revered by Muslims. They claim that the Prophet Muhammad saw a light over Mary's tomb during his "Night Journey" from Mecca to Jerusalem.

CHURCH OF MARY MAGDALENE

The striking Church of Mary Magdalene, a Russian Orthodox church close to the Garden of Gethsemane, is nestled in a tranquil garden adorned with Orthodox images and works of art. The church's seven gilded onion domes are representative of sixteenth- and seventeenth-century Russian architecture.

The Church of Mary Magdalene was originally built in 1886 by the Russian Tsar Alexander III to pay tribute to his mother, Russian Empress Maria Alexandrovna. It was later dedicated to Mary Magdalene, the grateful follower of Jesus from whom Jesus cast seven demons.

They went to a place called Gethsemane, and Jesus said to his disciples, "Sit here while I pray." He took Peter, James and John along with him, and he began to be deeply distressed and troubled… Going a little farther, he fell to the ground and prayed that if possible the hour might pass from him. "Abba, Father," he said, "everything is possible for you. Take this cup from me. Yet not what I will, but what you will." MARK 14:32–36

THE LORD'S PASSIONATE PRAYER AT GETHSEMANE IS HIS LAST ACTION PRIOR to His arrest. This is also the site of His final instructions to His disciples.

The peaceful Garden of Gethsemane, adorned with beautiful, ancient olive trees, sits at the foot of the Mount of Olives. *Gethsemane* means "oil press." Similarly, the weight of our sins pressed down upon Jesus like the heavy rock of the oil press, and His blood flowed from Him like olive oil. Scholars estimate the age of the olive trees at between one and two thousand years old. However, it is questionable if they would have survived the siege of AD 70.

CHURCH OF ALL NATIONS

The Catholic *Church of All Nations*, was built between 1919 and 1924. It is located at the foot of the Mount of Olives and encompasses the Garden of Gethsemane on its north side. Enshrined inside its chapel is a piece of flat bedrock referred to as the "Rock of Agony" where many believe Jesus prayed the anguishing prayer to *"let this cup pass me by"* if at all possible.

GARDEN TOMB

They came to a place called Golgotha (which means "the place of the skull").
MATTHEW 27:33

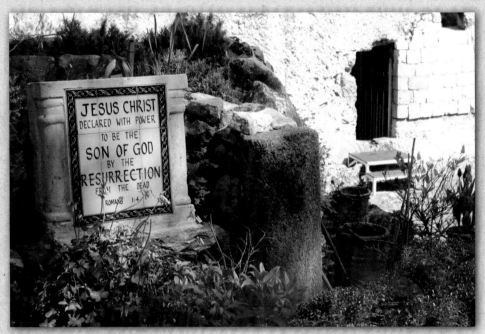

THE GARDEN TOMB IS AN ALTERNA-tive site to the Church of the Holy Sepulchre for the crucifixion, burial, and resurrection of Jesus. It essentially fits the description of the location and narrative in Scripture.

The site of the crucifixion is described as outside the city walls, close to a city gate (Hebrews 13:12), and along a busy thoroughfare—making it a credible place for a public execution. Also, the rock wall resembles *Golgotha* (Aramaic for "skull"), as depicted in the photo to the right. Sadly, in 2015, the bridge of the skull's nose collapsed during a storm.

Scripture relates the tomb was near a garden belonging to a rich man (John 19:41; Matthew 27:57–58). One of the best evidences for the Garden Tomb's authenticity is the 1924 discovery of a wine press, indicative of a nearby vineyard (a rich man's crop). The tomb also is carved out of a rock (Matthew 27:60), sealed with a rolling stone, has an entry through a low doorway (John 20:5), and a burial chamber is situated to the right of the entrance (Mark 16:5). *Note: The average stone size to cover the opening of a Jewish tomb would have been 4–6 ft (1–2 m) in diameter, about one thick (30 cm); it would have weighed between one and two tons.*

Today the site is a lovely, serene garden and the empty tomb is a fitting reminder of a risen, living Savior to a sinful, hurting world whether or not it is the actual site.

Church of Mary Magdalene

JUDEA

After Jesus was born in Bethlehem in Judea, during the time of King Herod,
Magi from the east came to Jerusalem and asked, "Where is the one
who has been born king of the Jews? We saw his star when it rose
and have come to worship him."

MATTHEW 2:1–2

*But you will receive power
when the Holy Spirit comes on you;
and you will be my witnesses in Jerusalem,
and in all Judea and Samaria,
and to the ends of the earth.*
ACTS 1:8

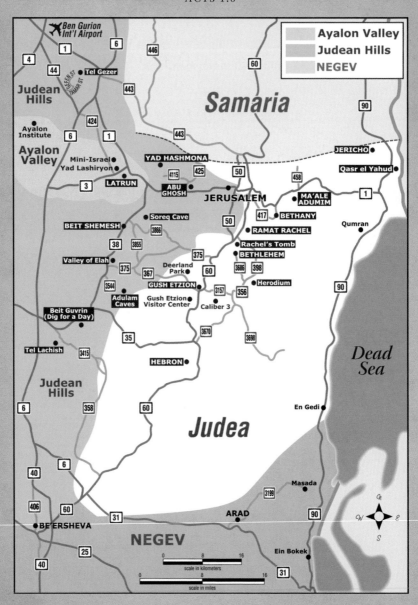

View additional site info online: Bethany, Ma'ale Adumim, Rachel's Tomb,
Ramat Rachel, Latrun, Mini-Israel, Gardens of Life, and Beit Shemesh.

Go to WalkAboutZion.com; click on Inspiration Israel.

Let it be known to the king that we went into the province of Judea, to the temple of the great God, which is being built with heavy stones, and timber is being laid in the walls; and this work goes on diligently and prospers in their hands.

EZRA 5:8 (NKJV)

JUDEA IS WEST OF THE JORDAN RIVER and south of Samaria. Its primary cities and communities are Bethlehem, Jericho, Gush Etzion, Hebron, and parts of Jerusalem. *Judea*, or the "land of the Jews," is a Greek and Roman adaptation of the word "Judah." After being released from Babylonian captivity, most Israelites belonged to the tribe of Judah. Thus, they came to be called *Jews*, and all the land west of the Jordan became known as *Judea*. In AD 70, the Romans slaughtered countless Jews and sold masses into slavery. Many of the remaining Jews fled Israel (the Jewish Diaspora), but Judea was never completely abandoned by the Jewish people.

Mount of Temptations in Judea Wilderness

Numerous biblical events took place in Judea. Most importantly, Jesus was born in Bethlehem of Judea, and He regularly ministered and performed miracles in the region. John the Baptist emerged from the wilderness of Judea and Jesus was led by the Spirit into the Judean wilderness where He was tempted by Satan for forty days.

Over the centuries, the borders of Judea have varied greatly and its boundaries have been debated among countless biblical scholars. However, Judea would have definitely included the territories of the tribes of Judah, Benjamin, Dan, Simeon, and part of Ephraim. According to Josephus, Judea's southern borders went as far south as (Saudi) Arabia and spread from Jaffa in the west to the Jordan River in the east. In biblical times, only three main regions of Israel existed: Judea, Samaria, and the Galilee; today there are many regions.

Geographically, Judea contains three primary sub-regions: the Judean Desert, the Judean Hills, and the Judean Lowlands also known as the Shephelah. The **Judean Desert**, known as the **"Wilderness of Judea,"** was the land situated between the Dead Sea to the east and the Judean mountains to the west. Judea's northeastern edge is where the Jordan River emptied into the Dead Sea. The desert topography included mountain cliffs, rolling hills adjacent to plateaus, and riverbeds set in deep canyons. Historically, Judea's rugged landscape and rock crevices have often served as fortresses and places of refuge.

The **Judean Hills** or **Judean Mountains** formed the heartland of the kingdom of Judah. From these hills the earliest Jewish settlements emerged. In ancient times, the Judean Mountains were the allotment of the tribe of Judah and the heartland of the former kingdom of Judah. The mountain range forms a natural division between the Judean Lowlands and the coastal plain to the west and the Jordan Rift Valley to the east. North of the Judean mountains are the hills of Samaria.

The territory of the **Judean Lowlands** or **Judean Foothills**, also known as the **Shephelah**, was originally assigned to the tribes of Judah and Dan. This transitional region of Judea, 12 to 15 miles (19–24 km) wide, spans the area between the Judean Mountains and the Coastal Plain. Four valleys make up the Shephelah: the Ayalon, the Soreq, the Elah, and the Lachish. In ancient times, each valley was guarded by a tel. Today, the Shephelah is predominantly rural farmland.

*But you, Bethlehem Ephrathah, though you are small among the clans of Judah,
out of you will come for me one who will be ruler over Israel,
whose origins are from of old, from ancient times. MICAH 5:2*

THE SMALL TOWN OF BETHLEHEM, located in Judea 6 miles (10 km) south of Jerusalem, is part of the **Area "A"** (see p. 27). The town is surrounded by Israeli checkpoints and roadblocks. A special permit is required for Bethlehem residents to travel into Jerusalem; Israeli citizens are barred from entering Bethlehem, unless they also have a special permit. Its population of roughly 25,000 has changed over the years. It is predominantly Muslim with only about 15% Christians; fifty years ago, Bethlehem residents were primarily Christian. Bethlehem's economy revolves around agriculture and tourism, especially crafting religious items made from mother-of-pearl and olivewood.

In Hebrew, *Bethlehem* means "House of Bread," and Jesus was *"the **bread** sent down from heaven to feed the souls of mankind"* (John 6:51). In about 700 BC, the prophet Micah prophesied that Bethlehem would be the birthplace of the Messiah (Micah 5:2). The Messiah would also be a descendent of King David, the "Shepherd-King" of Israel. Remarkably, Jesus would be born in the exact same, virtually unknown, tiny city as King David—Bethlehem!

Manger Square, Bethlehem's prominent plaza, encompasses two churches—the **Church of the Nativity** (operated by three feuding denominations: Greek Orthodox, Armenian Orthodox, and the Franciscan order) and the adjoining **Church of St. Catherine** (a Catholic church and Franciscan Monastery). The Church of the Nativity is the oldest continuously operating Christian church in the world.

The Church of the Nativity's entry **"Door of Humility"** (right) is only 2.3 ft (78 cm) wide and 4.3 ft (130 cm) high. The entryway was built during Ottoman times to prevent thieves from driving their carts inside and to respectfully force visitors on horseback to dismount prior to entering.

Beneath the church is a cave or *grotto* believed to be the birthplace of Jesus. This cave would likely have been used as both a storage area and a stable for horses, while the manger would have been a feeding trough for the horses. A silver star in the grotto allegedly marks the exact location of Jesus' birth.

THE SHEPHERDS' FIELDS IN THE Bethlehem vicinity are believed to be where **Ruth** and **Boaz** met while gleaning the fields (Ruth 2–4). Three excavated sites in these fields, dating back to the fourth century AD, are "rivals" for the location where the shepherds saw the star of Bethlehem and heard the angelic proclamation, *"Glory to God in the highest, peace on earth and good will to men"* (Luke 2:14).

The **Greek Orthodox** site has a fifth century church built over a cave. The **Roman Catholic** site has a Franciscan Chapel designed to resemble a shepherds' tent with a bronze angel on top. This chapel is a wonderful place for worship, as the echo of voices in the small chambers sound like the voices of angels!

The third "**evangelical**" site is located at the **YMCA** in the Christian village of Beit Sahour, just east of Bethlehem. This site encompasses a grove of pines, a cave, and a view toward Jerusalem and the desert.

It is awe-inspiring to note that in His providence, the Lord came down to the very place where the lambs were raised and provided for Temple sacrifice. Every first-born male lamb in the vicinity of Bethlehem was considered holy and set aside for sacrifice to atone for sins. At this same place amid the sacred Temple flocks, "the LAMB OF GOD who takes away the sin of the world" was born. The lambs and the Lamb of God were both born in Bethlehem and both put to death at the same place—Jerusalem. They both shed their blood and lost their lives as atonements for sin. However, the Lamb of God put an end to animal sacrifice once and for all when He sacrificed His own life to atone for man's sin: the one-time perfect sacrifice.

Greek Orthodox

Catholic

Evangelical

HERODIUM

"And after a long time he built a town on that spot in commemoration of his victory, and enhanced it with wonderful palaces...and he called it Herodion after himself."

JOSEPHUS

HEROD THE GREAT DEFEATED THE Parthinians and built a fortress and palace to mark the battle site. Herodium National Park is located on the highest hill in the Judean desert, only 3 miles (5 km) southeast of Bethlehem.

Herodium's massive circular structure, completed in 20 BC, had four defense towers—each with seven levels of rooms utilized for living space and storage. Several levels can be seen; the top two or three no longer exist. Additionally, visitors can walk through its sophisticated underground water network of cisterns and tunnels.

The palace had extravagant living quarters for Herod's guests: a banquet hall in which he threw intimate dinner parties (which the Zealots, *militant Jewish adversaries to Roman rule in Judea,* converted into a synagogue in AD 70), an

elaborate bathhouse complex, and a large courtyard. The courtyard encompassed beautiful gardens and roofed porticoes to the north and south to create shaded terraces.

Herodium is also the site where Herod chose to be buried. His tomb (photo below) was discovered in 2007 halfway up the hill to the palace—the precise location described by Josephus in his writings. The original tomb was recorded to stand about 80 ft (24 m) high. A scaled-down replica, standing 13 ft (4 m) high, was constructed on Herodium's hill.

At the foot of Herodium was its Lower City. 1970–1987 excavations revealed a colonnaded area with a large lake and island, a bathhouse, and an immense structure believed to have housed both the offices of the district capital and palace rooms for Herod's family and his many visitors.

"I can think of no battle in the annals of the Israel Defense Forces which was more magnificent, more tragic or more heroic than the struggle for Gush Etzion...If there exists a Jewish Jerusalem, our foremost thanks go to the defenders of Gush Etzion."

DAVID BEN-GURION, 1949

IN THE WAR OF INDEPENDENCE IN 1948, the community of Gush Etzion came under heavy siege. The heroic defenders of Gush Etzion blocked the road to Jerusalem with their own bodies. Eventually Gush Etzion was conquered by a combined force of the Arab Legion and local Arab men. Most of its defenders fell in battle on the eve of Israel's statehood on May 13, 1948, while the remainder of the defenders surrendered and were taken captive. 245 defenders tragically lost their lives; however, they saved Jerusalem!

Gush Etzion remained in ruins for nineteen years, until it was finally liberated again in the 1967 Six-Day War. Today Gush Etzion is home to about 70,000 Jews living in a cluster of 22 Jewish settlements in the Judean hills, officially part of **Area "C."** Its capital is the settlement of **Efrat**. The international community considers these Israeli settlements illegal, but the Israeli government, as well as the Abrahamic land covenant, emphatically dispute this conclusion.

If you're in the area, you can enjoy the delicious, healthy food and beautiful mountain ambience of **Gavna Restaurant** (p. 267) or drop by the **Gush Etzion Winery** (photo right). The family-run winery was established to allow visitors to relax and enjoy the fruits of about 150 acres (600 dunams) of vineyards planted throughout the settlement. Gush Etzion Winery offers a wonderful restaurant, daily wine tours and tastings, and an archeological garden that teaches about ancient wine making process. Call 972-2-930-9220.

GUSH ETZION VISITOR CENTER

Gush Etzion's Visitor Center is a memorial to the heroic defenders of Gush Etzion. "Mountain People" is a moving sound and light show that tells the story of the establishment of Gush Etzion—from its early beginnings, to its fall in 1948, and to its triumphant rebirth in 1967. Included in the show is an interview with the final defenders on the ruins of the original 1948 bunker. The museum includes documents, photos, films, and personal exhibits from the estate of the fallen defenders. The Visitor Center is near the Field School of Kibbutz Kfar Etzion. Phone: 972-2-993-5160; Email: orkoli@kfar-etzion.co.il

CALIBER 3

CALIBER 3, ISRAEL'S LEADING COUNTER TERROR & SECURITY training academy, was established in Gush Etzion in 2003 by Israeli Defense Forces (IDF) Col. Sharon Gat. The academy offers top security solutions and high threat protection as well as intelligence operations and tactical training to military, law enforcement, government agencies and commercial clients around the globe. Caliber 3 is certified by the Israeli Police, Defense Forces, Prime Minister's Office, Ministry of Defense, Ministry of Homeland Security, Ministry of Commerce and Industry, and Ministry of Foreign Affairs.

All clients train in techniques and skills with the best active military IDF officers in each security field. Caliber 3's strength lies in the fact that their training and security techniques are continually updated to address new and changing security threats. Tourists can be trained in urban combat paintball, Krav Maga, clay target shooting, combat rappelling, and survival and navigation.

Caliber 3's "Renowned"
ULTIMATE SHOOTING ADVENTURE

- Tour Caliber 3's facility.
- Interact with Israeli Security professionals.
- Shoot assault rifles and sniper rifles.
- Participate in a live counter-terror demonstration.
- Compete in a sniper tournament.

Reservations required; group discounts available.
www.caliber3range.com ▪ sharon@caliber-3.com ▪ 972-2-673-4334

PATH OF THE PATRIARCHS

Also, in Gush Etzion is the Path (or "Way") of the Patriarchs, a section of the ancient route that connected Hebron to Jerusalem. About two miles (three km) in length, the path is widely believed to be the one used by patriarchs Abraham, Isaac and Jacob when traveling between Hebron, Be'ersheva, Mount Moriah, Beit El, and Shechem. Additionally, during the First and Second Temple periods, Jews living south of Jerusalem would have traveled this path three times a year for their annual pilgrimage feasts in Jerusalem. The Path of the Patriarchs was also quite likely used by the Romans who conquered Israel following the AD 70 destruction of the Second Temple.

Three highlights of the Path of the Patriarchs are a **Roman milestone marker**, a **mikvah** (ritual bath), and the **Biyah Aqueduct**. **Roman milestone markers** were used to convey the distance from that marker to the Damascus Gate of the Old City. A Roman mile is .86 miles (1400 m) today.

To access the path, take Highway 60 South from Jerusalem until you reach the Gush Etzion junction. At the junction, make a right turn onto Route 367, heading toward Kfar Etzion. Soon you will make another right turn toward Rosh Tzurim where you will catch sight of a bridge ahead. About 650 ft (200 m) past the bridge, turn right onto a dirt road and you will see the **"Path of the Patriarchs" sign**. Drive a few more minutes on the dirt road and you will arrive at the beginning of the path the **Roman milestone marker**.

Continuing on the dirt road, you will reach an intersection; make a left at this intersection. To your immediate right, adjoining a rest area covered by arches, you will see a **mikvah** dating back to the Second Temple period. This well-preserved mikvah was likely used for the purification of travelers on their way to Jerusalem for the three annual feasts.

Finally, you will arrive at the **Biyah Aqueduct**. This aqueduct was used to transport water to Jerusalem during the Second Temple era. If you'd like to explore the ancient water system, you can walk down into it. Expect to get wet and muddy; bring water shoes, a change of clothes, and a flashlight.

DEER LAND PARK

- The longest zip line in Israel—visitors can zip through lush terrain above a 400 ft (120 m) high canyon for ¼ mile (400 m); shorter zip lines available for children and beginners.
- 4 x 4 ATV jeep adventure
- Nature reserve, petting zoo, and carousel for children
- Climbing wall, bungee trampoline, and 350° swings
- Paintball, archery, marksmanship, and horseback riding
- A rope course with ladder, snappling, and swings; acrobat rope walking

Deer Land is a hub of adventure for the entire family!
Contact them for hours, reservations, and directions
deerlandal@gmail.com ■ 972-2-570-9768

THE CITY OF HEBRON, ONE OF THE oldest continuously-occupied cities in the world, is located 19 miles (30 km) south of Jerusalem in the Judean Hills. Hebron is the largest city in Judea and Samaria with a population of over 200,000 Palestinians and roughly 750 Jews.

The Hebrew word *Hebron* originates from *haver* or "friend," referring to the patriarch, Abraham. Hebron has been a major site of religious worship for Jews, Christians, and Muslims alike for over two thousand years due to its connection to Abraham. Hebron is Judaism's second holiest city after Jerusalem as well as being the oldest Jewish community in the world, dating back to biblical times. Islam esteems Abraham as a prophet and considers Hebron its fourth holiest site, following Mecca, Medina, and Jerusalem.

Biblical events connected to Hebron include the following:

- David was anointed king of Judah in Hebron (II Samuel 2:1-4).

- David was later anointed king of all of Israel in Hebron, reigning in the city for seven years (2 Samuel 5:1–3).

- Joshua granted the city of Hebron to Caleb (Joshua 14:13–14).

- After the death of Joshua, Caleb led the tribe of Judah in conquering Hebron (Judges 1:1-20).

Abraham paid 400 shekels of silver to purchase a plot of ground in Hebron for a burial cave for his wife, Sarah (Genesis 23). This was the first parcel of land owned by the Jewish people in the Holy Land. It is traditionally believed that the bones of the patriarchs were discovered in a cave at this site. Over 2,000 years later, King Herod constructed an enclosure of stone to memorialize the burial cave of the revered patriarchs. The walls of the **Cave of the Patriarchs** measured 40 ft (12 m) high and 6 ft (1.8 m) wide. Abraham's and Sarah's tombs are in a center room, while a room to the east encloses the tombs of Isaac and Rebekah (which Jews may visit only ten days each year). A room to the west contains the tombs of Jacob and Leah. A mosque and synagogue within the cave are separated by bulletproof glass. Additional biblical sites in Hebron include the Tomb of Ruth and Jesse and the site of the Terebinths of Mamre from Genesis 18:1.

After Israel became a state in 1948, Hebron was captured and occupied by the Jordanian Arab Legion. From this time through the 1967 war, Jews were not allowed to live, visit, or pray at the Jewish holy sites in Hebron. The Jewish Quarter of the city was razed to the ground, the Jewish cemetery desecrated, and an animal pen was constructed on the ruins of their beloved Avraham Avinu Synagogue. The Jewish community of Hebron was re-established in 1967 when Israel reclaimed the "West Bank." Since 1997, the land of Hebron has been divided into two sectors: H1, controlled by the Palestinian Authority (80%), and H2, controlled by Israel (20%).

Is Hebron safe to visit? Even though Hebron is regarded as the city of the most turmoil within Israel, foreigners have never been the target of the occasional violence. So, yes, visiting the site is generally safe; however, it is advisable to check for safety and visit with a savvy local guide or a tour group.

YAD HASHMONA, NESTLED IN THE lush Judean Hills, is a small *moshav* (communal village) of about 280 diverse local and international believers in *Yeshua* (Jesus). Yad Hashmona members work both within the village and in various professions outside of the community, all contributing a portion of their salary into the collective fund.

The village was first settled in 1974 by Finnish Christians. *Yad Hashmona* means "Memorial to the Eight." It was given its name by the founding members in memory of, as well as an act of restoration and forgiveness to, eight Jewish refugees who escaped Austria to Finland in 1938, but subsequently were handed over by the Finns to the Nazi Gestapo in 1942. Seven were murdered at Auschwitz; the last lost his wife and baby in an extermination camp.

The property encompasses the popular Yad Hashmona Country Hotel and restaurant, the Biblical Garden, a bakery, stables, various ministry offices, and the homes of business professionals, artists, historians, and several tour guides who speak a variety of languages. The hotel is conveniently located: a short 20-minute drive to Jerusalem and 30-minute drive to the airport.

Their Biblical Garden gives visitors a glimpse into the spiritual, physical, and agricultural world of the Jewish people in the land of the Bible. A variety of biblical plants and trees, as well as reconstructed facilities from biblical times, are displayed. The garden includes an ancient wine press, an olive oil press, a mikvah, a burial cave, an agricultural watchtower, a Galilean-style synagogue, and a Bedouin tent. Forty-five-minute guided tours are available in various languages upon request. Tours elaborate on biblical stories such as Ruth and Boaz, the Ark of the Covenant's journey to Jerusalem, spiritual symbolism, parables of the New Testament, etc. Contact: 972-2-594-2000; info@yadha8.co.il.

ABU GHOSH

THE PREDOMINANTLY ARAB VILLAGE of **Abu Ghosh** has an estimated population of 7,500. Abu Ghosh is the unrivaled hummus capital of Israel! Their exceptional Middle Eastern cuisine makes Abu Ghosh a popular stop for locals, especially on Saturdays when most restaurants in Israel are closed for the Shabbat.

Abu Ghosh is believed to be the location of several significant biblical events:

- **Emmaus**, where Jesus appeared after the Resurrection (Luke 24:12-31)

- Kiryat Ye'arim, home of the **ark of the covenant** after leaving Bet Shemesh in Philistine captivity (1 Samuel 6:21)

- Anathoth, the **birthplace of the prophet Jeremiah**

Abu Ghosh is also known for its music festivals and beautiful churches. An impressive Crusader church has paintings of New Testament scenes embellishing its walls; some are among the world's oldest medieval frescos.

Abu Ghosh is renowned as a "model of coexistence" with a history of friendly relations with their Jewish neighbors and a strong support of Zionism. During the 1948 Arab-Israeli War, Abu Ghosh actively assisted the Israeli army; their village became the headquarters of the Har'el Brigade (a reserve brigade for the IDF). As a result, the Israeli army protected the village. The Israeli government invested in improving the town's infrastructure, and more recently donated land to them for their "Mosque of Peace," the second-largest mosque in Israel.

THE REMAINING SITES IN THIS CHAPTER ARE ALL PART OF THE *SHEPHELAH*, AN ancient border region between the kingdom of Judah and the Philistines. A coastal strip along the Mediterranean close to the hills of Judah was considered "Philistine country." Their three major cities were Ashdod, Ashkelon, and Gaza (where the temple of Dagon was located). The Shephelah was Samson's stomping grounds, as well as the setting of most of the Philistine-Israelite conflicts recorded in Judges, 1 and 2 Kings, and Samuel.

TEL GEZER NATIONAL PARK

Tel Gezer, a 33-acre (13-hectares) archaeological site, is one of the most excavated sites in Israel. In 1871, it was positively identified as biblical Gezer due to the discovery of Hebrew inscriptions engraved on thirteen **boundary stones** with the city's name. These first century BC inscriptions found close to the site read "boundary of Gezer."

Gezer was one of the most strategic cities in the Canaanite and Israelite periods because of its strategic position at the crossroads of two prominent trade routes: the Via Maris and the road to Jerusalem and Jericho.

Gezer in the Bible:

- Horam, king of Gezer, came to help Lachish, but Joshua smote him and his people (Joshua 10:33).

- The king of Gezer was named in a list of the kings of the land that Joshua and the Israelites conquered on the west side of the Jordan (Jordan 12:12).

- Gezer was part of the land of the tribe of Ephraim; the requirement for the Canaanites who wished to remain was forced labor (Joshua 16:10).

- The Kohathite clan of the Levites were allotted four towns from the tribe of Ephraim; one was Gezer (Joshua 21:20–21).

- King Solomon raised a levy for building Hazor, Megiddo, Gezer, and other projects (1 Kings 9:15).

- Pharaoh burned down Gezer, killing all of the Canaanites; he gave Gezer as a present to his daughter (1 Kings 9:16).

- Over the course of time, after Joab attacked Rabah and King David plundered Ammonite towns, war with the Philistines broke out at Gezer (1 Chronicles 20:4).

Tel Gezer discoveries indicate a mixed Canaanite/Philistine population. Some of the most impressive finds include:

- Ten **standing stones**, up to 10 ft (3 m) tall, likely from the Canaanite period (about 1500 BC) with a structure resembling an altar in the middle, possibly used for either a treaty alliance (Exodus 24) or a cultic "high place" (Leviticus 26)

- A **Middle Bronze Tower** 52 ft (16 m) in width, the largest structure in any defensive system found in this period

- An elaborate six-chambered **Solomonic gate** identical in construction to Solomonic remains excavated at Tel Megiddo and Tel Hazor

- A large **water system** similar to Hezekiah's tunnel.

- The **Gezer Calendar**, a tenth century BC Hebrew, seven-line inscription engraved on a limestone tablet which listed agricultural seasons

SOREQ CAVE

Approximately 12 miles (19 km) southwest of Jerusalem is Israel's largest cave, Soreq Cave, also known as **Avshalom Cave**. Soreq is a spectacular wonderland of stalactites and stalagmites in a rich variety of forms—possessing one of the most diverse and extensive collections in the entire world. The cave measures approximately 200 ft (61 m) in both length and width.

Soreq Cave was discovered accidentally in May 1968 while quarriers were using explosives. An explosion opened a crevice into a magical and wonderful world hidden beneath the ground. After its discovery, the location of the cave was kept secret for several years for fear of damage to its nat-ural treasures. Seven years later, in March of 1975, Soreq Cave was opened to the public.

A visit to the cave includes a slide show and a guided tour. To schedule a tour, call 972-2-991-1117.

VALLEY OF ELAH

The Valley of Elah, or the "valley of the terebinth," is the setting of the famous battle between young David and the giant Goliath recorded in 1 Samuel 17. This single combat essentially settled the ongoing war between King Saul's mighty Israelite warriors and the Philistines. Each of the two camps watched the fight from their side of the valley. Young David, armed with five stones and a sling, ran to the battle line to face the heavily armed giant, Goliath, who cursed David by his Philistine idol-gods. The young shepherd, drawing his strength from his faith in God, cast the rock into the center of the giant's forehead, knocking him to the ground. David then took Goliath's sword and cut off his head. Israel was the victor and the fleeing Philistines were chased out of the valley.

The Valley of Elah is a triangular-shaped open and flat fertile valley with a narrow trench strewn with pebbles running down its center. The valley is named after the large and shady terebinth trees indigenous to the area. On the west side of the valley stands a very large and ancient terebinth tree that marks the upper end of the valley.

It's awe-inspiring to scan the area today and visualize the Israelites stationed on the ridge to the north and the Philistines gathered for battle in front of the ridge to the south. Then imagine the thrill of the physical and spiritual victory of the legendary battle between young David and the giant Goliath.

Valley of Elah viewed from the top of Tel Azeka.

ADULAM CAVES PARK

David left Gath and escaped to the cave of Adullam. When his brothers and his father's household heard about it, they went down to him there.

1 SAMUEL 22:1

At the southeast end of Elah Valley are the hilltop ruins of Adulam Caves Park. The park spans an area of almost 10,000 acres (40,000 dunam) and can be accessed by Highway 38 southeast of Beit Shemesh.

This area is associated with the biblical city of **Adullam**, a royal Canaanite city which was named after one of the Canaanite kings defeated by Joshua. Adullam was fortified by King Rehoboam (2 Chronicles 11:7) and was referred to as the "glory of Israel" in Micah 1:5. David found refuge from the pursuit of King Saul in a cave in Adullam. The city bordered ancient Philistine land; 400 men, including 30 of David's mighty men, met him in a specific cave in Adullam (2 Samuel 23:13). Apparently, this cave was utilized as David's military base of operation against the Philistines who were encamped nearby. In the Second Temple era, Adullam and all the surrounding region thrived. However, it came to its end in the middle of the sixth century AD, following the Arab conquest of Israel.

The **Atari Ruins** are the remains of a first-century Jewish village that were found on one

Archaeological Remains of the Atari Ruins

Columbarium cave in park

of the Adulam Cave Park's hilltops. The ruins provide fascinating exploration for all ages. Among them are houses, a large building that could have functioned as a synagogue, a mosaic floor, water cisterns, three mikvahs, a 3,000-year-old winepress within an extensive agricultural complex, rock utensils, earthenware candles, underground caves and tunnels for hiding, and burial caves. *Also, the bone remains of fifteen people, as well as their belongings, were discovered buried here.* The ruins are complete with a 130 ft (40 m) underground "hiding" tunnel which one can crawl into and come out the other end. *Flashlight required.*

The village was believed to have been destroyed during the Great Revolt in AD 69 and then reestablished years later in preparation for the Bar Kokhba Revolt of AD 135. This preparation is evident from the fortified walls and the intricate systems created for hiding, gathering water, and preserving food for long periods of time. History records that the village was destroyed once again near the end of the Bar Kokhba Revolt.

BEIT GUVRIN NATIONAL PARK

Beit Guvrin, a 1,250-acre (506-ha) national park, was named a UNESCO World Heritage Site in 2014. The park contains 480 man-made chalk caves which are part of a broader area spanning from the Elah Valley almost to Be'ersheva. With an estimated 10,000 caves, this stretch of land is known as the "Land of a Thousand Caves." The caves range in size dramatically, with the largest one taking fif-

teen minutes to walk from one end to the other. Archaeological excavations began in the early 1900s.

Over the past 2,000 years, the caves have been used for diverse purposes such as quarries, stables, rooms for storage, water cisterns, work-spaces for pressing grapes and olives, cul-tic houses of worship, dovecotes, hideouts, and even gravesites.

Caves of special interest:

- **Columbarium caves:** 85 caves with 2,000 nesting niches once used for raising doves

- **Bell Cave complex:** 70 connected bell-shaped quarry caves with Arabic inscriptions from the early Islamic period

- **Sidonian Burial Caves:** used for Greek, Sidonian, and Edumite inhabitants of Beit Guvrin from the Hellenistic period

- **Maze cave:** 30 interconnected caves with an underground network of cisterns

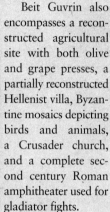

Beit Guvrin also encompasses a recon-structed agricultural site with both olive and grape presses, a partially reconstructed Hellenist villa, Byzan-tine mosaics depicting birds and animals, a Crusader church, and a complete sec-ond century Roman amphitheater used for gladiator fights.

The park provides visitors with a map of the sites which takes them from cave to cave with explanatory information about each cave's discovery and historical background. Private English-speaking tours can be arranged. Call 972-8-681-1020 for more information.

DIG FOR A DAY

Visitors of all ages can be an archaeologist for a day!

- Dig, sift, and examine pottery.
- Excavate an underground cave from the time of the Maccabees!
- Tour cave complexes.
- Crawl through an unexcavated cave (optional).
- View examples of important and rare finds.

Participate in three hours of fascinating activities.

Call at least one month beforehand
for reservations and directions: 972-2-586-2011

TEL LACHISH NATIONAL PARK

A few minutes south of Beit Guvrin (and an hour's drive south from either Tel Aviv or Jerusalem) is Tel Lachish National Park, the only archaeological tel owned by the Israel Antiquities Authority. Events in Lachish are recorded in over twenty Bible verses including Joshua 10:3, 5; 23:31-35; 12:11; 15:39, 2 Kings 14:19; 18:14-17; 19:8; 2 Chronicles 11:9, 25:27, 32:9; Nehemiah 11:30; Isaiah 36:2, 37:8; Jeremiah 34:7; and Micah 1:13.

Lachish was assigned to the tribe of Judah and is commonly considered the second most important city in the Kingdom of Judah due to its strategic location of defense against Israel's enemies approaching from the coast.

Heavily-fortified Lachish was one of only two Judean cities (along with Azekah) that remained following the Assyrian Siege of Jerusalem in 701 BC. At this time, King Hezekiah made a fatal mistake; he rebelled against Sennacherib, king of Assyria, and refused to pay him tribute. In the end, Lachish and 46 other cities were taken by Sennacherib and destroyed. The Jews returned to Lachish years later, but in 586 BC, they were exiled by Babylonian King Nebuchadnezzar. Some of them returned after this exile, but they were ultimately conquered by Alexander the Great in the fourth century BC. Lachish has remained uninhabited ever since.

Archaeological findings from 1932 to the present include the following:

- Nine "Lachish Letters" from the twelfth century BC including "Lachish Letter 4" discovered in 1935, indicating that only Lachish was left at the time of the writing (presently in the British Museum in London and Rockefeller Museum in Jerusalem)

- Two massive walls and a lower retaining wall that surrounded the city

- Sennacherib's 701 BC stone and dirt siege ramp built by the Assyrians, which ran up to the top of the wall and ended at a triple-chambered gatehouse, permitting soldiers to charge up the ramp and storm Lachish

- Hundreds of arrowheads on the ramp and at the peak of the wall, indicating the fierceness of the battle

- 1,500 skulls in a nearby cave

- The "Solar Shrine," a Hellenistic period temple with an entrance door facing to the east

- An extensive Iron Age "governor's palace" at the tel's summit

Of special interest is the recent discovery of a six-chambered gate, the largest unearthed from the First Temple period, measuring 13 ft (4 m) high and consisting of six chambers. Three chambers would have been positioned on each side of the ancient city's main road, the total square structure measuring 80 ft (24 m) x 80 ft. Benches were also discovered, giving credence to the city gates being used as a place of business for high ranking officials, judges, and kings. Two four-horned altars were found in the remains; the horns looked as if they were intentionally broken off, confirming King Hezekiah removing the high places of idol worship (2 Kings 18:4). Additionally, an ancient toilet was found in one of the rooms, perhaps related to the biblical account in 2 Kings 10:27 of Jehu turning one of the temples of Baal into a latrine. Finally, grain scoops, jars, and jar handles stamped with the seal "lmlk," marking them as property of the king, were unearthed.

SAMARIA

Again you will plant vineyards
on the hills of Samaria;
the farmers will plant them
and enjoy their fruit.

JEREMIAH 31:5

"Don't be afraid," the prophet answered. *"Those who are with us are more than those who are with them."* And Elisha prayed, *"Open his eyes, Lord, so that he may see."* Then the Lord opened the servant's eyes, and he looked and saw the hills full of horses and chariots of fire all around Elisha...After they entered the city, Elisha said, *"Lord, open the eyes of these men so they can see."* Then the Lord opened their eyes and they looked, and there they were, inside Samaria.

2 KINGS 6: 16,17,20

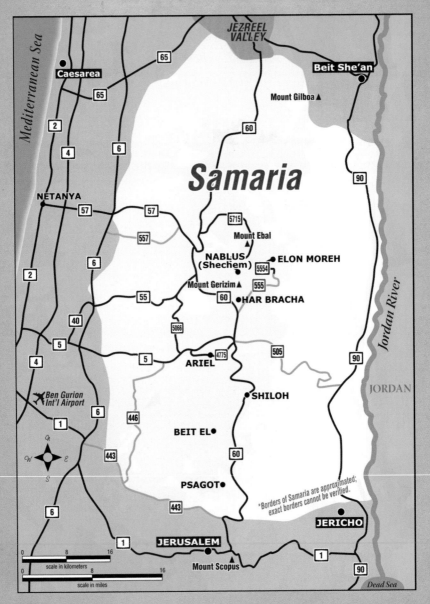

SAMARIA AND ITS CAPITAL SHECHEM was the central region of ancient Israel. It encompasses about 40 miles (65 km) from north to south (between the lower Galilee region and Judea) and about 35 miles (56 km) from east to west (from the Jordan River to the Mediterranean Sea).

In biblical times, ancient Shechem served as the crossroads as well as the religious and political center and capital of Samaria. This parcel of land, assigned to the house of Joseph, was ultimately bequeathed to Jacob's two sons, Ephraim and Manasseh.

In 722 BC, Samaria was conquered by Assyria, and a large segment of its population was carried away into captivity. The king of Assyria then sent Assyrians to inhabit the region. Many came from Babylon and other nations east of Israel (the vicinity of modern-day Iraq). These foreigners intermarried with the Israelites who had remained in Samaria, resulting in the people group known as the "Samaritans." Initially, the foreigners brought in their practices of idol worship, while the Samaritans instructed them in the *Torah* (the first five books of the Bible). They eventually accepted the Torah but retained many of their idolatrous practices (2 Kings 17:26-28). Through the ages, Samaritans have accepted *only* the first five books of Moses, while rejecting the rest of the *Tanach* (the Jewish Bible—the Old Testament). Samaritans do not participate in Jewish traditional feasts or customs outside of the Tanach. In the fifth century BC, the Samaritans built and worshiped at their own temple on Mount Gerizim—as opposed to worshipping at the Jerusalem temple, as instructed by the Lord in Scripture. Due to this unfavorable mix of idol worship and rejection of much of the Jewish Bible, Samaritans were largely considered "half-breeds" and despised by the Jews.

SUGGESTED ITINERARIES FOR ONE DAY IN SAMARIA

Heading north from Jerusalem, the first interesting site would be Psagot. You can take a tour of the Psagot winery or you may want to just stop here and pick up some wine for your group for later in the day. Don't forget your wine glasses, napkins, and cork screws!

BIBLICAL SAMARIA ONLY:

- Psagot winery or Har Bracha winery
- Beit El "Lift Your Eyes" Observation Tower and Cultural Hall
- Tel Shiloh and Seers Tower; lunch
- Mt. Gerazim—view and wine with Scripture reading
- Elon Moreh if time allows

BOTH BIBLICAL AND MODERN-DAY SAMARIA:

- Psagot Winery
- Shiloh
- Mount Gerizim, HaYovel, OR Elon Moreh—view with lunch and wine
- Ariel: National Center for Leadership and Development and either Ariel Industrial Park OR the Randolph A. Hearst Sheltered Workshop

PSAGOT IS AN ISRAELI SETTLEMENT established in 1981 with a current population close to 2,000. Psagot is in the Binyamin region of Israel, renowned for its exceptional vine-growing conditions. The eastern side of the settlement displays breathtaking scenery highlighting stretches of picturesque vineyards and orchards. Palestinian Arabs and Israeli Jews work in the vineyards side by side in peaceful coexistence. HaYovel, an American evangelical Christian organization sends volunteers to tend and harvest their vineyards.

Psagot is best known for its winery founded in 2003. The Psagot Winery produces 350,000 bottles of wine per year, 70% of which is exported worldwide. This number encompasses eleven varieties with the Bordeaux blend named "Edom" being its best seller. Psagot Winery was chosen by the London-based *World Finance* magazine as Israel's top wine producer for 2018; the competition featured the magazine's list of the best brands from fourteen of the top wine countries in the world.

The winery utilizes a modern barrel cellar as well as oak Bordeaux barrels stored in a cave that dates back to the Second Temple era. This cave was part of an ancient cluster of caves that was discovered during the construction of the winery. Some archaeologists believe the location of these caves was the site of the biblical city of Ai, a Canaanite city conquered by the Israelites while under the leadership of Joshua, successor to Moses.

The Psagot Winery offers informative tours about the region's rich winemaking tradition that began 3,000 years ago and how the Psagot Winery combines advanced production methods with biblical-era winemaking traditions. Visitors hear the story of the Binyamin region, its distinct role in biblical times, and its deep connection to the roots of Hebrew settlement, agriculture, and winemaking. The one-hour tour includes audiovisual displays, balcony views of the vineyards, and a select tasting of Psagot's fine wines. Call 972-2-997-9333 for more information and reservations.

He [Jacob] had a dream in which he saw a stairway resting on the earth, with its top reaching to heaven, and the angels of God were ascending and descending on it. There above it stood the Lord, and he said: "I am the Lord, the God of your father Abraham and the God of Isaac. I will give you and your descendants the land on which you are lying. Your descendants will be like the dust of the earth, and you will spread out to the west and to the east, to the north and to the south. All peoples on earth will be blessed through you and your offspring."

GENESIS 28:12-14

BEIT EL IS AN ORTHODOX JEWISH settlement in the hills of Samaria with a population of approximately 6,500. The site has much to offer Bible-believing visitors. First, the **"Lift Your Eyes" Observation Tower** (atop the town's water tower) at the summit of Jacob's Peak, provides a spectacular view. The entire Promised Land can be viewed in all directions. In the center of the floor of the tower is a unique mosaic map of the "Promised Land of Israel" featuring Bible verses regarding the Land promised to Abraham and Jacob.

BIBLICAL SIGNIFICANCE:

■ Jacob slept with a stone pillow under his head and dreamt of a ladder to the sky with angels ascending and descending. The Lord reiterated the Land promise to his offspring in the dream. After waking from his dream, Jacob erected an altar and named the place *Beit El*, meaning "House of God" (Genesis 28:10-22). This place is called **Jacob's Rock.**

■ Abraham erected an altar to God and called upon the "name of the LORD" (Genesis 12:8).

■ Jacob proclaimed, *"How awesome is this place! This is none other than the house of God; this is the gate of heaven"* (Genesis 28:17).

HIGHLIGHTS FOR VISITORS:

Archaeological finds include ruins from the First Temple period believed to be the altar of Jeroboam, son of Nevat, in 1 Kings; Hasmonian Jewish burial caves, a site from the time of King Yannai, and an ancient olive press cave with presses from the Second Temple period with a nearby Wine Press Trail to explore.

A 1,000-year-old wormwood oak tree, the oldest of its kind in Israel, is nicknamed **Oak of Tears** from Genesis 35:8. Wormwood, often mentioned in the Bible, connotes bitterness.

Beit El's **Cultural Hall** encompasses two 15-minute "Beit El Through the Ages" timelines. The first biblical timeline shows the history of the Jewish people from Abraham's birth through the destruction of the Second Temple and Beit El. The second timeline relates the modern story of Beit El.

Beit El's unique **Tefillin Factory**, which produces the vast majority of the tefillin sold in Israel, showcases the remarkable artistry that goes into these humble black leather boxes and straps that contain Hebrew parchment scrolls for prayer.

Other notable establishments include the boutique **Beit El Winery** and the **"Jacob's Ladder" Gallery and Gift Shop** where artwork of local artists can be viewed and/or purchased.

But go now to My place which was in Shiloh, where I set My name at the first.

JEREMIAH 7:12 (NKJV)

SHILOH, AN ANCIENT SAMARIAN CITY, is one of the most significant archaeological and biblical sites in Israel. It is a short 10-mile (16 km) drive from Beit El. **Tel Shiloh** is just west of modern Shiloh.

BIBLICAL SIGNIFICANCE:

- Shiloh was the religious center of Israel prior to Jerusalem. The *mishkan* (portable tabernacle), built to house the **ark of the covenant,** was built according to Moses' direction from God; it traveled with the Jewish people for forty years in the wilderness. It was then transferred to Gilgal for fourteen years. After this, the ark of the covenant remained in the tabernacle at Shiloh for 369 years.

- Jeremiah 7:12-15 and 26:5-9 relate that Shiloh was reduced to ruins. Jeremiah used the example of Shiloh to warn Judah and Jerusalem what Yahweh could do to the "place where I caused my name to dwell." He warned them that their holy city Jerusalem (like Shiloh) could fall under divine judgment.

- Joshua chose Shiloh for a central gathering place for the Israelites to prepare for battle.

"The whole assembly of the Israelites gathered at Shiloh and set up the tent of meeting there."
JOSHUA 18:1

- Shiloh was the destination of regular pilgrimages for major Jewish feasts and sacrifices. Judges 21 records Shiloh as the site of an annual "fifteenth of Av" celebration dance of maidens among the vineyards.

- 1 Samuel chapters 1 and 2 gives the account of barren Hannah praying for a child. She travelled to the tabernacle at Shiloh to pray for a son that she would give to the Lord. God answered Hannah's prayer and she gave birth to Samuel in Ramah. Once Samuel was weaned, Hannah and Samuel travelled to Shiloh, bringing a sacrifice with them. After the sacrifice was offered, Hannah presented Samuel to Eli,

"I prayed for this child, and the LORD has granted me what I asked of him. So now I give him to the LORD. For his whole life he will be given over to the LORD."
1 SAMUEL 1:27–28

- Eli and Samuel both ministered at Shiloh (1 Samuel 3:15) and this is where Samuel's prophetic ministry began.

HIGHLIGHTS FOR VISITORS:

At the entrance of Tel Shiloh is a state-of-the-art **Visitor Center** with a café, a captivating movie of Shiloh's history, touring information, and a gift shop with items made by local artisans. The tel is a working archaeological site; excavations have uncovered significant remains from the Middle Bronze, Late Bronze, and Iron ages. To book a tour or an archaeological dig, call 972-2-578-9111 or email visit@telshiloh.org.il.

A new **Seer's Tower** observation site offers a fascinating light-and-sound presentation which uses innovative multimedia technology to vividly re-enact life in the days of the Tabernacle. On the bottom floor of the tower, the **Days of Shiloh** museum displays archaeological discoveries found at the site. Of special interest are jars from the time of Joshua and Shiloh inscriptions.

During your visit, you might want to grab a bite to eat at the popular, new **Merlot Restaurant** in ancient Shiloh.

ARIEL, FIRST ESTABLISHED IN 1978, IS A thriving city of nearly 20,000, 40% of which are new immigrants. Ariel provides employment, health care, and education to both Jews and Arabs. It is one of Israel's exceptional communities where Jews and Arabs co-exist and strive for peace. In 2010, Prime Minister Netanyahu emphasized the importance of Ariel, *"Everyone who understands the geography of Israel knows how important Ariel is. It is the heart of our country. We are here where are forefathers were, and we will stay here."* Ariel is one of the only cities located between Tel Aviv and Jerusalem, and it creates a pivotal line of defense for both Israel's east and west borders.

BIBLICAL SIGNIFICANCE:

- The name *Ariel* means "Lion of God." *Ari* represents "lion" in Hebrew, denoting bravery and courage; it is also the symbol of the tribe of Judah.

- King David encamped at Ariel.

- Joshua and Caleb are buried opposite the foot of modern-day Ariel.

- Sadly, Isaiah refers to Ariel as a place of mourning and lamentation (Isaiah 29:1–7).

- Ariel fulfills prophecy: it is home to a budding vineyard and ground-breaking wine research at Ariel University.

> *"Again you will plant vineyards on the hills of Samaria; the farmers will plant them and enjoy their fruit."*
> JEREMIAH 31:5

HIGHLIGHTS FOR VISITORS:

Ariel National Center for Leadership Development (ANCLD) is Israel's foremost education leadership center. It is a joint project between the city of Ariel and U.S. Christians including JH Ranch of California and Pastor Ray Bentley of Maranatha Chapel. ANCLD trains over 6,000 young people per year in leadership, teamwork, and communication skills. They utilize innovative outdoor challenge facilities and obstacle courses—while drawing inspiration from biblical values. Contact ANCLD if you are interested in booking leadership training: info@friendsofariel.org. Allot 30–45 minutes for a brief introduction to the site and 3–4 hours if you'd like a training session. You can also visit their website at www.friendsofariel.org.

Ariel Industrial Park is a place where Israelis and Palestinian Arabs work side by side. Allot 45 minutes for a driving tour and 1½ hours for a factory tour which includes information regarding the threats, failures, and ramifications of the boycott movement.

Ariel University is Israel's newest university with 16,000 students. Visitors have the opportunity to meet faculty and students while touring the campus to discover groundbreaking, one-of-kind research projects.

The **Holocaust and Heroism Memorial Museum** is a unique museum that preserves the individual stories of Holocaust survivors through personal insights, access to rare artifacts, and home hospitality.

The **Randolph A. Hearst Sheltered Workshop** is a pioneering facility, successfully integrating the elderly and disabled into the workplace as factory employees in a shared workspace. See the value of self-worth and personal dignity in action. Allot ½ hour.

The **Ariel Pioneers Museum** and **Ron Nachman Legacy Center** highlights the dream of Ron Nachman, Ariel's founding father and longstanding mayor, who envisioned Ariel as a regional hub and a full-fledged city. Ron passed away in 2013, a few short weeks after Ariel University was recognized as Israel's eighth and newest university. The Museum and Center provide an overview of the city's modern history, with a beautiful view of Ariel and its surroundings. Allot 45 minutes to one hour.

> *When you have crossed the Jordan, these tribes shall stand on Mount Gerizim to bless the people: Simeon, Levi, Judah, Issachar, Joseph and Benjamin. And these tribes shall stand on Mount Ebal to pronounce curses: Reuben, Gad, Asher, Zebulun, Dan and Naphtali. The Levites shall recite [the curses] to all the people of Israel in a loud voice...*
>
> DEUTERONOMY 27:12-14

TWO SIGNIFICANT MOUNTAINS IN Samaria are Mount Gerizim to the south and Mount Ebal to the north. Mount Gerizim is known as the "Mount of Blessing" and Mount Ebal as the "Mount of Cursing." In biblical times, Sychar (a small village near Shechem) lay right between Mount Gerizim and Mount Ebal. Here, right in the midst of these two mountains, the tribes would gather to receive blessings and curses tied to the Mosaic covenant (Deuteronomy 11:29, 27:12-14, Joshua 8:33). According to tradition, lush and fertile Mount Gerizim and rocky and barren Mount Ebal represent the ramifications of our choices—follow God and be blessed or depart from God and embrace evil, resulting in an empty and cursed life.

Mt Gerazim (Blessing)   Mt Ebal (Cursing)

Mount Gerizim was the ancient center of Samaritan worship; it is here where the temple was built to rival that of Jerusalem. It is Mt. Gerizim that represented "this mountain" pointed to by the Samaritan woman's conversing with Jesus. "*Our ancestors worshiped on this mountain, but you Jews claim that the place where we must worship is in Jerusalem*" (John 4:20).

Har Bracha ("Mount Blessing") is a small Israeli settlement of about 2,500 located on the southern ridge of Mount Gerizim. Har Bracha is named after Mount Gerizim. Of interest is a group of evangelical Christians known as **HaYovel** (next page), who have joined the community with the support of

Har Bracha's chief rabbi. Their presence has proved controversial for some, but most appreciate their diligent work in the vineyards.

Mount Gerizim Archaeological Park is located on the top of the mountain. The most important remains are those of Justinian's fortress, built in AD 533 in order to protect the church which had been built in AD 475.

Some visitors like to travel to the top of Mount Gerizim for the impressive view and enjoy a glass of wine from the **Har Bracha Winery** while giving thanks to God for His many blessings. Groups can "re-enact" Deuteronomy 27–30: half of the group can stand to one side (facing Mount Ebal) while the other half stands across from them. The Mount Ebal group can holler out the curses in Scripture and the Mount Gerizim group can do the same with the blessings in Scripture, while every curse and blessing is concluded with a universal "AMEN!"

Elon Moreh, an Orthodox Jewish settlement 12 miles (19 km) from Mount Gerizim, would also be a great place to take turns reading the blessings and curses; it provides an awesome view of biblical Shechem, Mount Gerizim, and Mount Ebal. Elon Moreh was the first place Abraham travelled to in the land of Canaan (Israel). Here he built an altar under an oak tree (Elon Moreh) and was told by the Lord, "*To your offspring I will give this land...*" (Genesis 12:7).

They will rebuild the ancient ruins and restore the places long devastated;
they will renew the ruined cities that have been devastated for generations.
Strangers will shepherd your flocks; foreigners will work your fields and vineyards.

ISAIAH 61:4-5

HAYOVEL IS A NON-PROFIT ORGAN-ization based in the hills of Samaria that brings Christian volunteers from all over the world to serve Jewish farmers in Judea and Samaria, in fulfillment of prophecy: *"You shall yet plant vines on the mountains of Samaria…"* *(Jeremiah 31:5).* Jewish farmers, inspired by the words of the prophets, have planted vineyards and olive groves. Some planted in faith, not knowing where they would find laborers to bring in the harvest. Today, many farmers depend on the yearly HaYovel volunteers to keep afloat. For ten years, this multi-generational and family-oriented organization has strived to unite Jews and Christians to work together toward one common goal—the restoration of Israel through tending the land.

Almost every country in the world has turned its back on Judea and Samaria—the historical and spiritual heartland of Israel where 80% of the Bible was either written or occurred. HaYovel serves because of God's deep, unfailing love for Israel. Their stated mission is "to strengthen and undergird the often-overlooked small independent farmer in Israel through creative networking, education, tourism, and activism." Their goal is to equip every volunteer to be an educated, effective, and positive ambassador for Judea and Samaria—and part of the prophetic RESTORATION of the land of Israel that is happening TODAY!

HaYovel invites believers worldwide to *"by faith, to leap into the prophetic pages of the Holy Scripture and join us as we sink our hands into the soil of God's beloved Israel. Experience the incredible restoration of the Land and People God has never forgotten."*

Volunteers have the opportunity to participate by harvesting and/or pruning vineyards and olive groves. They will also have the perks of gaining a first-hand experience of Israel's heartland through professional tour guides and learning from many important guest speakers. HaYovel is serious about providing the best hands-on educational experience for anyone willing to become an effective advocate for Judea and Samaria. Visit www.hayovel.com for more information regarding visits or volunteering.

AT THE FOOT OF MOUNT GERIZIM lies the modern town of **Nablus**, the site of ancient Shechem (also referred to as *Sychar* in the Bible). In biblical times, Shechem was the main settlement of the Samaritans whose religious center stood on Mount Gerizim, right outside of the town. The historian Josephus wrote that Shechem lay between Mount Ebal (to its left) and Mount Gerizim (to its right). He said this was the setting where the twelve tribes gathered on the two mountains to recite God's Law and the blessings and curses that accompanied obedience and disobedience. According to archaeological evidence, the city was destroyed and rebuilt at least 22 times over the years.

BIBLICAL EVENTS IN SHECHEM:

- After Israel split into the two separate kingdoms of Israel and Judah, Shechem became the first capital of the kingdom of Israel.

- Shechem is the site of Jacob's well, where Jesus spoke to the Samaritan woman.

- God appeared to Abraham here and confirmed His covenant with him; Abraham built an altar to the Lord in gratefulness (Genesis 12:6-7).

- Jacob bought a plot of land, and his sons tended sheep (Genesis 33:8-9; 37:12).

- Jacob's sons avenged their sister Dinah's rape in Shechem (Genesis 34:2).

- Shechem was set aside as a city of refuge for those accused of murder (Joshua 20).

- Joshua assembled the Israelites in Shechem and encouraged them to reaffirm their adherence to the Torah (Joshua 24:1).

- Shechem is the burial place of Joseph (Joshua 24:32).

- Rehoboam was declared king in Shechem, and here the ten tribes rejected him as king (1 Kings 12).

Jacob's well, 1934

- The bodies of Jacob's ancestors were brought to Shechem and "placed in the tomb that Abraham had bought..." (Acts 7:15-16).

Jacob's Well still exists today within the monastery complex of the Eastern Orthodox Church in Nablus. It is about 250 feet from the archaeological ruins of ancient Shechem.

Ancient Shechem archaeological ruins include the remains of the fortified Temple of Baal Berith with 17 ft (5 m) thick walls from the Middle Bronze and Late Bronze eras, a Middle Bronze wall, and the stone foundation of a Middle Bronze gate which would have been the main gate of the city during the reign of King Abimelech. It was most likely used in the time of Jacob (Judges 9).

Although not backed by archaeological evidence, **Joseph's Tomb** is a monument located on the outskirts of Nablus. The tomb is a memorial to Joseph whose bones were carried from Egypt to Shechem by the children of Israel.

DEAD SEA

When I arrived there, I saw a great number of trees on each side of the river.
He said to me, "This water flows toward the eastern region and goes down into
the Arabah, where it enters the Dead Sea. When it empties into the sea,
the salty water there becomes fresh. Swarms of living creatures will live wherever
the river flows. There will be large numbers of fish, because this water flows
there and makes the salt water fresh; so where the river flows everything will live.
Fishermen will stand along the shore; from En Gedi to En Eglaim there will be
places for spreading nets. The fish will be of many kinds—
like the fish of the Mediterranean Sea."

EZEKIEL 47:7–10

Masada in the foreground of Jordanian mountains and the Dead Sea.

So when the people broke camp to cross the Jordan,
the priests carrying the ark of the covenant went ahead of them.
Now the Jordan is at flood stage all during harvest. Yet as soon as
the priests who carried the ark reached the Jordan and their feet touched the
water's edge, the water from upstream stopped flowing. It piled up in a heap
a great distance away, at a town called Adam in the vicinity of Zarethan,
while the water flowing down to the Sea of the Arabah (that is, the Dead Sea)
was completely cut off. So the people crossed over opposite Jericho.

JOSHUA 3:14-16

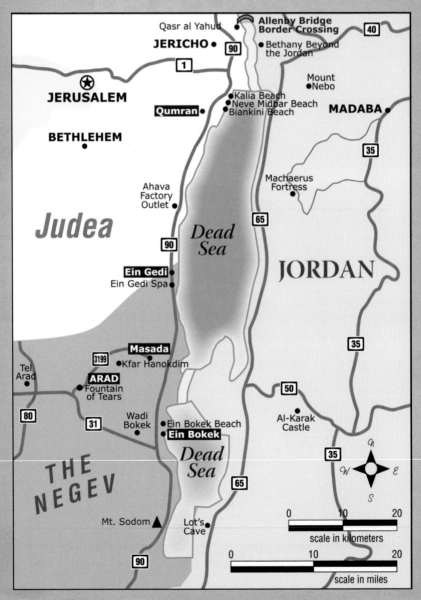

AT 1,300 FT (400 M) BELOW SEA LEVEL, the Dead Sea is the lowest spot on earth. Its full length is 40 miles (65 km) and its maximum width is 10 miles (16 km). Its depth spans a wide range from 16 ft (5 m) to 1,420 ft (433 m). Geographically, the west side of the Dead Sea belongs to Israel, and the east side to Jordan. The Israeli side was bequeathed to the tribe of Judah, while the Jordanian side was part of Reuben's inheritance.

The Dead Sea is aptly named because its high mineral content and salinity do not allow plants or animals to survive in its waters. While the Jordan River feeds into the Dead Sea, no water flows out. Sadly, the Dead Sea's water level has been declining 3–5 ft (1–1.5 m) each year due to several factors. First, the Dead Sea relies upon water from other natural sources, such as the Sea of Galilee and the Jordan River basin. However, since the 1960s, some of these water sources have been diverted. Additionally, mineral extraction industries for Dead Sea health and beauty products have taken a major toll on the water level. And then, of course, the Middle East's hot, dry climate makes it difficult for the lake to replenish itself.

Reduced amounts of fresh water results in elevated salt levels. Hence, the Dead Sea is also known as the "Salt Sea"; its high salinity content (about 33%) is more than eight times that of ocean water. Due to this high concentration of natural salt, the density of Dead Sea water is almost 24% greater than regular water, causing objects that would not normally float (like people) to become buoyant and float!

The Dead Sea's greatest draw for tourists is the opportunity to float on the water and cover their skin with its renowned therapeutic mud. Its water is a very comfortable temperature (72° F or 22° C) and the high concentration of minerals make it a rich source of healing.

DEAD SEA BEACHES

Three popular Dead Sea beaches are close to one another on the northwest tip of the Dead Sea, and two are in the southern region of Ein Bokek (following page). All include beautiful private beaches, natural mud areas, beach chairs, sunshades, restrooms, and showers. The three northern beaches do charge entrance fees.

Driving south on the 90, west of the Lido junction gas station, the first beach will be **Kalia Beach.** Extra amenities include dressing rooms with lockers, barbecues, a Bedouin-style restaurant, and food stands offering falafel, hot dogs, and crepes. The beach is located next to Kibbutz Kalia. Phone: 972-2-994-2391; Email: hofkalia@kalia.org.il

Kalia beach

Immediately south of Kalia Beach is **Biankini Beach**, a Moroccan-style oasis and resort, which also offers cabins, suites, and camping. Biankini also has a Moroccan restaurant, a mini-market, two swimming pools (one for adults and one for children), a spa, billiards, ping-pong, and a "kids club." Phone: 972-2-940-0266; Email: biankini10@gmail.com

Neve Midbar Beach is off the same access road as Biankini. Additional amenities at Neve Midbar include a lawn area with barbeques, a bar, and a gift shop. The beach closes at sunset. Phone: 972-2-994-2781; Email: ayelet.neve@gmail.com

TEN TIPS FOR SWIMMING IN THE DEAD SEA

1. Avoid acute stinging; don't shave for several days before entering the water.

2. Open cuts or sores will cause serious stinging; wrap them in waterproof bandages.

3. Wear an old, dark bathing suit (salt water and dark mud can permanently stain); Water shoes are highly recommended, as your feet will likely encounter uncomfortable rocks.

4. Take photos *before* entering the water; don't ruin your camera.

5. Don't swim, float!

6. Move slowly and make sure not to get water in your eyes.

7. Close your mouth as much as possible; you will likely not appreciate the taste of strong salt water!

8. Do not stay in the water for more than ten minutes at a time to avoid stinging.

9. For amazing skin, put the Dead Sea mud all over your body and face; let it dry in the sun and work its magic!

10. Use outdoor showers to rinse off thoroughly as soon as you leave the water.

EIN BOKEK, JUST SOUTH OF MASADA, is the hub of the luxurious Dead Sea resorts with easy access to the Dead Sea, some with their own private beaches. Nearby stores and factories offer a plethora of health and beauty products manufactured from Dead Sea minerals. Visitors will also find a great selection of unique jewelry handcrafted by Israeli designers.

The **Ein Bokek Beach**, fifteen minutes south of Masada, encompasses a central beach and a south beach (Neve Zohar) with fabulous views. These excellent, free public beaches are rarely crowded. Visitors can enjoy a therapeutic mineral spring, the *Ein Bokek Solarium* skin care clinic, barbecue grills, and a snack bar. The central beach is a one-minute walk southeast from the Isrotel Ganim Hotel. Neve Zohar is a few minutes south, about ½ mile (1 km) north of where highways 90 and 31 converge.

Wadi Bokek is one of three wadis (valleys) fed by springs in the Dead Sea region; the other two are at Ein Gedi. The site offers an easy one-hour walk through beautiful lush scenery, narrow gorges, and gushing springs which contrast the sheer, towering cliffs above. Wadi Bokek can be accessed by foot through a pedestrian tunnel between the Leonardo Inn and the David Dead Sea Resort, or parking is available at the trailhead.

QUMRAN NATIONAL PARK IS 13 MILES (21 km) east of Jerusalem, on the northwest shore of the Dead Sea. The Dead Sea Scrolls, primarily dating back to 152–63 BC, were discovered in eleven different caves in this vicinity, all within a radius of about 3 to 4 miles (5–6 km). Bedouin discovered the first five caves and archaeologists the other six.

Excavations from 1947–1956 uncovered thousands of fragments of scrolls, comprising the oldest surviving biblical manuscripts today. They include portions of every book of the Old Testament (except Nehemiah and Esther) as well as various writings that describe life during the time of Jesus. The texts from the Qumran scrolls were found to be word-for-word identical to our Hebrew Bible in more than 95 percent of the text. The remaining 5% was primarily slips of the pen and spelling adaptations. The restoration of the scrolls was completed and published in 2001.

The scrolls had been hidden inside jars by the **Essenes**, a Jewish mystical sect who lived in Qumran from about 150 BC until AD 68, when the community was destroyed by the Romans. The Essenes led lives of ritual purity, poverty, separation, and abstinence from worldly pleasures. Their communal life centered around one large main square building, which held the scriptorium (the room used by Essene scribes), a large refectory (a dining room for communal meals where the Essenes ate in silence), and an assembly hall. This structure and adjoining buildings also housed baths and latrines, storerooms, mikvahs, a flour mill, stables, furnaces, workshops, and an elaborate cistern and conduit system for retaining water. The entire community was fortified by three-foot walls.

An audiovisual presentation at the site provides a valuable overview of the community and the scrolls. A large gift shop, a snack shop with great ice cream, and restaurant are onsite. You may want to ask if you can visit one of the caves where scrolls were discovered. Phone: 972-2-994-2235

THE COPPER SCROLL

The Copper Scroll is the most mysterious discovery of all the Dead Sea Scrolls. In the spring of 1952, this intriguing scroll was unearthed inside Cave 3 in Qumran.

Rather than papyrus or leather, the Copper Scroll is inscribed on thin sheets of almost 100% pure copper. Copper was particularly valuable in ancient times and much more strenuous and time-consuming to inscribe. Each letter had to be hammered out individually with a chisel. The choice of copper indicated that the contents of the scroll were of such importance that the scribe wanted to be sure it could withstand the ravages of time. Originally measuring over 7 ft (2 m) long and 1 ft (30 cm) wide, the Copper Scroll is one of the largest ancient metal documents ever found.

The inscription lists over fifty locations that purportedly store vast amounts of buried gold, silver, coins, and vessels. Because there was no accompanying narrative to the list, questions concerning the context of the Copper Scroll have plagued archaeologists and historians alike. Who from ancient times inscribed this treasure map and why? And most important, *what* are the treasures and precisely where were they buried? There is one potential and intriguing possibility: could the Copper Scroll be a vital witness to an undercover operation to rescue temple tithes and vessels before the siege of Jerusalem in AD 70?

For fascinating details of this discovery and its aftermath, read the recently written book, *The Copper Scroll Project: An Ancient Secret Fuels the Battle for the Temple Mount*. The book, written by Shelley Neese, in cooperation with project director Jim Barfield, is available on Amazon.

My beloved is to me a cluster of henna blossom from the vineyards of En Gedi.
SONG OF SONGS 1:14

EIN GEDI NATURE RESERVE IS A SPECtacular oasis known for its scenic hiking trails, high cliffs with caves, waterfalls, lush foliage, superior dates and therapeutic plants. The reserve has several springs used for agriculture and bottled drinking water, while serving as a sanctuary for diverse plant, bird, and animal species including the **Nubian ibex** and the **coney**, or "**rock hyrax**." Psalm 104:18: *"The high mountains belong to the wild goats; the crags are a refuge for the hyrax."* The name *En Gedi* is composed of two Hebrew words, *en* meaning "spring" and *gedi* meaning "young goat-kid."

The remains of an ancient synagogue on the reserve bears an inscription warning the community against "revealing the town's secret." Many believe this "secret" referred to the community's method of extraction and preparation of their much-prized balsam resin (ancient persimmon)—possibly made into expensive perfume.

Ein Gedi is best known for serving as David's refuge from the pursuit of King Saul (**Wadi David** or "Valley of David"). *"And David went up from there and lived in the strongholds of En Gedi. After Saul returned from pursuing the Philistines, he was told, 'David is in the Desert of En Gedi'"* (1 Samuel 23:29–24:1).

The good news of the Bible is that after the return of Jesus Christ, the Dead Sea will become fresh and that fish and fruit trees will thrive at En Gedi (Ezekiel 47:8–12).

EIN GEDI TRAILS

Ein Gedi's two most popular and scenic trails are distinct; each follows its own spring. If you can arrive early in the morning for your hike, you have a good chance of viewing an ibex or a coney.

The basic walk follows the **Nahal (Wadi) David** trail. This fairly easy hike is on a dirt path, walking through some reed tunnels, passing the lower falls, and culminating at *David's Waterfall* gushing out from a rock and surrounded by lush green foliage. Allot at least an hour for this hike, preferably more. The first ¼ mile (400 m) of the trail includes the first (lower) waterfall; this initial part of the path is fully wheelchair accessible.

The **Nahal (Wadi) Arugot** trail follows the *Arugot Stream*. This hike is longer, more strenuous, and less crowded than the Wadi David hike; allot two to three hours or more. If you have some extra time, stop first at the fifth-century AD synagogue northeast of the wadi entrance to view an exquisite mosaic pavement with inscriptions, one of which calls down a curse on any person who is quarrelsome and slanderous! A small model shows what the synagogue

would have looked like in its time. The Wadi Arugot trail takes you through a stream; you *will* get wet, so wear water shoes. The walk back is on a dry path. You'll see amazing views, caves, and a waterfall. Enjoy wonderful refreshment soaking in the upper pools at the head of the stream. When you reach a T-junction after a small stream, head right for a treat. At the head of David's Waterfall is *Dodim Cave*, also known as *Lovers' Cave*, an intimate and picturesque cave and water pool (photo above).

Snacks and light lunches, as well as a small store and gift shop, are available at the entrance of Ein Gedi. Phone: 972-8-658-4285

AHAVA FACTORY OUTLET

The settlement of Mitzpe Shalem, about 15 minutes north of Ein Gedi, is home to the Ahava Visitors Center and Factory Outlet that sells cosmetics and skin care products featuring the mud, minerals, and salts of the Dead Sea. The center includes a gift shop, a cafeteria, and an opportunity to view the manufacturing process. Phone: 972-2-994-5123

EIN GEDI SPA

A few minutes south of the Ein Gedi Nature Reserve is the Ein Gedi Spa, a wellness center fed by the waters of the Dead Sea. The spa offers two Thermo-Mineral hot water pools, mineral mud straight from the Dead Sea, massages, a restaurant, and a private beach. Phone: 972-8-620-1030

MASADA IS HEBREW FOR "FORTRESS." According to Josephus, **Herod the Great** began building the fortress of Masada in 37 BC. Six years later, after three separate periods of construction, King Herod completed Masada "as a refuge for himself."

Jewish rebels, known as "**Zealots**" or "**Sicarii**," captured Masada in AD 66. After Rome destroyed Jerusalem and the Second Temple in AD 70, the Great Revolt ended—except for the surviving Zealots who had fled from Jerusalem to Masada. For three years, they prevailed over the substantial Roman garrison of 10,000 (5,000 soldiers and thousands of Jewish prisoners of war).

The Romans constructed a massive rampart of stones and earth on Masada's western slope. In the spring of AD 73, following four to six months of siege, the rampart was completed. The Roman army was now able to breach the fortress wall with a battering ram hoisted to the top of the rampart.

Nine-hundred and sixty men, women and children (made up of both Sicarii and probably the remaining Essenes from Qumran), led by Sicarii leader **Eleazar ben Ya'ir**, came to a heartbreaking joint decision. They resolved to burn the fortress and end their own lives rather than be taken alive. They burnt everything except the storehouses, sending a clear message to the Romans that it was not hunger that led to loss of life, but the preference of self-sacrifice to a brutal life of slavery and abuse. According to Josephus, two women and five children managed to hide themselves in a cistern and survive to tell the story.

The Masada Fortress covered 23 acres (9 hectares) with a casemate wall surrounding the plateau. It encompassed storehouses, barracks, palaces, an arsenal, large cisterns filled with rainwater, and a synagogue. Under the synagogue's treasury was a storeroom where large portions of two biblical scrolls were discovered in 1964: one from Deuteronomy 33–34; the other, Ezekiel 35–38. The Ezekiel portion of Scripture speaks of the dry bones coming back to life!

Moshe Dayan, while serving as the Chief of Staff of the IDF in the 1950s, launched a new tradition. He used the summit of Masada for the swearing-in ceremony of the IDF soldiers who had completed their basic training. Each ceremony concluded with the resolute declaration: "*Masada shall not fall again.*"

The large **Masada Visitor Center** encompasses a cafeteria, snack shop, a movie about the Masada story, a model of the site, an exhibit of many of the archaeological finds, and an upscale gift shop with souvenirs, skin products, and (typically) some the most beautiful jewelry in Israel at competitive prices. Phone: 972-8-658-4207

MASADA MUSEUM

The Masada Museum that opened in 2007 is a "must-see!" It is the culminating exhibition from the vision of the recently retired, long-time Masada Director, Eitan Campbell. Masada's story is brought to life through authentic artifacts, multimedia, and stories of everyday lives of individuals who lived on Masada. Sounds and images portray their poignant emotions as they seek to escape persecution by the Romans.

The museum tour begins with first century Roman historian Josephus Flavius and presents three main themes: Herod, the Jewish Rebels, and the Roman Army. Nine scenes recreate a setting and a theatrical background for the presentation of historic artifacts, most of which are authentic dating back almost 2000 years. Displays are three-dimensional and designed to reflect the spirit of the times; even Herod's palace is recreated. Life-size statues of figures from Masada's past stand throughout the museum, introducing visitors to the remarkable tales of Masada. Thirty-minute audio guides are available at the front desk. Phone: 972-8-658-4207

SUNRISE HIKE TO MASADA

Sunrise at Masada is a magical, unforgettable experience! *See photo on previous page.* Watching the brilliant sun emerge behind the Jordanian mountains over the crystal-clear, turquoise Dead Sea below is a sight to behold. Two Masada entrances are available for sunrise hikes to Masada's summit; both open one hour before sunrise.

The easier of the two hikes is the **Roman Ramp Path**, located on the back, western side of Masada. Expect a 20-minute hike on a steep, dirt path with many steps. If you're staying at one of the resorts in Ein Bokek, getting to the back of Masada is a significant drive: allow 30 minutes to the town of Arad, then another 30 minutes along the narrow, windy Road 3199 from Arad. This hike is ideal for travelers spending the previous night in an Arad hotel or Kfar Hanokdim (p. 241).

The most popular path, and arguably the most rewarding, is the **Snake Path** on the eastern side of Masada, off Route 90. This path begins almost 1,000 ft (300 m) below sea level and ends over 1,300 ft (400 m) above sea level. The 700-plus step winding path is a mix of hard dirt with some loose rocks and countless switchbacks. This hike should take somewhere between 45 and 75 minutes, depending on your fitness level.

Dress comfortably with breathable layers; weather can quickly change from cold and windy to scorching hot. Good walking shoes, sunscreen, and a large bottle of water (which can be refilled at the top) are essential! Other options are snacks, a good lightweight camera, and a headlamp for the darker, early morning hours. Coffee is available partway up the mountain.

Masada's summit provides one of the best views in the world! You can sing hymns, have a Bible lesson, share with one another, pray, have private devotions, or just walk around the ruins. If you plan to hike back down, don't forget to fill up your water bottle and give yourself a good hour for the descent. Be sure to inquire as to when the Snake Path closes, which is often around 10:00 AM due to the extreme heat. If you're done hiking, you can pay for a one-way cable car back (starting at 8:00 AM).

THE ARAD EXPERIENCE

Arad is only 30 minutes inland from the Dead Sea. If you are spending the night near the Dead Sea or travelling in southern Israel, try to allot a half-day for the fascinating ARAD EXPERIENCE. Read more on pages 240–243.

Experience Arad from ancient times to its modern-day wonders!

The region of Arad is of great significance. Located on the border of the Negev and Judean Deserts, the city of Arad is literally the southern border of biblical Judea. Ancient Arad was the main center of community life in all of southern Israel during biblical times. Today, the area encompasses important biblical, historical, and modern tourist sites.

Drive north on Highway 80 from Highway 31 to begin your experience with a short visit to **TEL ARAD** where you will be able to view the ruins of the **only recovered Judean temple in all of Israel**, where a "House of Yahweh" inscription was found. View the inner courtyard, a square room that would have been the Holy of Holies, complete with an altar of burnt offering, two incense altars, two standing stones, and channels to drain the blood of the sacrifices.

Continue north two miles to **TEL CRIOT**, identified as the biblical *Kerioth* ("Man from Kerioth") **birth place of Judas Iscariot**, the disciple who betrayed Jesus. View the ruins of the large ancient settlement where the inhabitants lived in underground caves.

Drive back to the modern town of Arad to visit the **FOUNTAIN OF TEARS** sculpture exhibit, **an incredibly impactful memorial to the Holocaust, Yeshua, and the modern state of Israel.** *"Oh, that my head were a spring of water and my eyes a fountain of tears! I would weep day and night for the slain of my people."* JEREMIAH 9:1

After a time of reflection, conclude your time in Arad at the spectacular Bedouin oasis of **KFAR HANOKDIM** where you can immerse yourself in the Bedouin life and culture by participating in a short **camel trek** overlooking a beautiful mountain range and Bedouin village, and partake of either Bedouin hospitality or a **traditional, lavish "Hafla" lunch**, hosted by local Bedouin.

For more information about the Arad Experience and special group rates, contact info@arad365.com.

A NEW NIGHT SHOW
"MASADA FROM DUSK TO DAWN"

*If you're in the area, come and experience
the thrilling and dramatic story of Masada told like never before,
right in the heart of the desert!*

The spectacular "Masada from Dusk to Dawn" takes place on the back of Masada, just a fifteen-minute drive from Kfar Hanokdim. Take yourself back in time to relive the authentic, heartbreaking story of Masada through remarkable special effects using the majestic Masada mountain as its backdrop.

Participate in the innovative and unforgettable saga of Masada and its heroes through video mapping, unique lighting effects, and a stirring sound track written by renowned Israeli musician Shlomo Gronich, complete with a full orchestra and a rousing choir.

Winter performances begin at 7:30 PM and summer performance at either 8:30 PM or 9:00 PM. Arrive an hour before the show begins for the full Masada experience as sunset and dusk turns to darkness. The 45-minute show is displayed on Tuesday and Thursday evenings; special group showings can be arranged for Sunday, Monday, and Wednesday evenings. Reservations are required; either email masadaevents@npa.org.il or call 972-8-995-9333.

BEFORE THE SHOW: Prepare yourself for what you about to experience. Step into the Masada story through "RADIO MASADA," listening to the "The Way to Masada" podcast at www.ranlevi.com.

AFTER THE SHOW: Consider staying nearby and hiking Masada at sunrise to round out your entire Masada experience!

THE MODERN TOWN OF ARAD WAS founded in 1961 and is technically part of the Negev. It is included in this chapter because of its proximity to the Dead Sea.

Arad is best known for its important Tel Arad archaeological site. To reach the site from Arad, drive about seven miles (11 km) west on Route 31, then north on Route 80. The tel encompasses two archaeological sites: the *lower city* and the *upper hill*.

The lower city was first settled around 4000 BC. Excavations date back to the Bronze Age, about 2650 BC. Ancient Arad was the urban center for the entire Negev. Canaanite Arad was a planned city surrounded by a wall, divided into public buildings and residential areas. The community earned their living from agriculture, breeding sheep, hunting, and the international trade of olive oil and asphalt from the Dead Sea.

Today, the lower city includes remains of a water reservoir and well, the foundations of a residential quarter of uniform houses dubbed "Arad Houses," a large complex of many rooms, cubicles, and courtyards known as "The Palace," a temple complex (indicating worship of several gods), and the remains of a long stretch of fortified walls which orig-

inally would have been reinforced by round towers which extended up to the fortress.

The site was apparently deserted for over 1,500 years, then resettled in the tenth century BC on the upper hill—the location of the "**Israelite Fortress**" that would have been built during the reigns of King David and King Solomon.

The most important remains are those of a Judean temple and altar in the northwest of the fortress. These remains are believed to have been in use from the ninth century BC to the end of the eighth century BC—concurrently with the First Temple in Jerusalem (the Iron Age). Since excavation has been prohibited on the Temple Mount platform in Jerusalem, the Arad temple is the only "House of Yahweh" uncovered by excavation in Israel. Hence, the site is of great importance to the archives of archaeology and biblical history.

The temple was built in three sections according to precise biblical instructions: the inner courtyard, the temple, and the Holy of Holies. Three steps lead up from the temple to the Holy of Holies, where two incense altars and a "standing stone" flank the entrance. *Ostraca* (pottery shards with inscriptions) were discovered inside. The inscriptions bore names of two priestly families mentioned in the Bible, *Meramot* (Ezra 8:33) and *Pashkhur* (Jeremiah 20:1). In the heart of the courtyard is the square sacrificial altar built of small stones and faced with unchiseled stones, compliant with the biblical prohibition against building an altar of stones chiseled by means of a metal tool.

If you have time, the **Arad Historical Museum** at Aviv St. 2 in modern Arad is highly recommended, as it houses many of the most important artifacts from Tel Arad. Phone: 972-50-858-9373

SOME TOUR GROUPS OPT TO LODGE at Kfar Hanokdim instead of the Dead Sea. Kfar Hanokdim is a center of Bedouin hospitality located halfway between Arad and the back side of Masada (only a 15-minute drive to the Masada Night Show or a sunrise hike).

The Kfar is a green oasis shaded by palm trees amid the tranquil beauty of the Judean desert. The picturesque desert resort offers goat-hair, Bedouin-style tents, spacious lodges made of local stone, and numerous relaxing spots to unwind. Its structures are built from natural stone and decorated with rugs and materials woven from goats' hair.

Visitors have many options. They can hike or cycle one of the six trails surrounding the Kfar, take a camel trek overlooking the Bedouin village and surrounding mountains of the Kana'im Valley, participate in an evening bonfire, or simply chill out in one of their many hammocks strewn across the property.

Bedouin hospitality and delicious food abound at the Kfar. Guests can enjoy **traditional Bedouin hospitality** within a spacious Bedouin tent surrounding a campfire where they can sip on tea, observe the traditional coffee-making ritual, and hear explanations and stories about the Bedouin way of life. The Kfar also offers two levels of feasts: a lavish, **traditional Bedouin "Hafla"** lunch or dinner served by Bedouin hosts and an even more elaborate **"Sheik-style"** meal.

Guests can choose from three types of overnight accommodations: 1) a large, **traditional Bedouin tent** made of black goat's hair with soft mattresses (minimum of fifteen guests in each tent, with restroom facilities nearby), 2) a desert-style lodge, or **sukkah,** for four to eight guests sleeping on futons (includes coffee-making facilities, a small cooking area, and nearby bathroom facilities), or 3) a **desert cabin** with indigenous, handcrafted furniture, a private bathroom, bed linens and towels, coffee-making facilities, and a cooking area (accommodates one couple with up to three children or additional guests). All overnight visitors are served a plentiful Israeli breakfast. Phone: 972-8-995-0097

Oh, that my head were a spring of water and my eyes a fountain of tears!
I would weep day and night for the slain of my people. JEREMIAH 9:1

THE FOUNTAIN OF TEARS IS A SCULP-ture exhibit in Arad. If you're anywhere near Masada or Arad, don't miss this powerful exhibit! It symbolizes a dialogue of grief between the Holocaust and the Crucifixion and it portrays how Yeshua, through the course of agonizing unto death, identifies and empathizes with His Jewish brothers and sisters who acutely suffered during the Holocaust. The Fountain of Tears is based on Jeremiah 9:1 (above) in which Jeremiah laments the devastation and slaughter of his people as they are marched off to their deaths.

Artist Rick Wienecke has created seven sculptured relief panels of Jerusalem stone (representing the last seven statements from the Crucifixion) and seven life-size bronze figures (representing the response and reflection of a Holocaust survivor). This becomes the dialogue in which the Holocaust survivor identifies, within his own pain, the words that he hears Yeshua speaking.

In the Bible, pillars of stone represented memorials. The panels are separated by six pillars of field stones, a memorial to the six million who perished. Water, symbolizing tears, continually runs down the stones of each pillar. This continual flow of water exemplifies the day and night intercession of the prophet Jeremiah crying out to God on behalf of His people.

After the seven panels is a sculpture of a child, inspired by a child's poem written during the Holocaust, *I Never Saw another Butterfly*. The child, representing all the children at Auschwitz, is leaning against the inside of a crematorium door in a fetal position, feeling totally abandoned. Most of the children from Terezin, in the Czech Republic, were sent to the Auschwitz concentration camp. Roughly 15,000 children from Terezin entered; only about 100 survived.

The arm of the child penetrates the closed door and clutches a small piece of ground. The ground represents the land of Israel. Here, the land and the butterfly become one. The hand of the child possesses the land, but it becomes the butterfly that the child never sees. The ground is covered with olive leaves, symbolizing the oil that brings healing and anointing—the beginning of the resurrection.

Visits to the Fountain are
by appointment only.
For booking or more information,
email Dafna at castingseeds@gmail.com.

MOUNT SODOM IS WEST OF THE southern Dead Sea basin. Many biblical archaeologists believe this to be the location of the depraved cities of Sodom and Gomorrah described in Genesis chapter 19—the cities upon which the Lord sent down fire and brimstone because of their great wickedness. Remarkably, 95% of Mt. Sodom is made entirely of *halite* (rock salt). This composite prevents any type of vegetation growth on the mountain and creates a lunar-like landscape.

The Lord instructed Lot's family to leave because He was going to destroy the city, and He warned them not to look back. However, Lot's wife *did* look back, and she became a pillar of salt (Genesis 19:26). One of Mt. Sodom's rock fragments that has separated off (photo to right) due to weathering has been nicknamed "Lot's Wife." As promised, the cities were destroyed.

Beneath the "Lot's Wife" formation are many fascinating caves full of extraordinary rock formations created by layers of salt. One of the caves known as the "Malch'am Cave" is Israel's longest known cave as well as the longest solitary natural salt cave in the world. Its entrance leads to a passageway that penetrates deep into the mountain; it is roughly 3½ miles (5,500 m) long!

The caves are permanently closed to visitors for safety reasons. However, Mount Sodom is a popular site for hiking and mountain biking!

FASCINATING DISCOVERY

Recently, Christian archaeological researchers have explored the land along the western shore of the Dead Sea and Jordan River where they believed the four cities God judged were located: Sodom, Gomorrah, Admah, and Zeboiim (Deuteronomy 29:23).

Apparently, these locations are made up of almost entirely white ash. They believe the heat of the fire God rained down was so hot that it burned the limestone that would have been used for construction. The ash there today is composed of calcium sulfate and calcium carbonate, both potential by-products of burnt limestone and sulfur.

The men also found numerous round, golf ball-sized balls of brimstone (sulfur), some with burn marks around them. The brimstone was analyzed by a professional lab and was confirmed to be composed of 96 to 98 percent sulfur—a composition unknown anywhere else. Read more at www.arkdiscovery.com/sodom_&_gomorrah.htm.

THE NEGEV

Restore our fortunes, Lord, like streams in the Negev. Those who sow with tears will reap with songs of joy. Those who go out weeping, carrying seed to sow, will return with songs of joy, carrying sheaves with them.

PSALMS 126:4–6

Solomon's Pillars

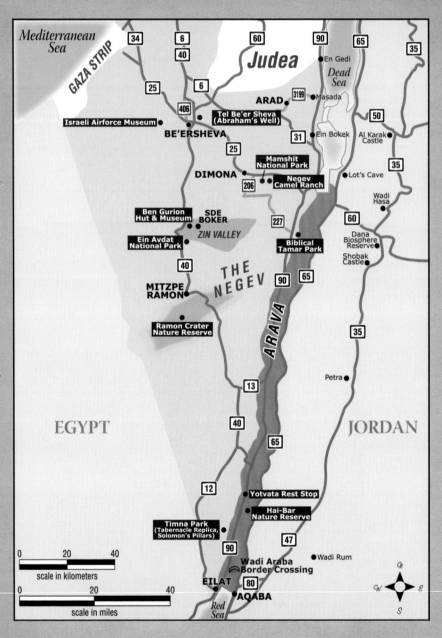

View additional site info online: Israeli Airforce Museum, Dimona, Mamshit, Ben Gurion Hut and Museum, and Biblical Tamar Park.

Go to WalkAboutZion.com; click on Inspiration Israel.

"It is in the Negev that the creativity and pioneer vigor of Israel shall be tested."

DAVID BEN-GURION

THE HEBREW WORD *NEGEV* DENOTES "dry." The Negev of Southern Israel is defined as a desert due to the small quantity of rain the regions receives—less than 8 inches (20 cm) annually. However, when the occasional heavy storm materializes, flash flooding can occur along the riverbeds.

In 2010, the Negev was home to some 630,000 people (8.2% of Israel's population); approximately 75% are Jews, 25% Bedouin. The population is expected to reach 1.2 million by 2025. Its four largest cities, along with their "rough" population statistics as of 2018, are: Be'ersheva (187,000), Eilat (45,000), Dimona (34,000), and Arad (25,000). Additionally, smaller cities, Bedouin communities, and kibbutzim scattered across the Negev. *Arad sites are included in the Dead Sea chapter on pp. 220–222.*

Israel is unique because of its desire, spurred by Bible prophecy, to "make the desert green." The land of the Negev, mentioned 39 times in the Bible, first belonged to the tribes of Judah and Simeon. Later it became part of the kingdom of Solomon, and then part of the kingdom of Judah. The Negev has the distinction of being the only desert in the world dedicated to reversing the global trend of desertification! In the midst of its large expanses of dirt and rocks, this land possesses remarkable landscapes of unique beauty: canyons, waterfalls, caves, wadis (dry riverbeds), archaeological sites, and three enormous craters.

Although sparsely populated, the Negev covers over half of Israel's total land area (over 4,700 sq mi or 13,000 sq km). Flanked by Jordan and Egypt, its northern border is the Be'ersheva and Arad rift and its southern border is Israel's southernmost tip, the resort city of Eilat.

For at least 4,000 years, the Negev has been home to the Bedouin—who are increasingly giving up their nomadic lifestyle and settling in permanent houses. Half live in virtually unknown cities, while the other half live in towns that were built for them by the Israeli government between the 1960s and 1980s.

The modern Israeli settlement of the Negev began when the British forces took it from the Ottoman empire in 1917. It was later added to the proposed area of "Mandatory Palestine," and eventually became an official part of Israel.

When David Ben-Gurion became Israel's first prime minister in 1948, he held a passionate dream that the Negev would thrive. Ben-Gurion believed the Bible and had faith that the land would become a place where Jews could settle and prosper. He was convinced the Negev was critical to the well-being of the new nation. In 1948, his dream began to take root. Today, Ben Gurion's vision has been realized. Along with its growing towns and cities, the Negev is increasingly being utilized for the Israel Defense Forces' primary bases. By 2020, four more major military bases in the Negev are expected to be established.

BE'ERSHEVA IS BOTH THE GATEWAY to the Negev and the region's largest city and administrative capital. A significant portion of Be'ersheva's original population were Jewish immigrants from Arab countries. Since 1990, most of the city's growth has come from immigrants of the former Soviet Union and Ethiopia.

Be'ersheva has been dubbed "the new Silicon Valley." It is the high-tech hub of Israel and home to the Ben-Gurion University of the Negev, a center for teaching and research with five campuses and over 20,000 students. Some of its research institutes include the National Institute for Biotechnology in the Negev, two schools of desert research, and another school that focuses its research on Israel and Zionism.

Be'ersheva's history began in Bible times when it was known as both *Beersheva* and *Beersheba*. In the phrase *"from Dan to Beersheba," Beersheba* symbolized the southern boundary of the land of Israel (Judges 20:1; 1 Samuel 3:19-20). Beersheba is where Hagar wandered in the wilderness and God opened her eyes to see a well of water from which her son Ishmael could drink. The name *Be'ersheva* is derived from the Hebrew words *be'er* (well) and *shvu'a* (oath). During the time of Abraham, when Abimelech was king, he pursued a covenant with Abraham because he knew "God was with Abraham." He wanted Abraham to make a pact with him, promising to show kindness to both him and his descendants. Since Abraham had dug a well that had been unknowingly seized by Abimelech's servants, Abraham requested that Abimelech accept sheep and cattle from him, including seven lambs, to be witness to the fact that the well that was seized belonged to Abraham. *"So that place was called Beersheba, because the two men swore an oath there"* (Genesis 21:22-31).

In the early twentieth century, Ottoman Turks settled in Be'ersheva. Then in October 1948, following the announcement of Israel's independence, the city was conquered by the Israeli Defense Forces during the "Battle of Be'er Sheva."

Tel Be'er Sheva, the archaeological site of biblical Beersheba, is a World Heritage Site located a few miles east of the modern city. The site dates back to the early Israelite period, around tenth century BC. It is believed to have been the first planned settlement in the region. Biblical Beersheba had many homes squeezed together in tight quarters, all surrounding a central square which housed their livestock. The community was built around an elaborate water system with evidence of numerous ancient wells, many likely dug by Abraham and Isaac.

Other remains that can be viewed are a city gate, several streets, a lookout tower, and storehouses. Of special note, a large horned altar made of sandstone was uncovered at the site. The altar attests to the existence of a temple or cult center in the city, which was probably dismantled during the reforms of King Hezekiah (1 Kings 18:4). One of the stones in the altar bore the image of a deeply incised serpent.

Tel Be'er Sheva

At the gates of Tel Be'er Sheva is the **Abraham's Well International Visitor Center**. Here you can view a 3,800-year-old well and enjoy a 3D presentation of the old and the new: Abraham's story and Israeli innovations for water in the desert. Phone: 972-8-623-4613

THE IMPRESSIVE ZIN VALLEY OR **Wilderness of Zin** spans ten miles (16 km). Zin Valley is breathtaking. It is a favorite of nature lovers and hikers! The top of the valley provides incredible panoramic views across the desert landscape.

Zin is mentioned several times in the Bible. It was the southern border of the land of Canaan promised to the Israelites (Numbers 34:3-4). The wilderness of Zin was the desert from which the twelve spies were sent out by Moses to explore the Promised Land (Numbers 13:21). And the Israelites crossed the

Wilderness of Zin while journeying from Egypt to the Promised Land (Numbers 27:12-14).

EIN AVDAT NATIONAL PARK

EIN AVDAT NATURE RESERVE, THE pristine narrow canyon of the Zin Valley, is only a ten-minute drive south from Sde Boker.

In the 1950s, after the establishment of Kibbutz Sde Boker, this once-remote area became easily accessible to visitors. Today it is part of the Israel National Trail, which winds through its canyon.

The Ein Avdat Nature Reserve is home to the ibex and many birds of prey. At the southern opening of the canyon, water from numerous springs empty into two deep pools, making its way through a series of waterfalls. When the springs in the canyon emerge from between horizontal layers of rocks, a Byzantine fortress can be seen overhead. At this spot, a stairway leads up to the beginning of the 50 ft (15 m) Avdat waterfall that flows into a 26 ft (8 m) deep pool of very cold water—a great swimming spot for the hearty!

As the trail continues upward, it crosses and re-crosses a stream, ultimately reaching a lovely grove of Euphrates poplar trees. At the trail's end, hikers will enjoy observation terraces with commanding views of the magnificent canyon.

THE TOWN OF **MITZPE RAMON**, WITH about 5,000 residents, sits at an elevation of 2,800 ft (860 m) overlooking a large erosion valley. This valley is Israel's largest national park known as the Ramon Nature Reserve. Mitzpe Ramon is a convenient place to stay while exploring the region in and around the Ramon Crater.

The Ramon Crater is the world's largest erosion "crater," or *makhtesh* in Hebrew. It is a natural wonder made by the Creator Himself that measures 24 miles (40 km) long, 5 miles (8 km) wide, and 1600 ft (500 m) deep. Its unique geology is fascinating; numerous one-of-a-kind geological formations can be seen in all directions.

The **Mitzpe Ramon Visitor Center** is the gateway to Ramon Crater. A film inside the visitor center provides the history of the crater and a three-dimensional interactive model provides a visual display of the crater's topography. Visitors ascend a ramp bordered by exhibits explaining local geologists' theories regarding the crater's formation as well as the region's history, geography, geology, flora, and diverse wildlife. At the top of the ramp are floor-to-ceiling windows imparting a breathtaking view of the Ramon Crater.

Sixteen miles (26 km) of underground galleries of gypsum mine quarries span Ramon Canyon. The valuable **Gypsum Quarry Restoration** processing factory operates right in the middle of the Ramon Crater! Just one mine at Mitzpe Ramon produces 10,000 tons of gypsum every year.

Ramon Nature Reserve is a hub for desert fun and adventure by car, hike, jeep, or bike. Two impressive crater lookouts, the **Camel Lookout** and the **Albert Promenade**, are a short drive from the Visitor Center. Hikers can inquire at the center about two recommended trails: the **Har Ardon Trail** and the **Negev Highlands Trail**. For those who enjoy camping, the **Be'erot Campground** provides a beautiful setting to camp out under the stars or in Bedouin tents. The Bedouin hospitality experience includes coffee, tea and pita bread. Group reservations are required.

THE ULTIMATE WAY TO EXPERIENCE the Ramon Crater is to take a jeep tour with an experienced local guide. The author of this travel guide can wholeheartedly recommend Dr. Haim Berger with Negev Jeep Eco Tours. Dr. Berger has a doctorate in Ecology and Animal Behavior, along with seventeen years of teaching experience on the topics of "nature" and "desert animals."

NEGEV JEEP ECO TOURS:

Tour # 1. Zin Valley

This tour begins with a drive to the Zin Valley nature reserve, where most of the natural springs within the Negev are concentrated. Stop at several beautiful observation points on the way and visit Ein Aqev spring, a high waterfall cascading into a deep pool where passengers can swim. Next, drive to the upper Zin Valley for a glimpse into the hidden and secret world of the **Nabatean** kingdom. Find out how this people group managed to collect and hide their water, how they grew vineyards in ancient times, and much more. Continue to a site filled with **ancient rock art** that gives clues to the spiritual world of the nomadic people of the Negev. Finally, observe their transition of writing over the years—depicted first in hunting scenes, next in symbols, then to the world's first alphabet from which modern Hebrew and Latin evolved.

Tour # 2. Ramon Crater

Take a tour through the dramatic landscape of the Ramon Crater and view ancient dwellings, graves, water systems, and old trade routes. Observe the diverse Negev wildlife and explore the highlights of the crater: its colorful rocks, geological formations, medicinal plants, animal footprints, and more. Along the way, stop for desert tea and/or coffee and a picnic lunch.

Tour #3: Night Safari

This adventure is for all ages! Board the 4WD jeep for a nighttime excursion using the vehicle's spotlight. Search for animal burrows and footprints as well as desert wildlife such as wolves, hyenas, foxes, hares, porcupines, and scorpions. Stop for desert tea and/or coffee over a warm bonfire under the stars.

For more information, visit the website at www.negevjeep.co.il or contact Dr. Berger directly. Phone: 972-54-534-3797; Email: negevjeep@gmail.com

THE NABATEANS

THE NABATEANS WERE ARAB NOMADS who first appeared in the Negev in the fourth century BC. These nomads knew how to find and preserve water like no one else, earning them the title, "lords of the desert." The Nabateans dominated the international spice trade and accumulated great wealth. They established a trade route, known as the **Spice Route**, across the Negev. Caravans of camels would regularly cross this route carrying spices, perfumes, salt, gems, silks, metals, medicinal plants, and resins like frankincense and myrrh. The Nabateans traveled from Yemen in the East to the Mediterranean port city of Gaza in the west. They passed through Petra, Jordan, and various locations across Israel; they built six cites in the Negev. The Nabatean culture came to an end when they were conquered in the second century AD. Remains of ancient Nabatean cities can be found between Be'ersheva and the Mizpe Ramon region.

THE BIBLE MENTIONS TWO NORTH-to-south plains referred to as *Arabah* (Arabic) or *Aravah* (Hebrew), meaning "desolate and dry area" as in the photo above. The region most frequently referred to in Scripture is today's Jordan Valley, which extended from the southern end of the Sea of Galilee to the Dead Sea. Only in Deuteronomy 2:8 does it refer to land *south* of the Dead Sea.

In biblical times, the Aravah was the center of copper production, focused primarily in its southern portion. It is believed that King Solomon would have had copper mines here. The northern area was at one time irrigated and cultivated by the Nabateans, evidenced by the remains of its ancient agricultural systems.

However, over time, the Arava has come to represent only this second, southern strip of land stretching 112 miles (180 km) from the southern shore of the Dead Sea to the Gulf of Aqaba (Israel's southern tip).

In Israel, a relatively small population of around 5,000 live in small towns, moshavim, and kibbutzim north of Eilat, encompassing about 150 farmsteads. However, the Arava straddles both Israel and Jordan. The more beautiful southern region has the densest population. While over 100,000 Jordanians live in the *Arabah*; over 90% of this number resides in the resort city of Aqaba. In Israel, the region's largely Jewish population of roughly 52,000 reside in the resort city of Eilat.

The resort cities of Eilat and Aqaba, across the Red Sea

DRIVING SOUTH FROM THE DEAD SEA on Highway 90 is a long stretch of barren land. Thirty minutes prior to reaching Eilat is a welcome rest top—the **Yotvata Rest Stop,** part of the **Yotvata Kibbutz,** open 24/7. Yotvata offers a convenience store, a gift shop, a play area for kids, a kosher restaurant, and light meals and snacks. They're also happy to host groups for one of their delicious, fresh Kosher meals.

The rest stop adjoins **Yotvata Park,** a new center which utilizes play equipment and advanced technology to introduce visitors to the history of the kibbutz, the desert, and renewable energy. Guests can visit the **Yotvata Cowshed** to learn all about their dairy, play some milking games, and meet and greet the cows up close!

The Yotvata Kibbutz, which encompasses the rest stop and park, was founded in 1957. It is the Arava's first and largest kibbutz with 170 families. It also serves as the hub of the region's schools, council offices, community center, etc. In 1962, Yotvata started a dairy farm which is now one of Israel's primary dairies, controlling roughly 63% of the Israeli dairy beverages market. The dairy farm is the main source of income for the kibbutz. Their secondary source of income comes from agriculture; Yotvata plants and harvests a variety of vegetables and herbs, while additionally maintaining plantations of dates and mangos. Yotvata Kibbutz is a cooperative community; nearly all adults work on the kibbutz either in production, services, or education; revenues are distributed equally among the members. Phone: 972-8-979-8516

Don't miss Yotvata's famous chocolate milk and ice cream, now in 72 flavors!

YOTVATA HAI-BAR NATURE RESERVE

TEN MINUTES SOUTH OF YOTVATA IS the 3,000 acre (12 sq km) Hai-Bar Nature Reserve. The reserve was established to breed animals specific to the Bible, as well as other endangered desert animals, with the goal of reintroducing them into the Negev desert. Animal species include the oryx, ostrich, sand cat, gazelle, Arabian wolf, and many others.

Hai-Bar Nature Reserve is divided into three main sections. The first is the **Open Area** with conditions comparable to the wild; this section is dedicated to desert herbivores which rely on acacia trees for shade and food.

The second section is the **Predator Center** where visitors can observe carnivorous animals in their enclosures: birds of prey, reptiles, small desert animals, and larger animals such as leopards and hyenas. The final section is the **Desert Night Life Exhibition Hall** where nocturnal animals can be observed during their active hours.

Hai-Bar Reserve can easily be reached by car. Various tours are available, including an hourly drive-through tour of the Open Area. For more information, call: 972-8-637-3057 or email: haibar-yotvata@npa.org.il.

ANIMALS OF
HAI-BAR
NATURE
RESERVE

TWENTY-FIVE MINUTES SOUTHWEST of Hai-Bar is Timna Park, a 15,000-acre majestic desert setting framed within a horseshoe-shaped valley and surrounded by sheer cliffs.

Timna is home to some of the most ancient **copper mines** in the world—mines that were developed by the Egyptians 6,000 years ago. An inscription nearby depicts Pharaoh Ramses III offering gifts to the goddess *Hathor*. More than 10,000 mining shafts have been discovered in the park. Although not specifically mentioned in the Bible, this area was a location for copper mining during biblical times, and some believe it to be the location of King Solomon's copper mines (Deuteronomy 8:9).

Solomon's Pillars (photo above), named after King Solomon, are spectacular natural geological formations of red sandstone found across the park. The distinct pillar shapes, such as "the mushroom" (right), were formed over the centuries by wind and water erosion through cracks in the sandstone cliff.

Timna Park offers the following:

- A small Egyptian temple dedicated to the goddess *Hathor* (goddess of copper), where thousands of artifacts were unearthed, nearly all offerings to the goddess
- Areas for fossil hunting and rock-climbing
- Diverse hiking trails throughout the park: long hikes, short hikes, some through canyons, Roman paths, and sand dunes
- A small lake with pedal boats for rent
- Sand bottling and other craft activities for kids
- A restaurant and a campground
- A multimedia display relating the history of the site and stories of Egyptian goddesses and pharaohs
- Exodus tabernacle tent replica (following two pages)

The site is best reached by car, tour bus, or the Timna Safari Shuttle in Eilat. Tickets and entry hours can be found on their website, www.parktimna.co.il.

The Lord said to Moses, "Tell the Israelites to bring me an offering. You are to receive the offering for me from everyone whose heart prompts them to give. These are the offerings you are to receive from them: gold, silver and bronze; blue, purple and scarlet yarn and fine linen; goat hair; ram skins dyed red and another type of durable leather; acacia wood; olive oil for the light; spices for the anointing oil and for the fragrant incense; and onyx stones and other gems to be mounted on the ephod and breastpiece. Then have them make a sanctuary for me, and I will dwell among them." EXODUS 25:1–8

A FULL-SCALE REPLICA OF THE BIBLI-cal tabernacle has been created in Timna Park. It stands in the same wilderness where Moses and the children of Israel wandered for forty years, assembling and dismantling the tabernacle 42 times (Numbers 33). Its dimensions are roughly 150 ft (50 m) long, 75 ft (25 m) wide, and 7.5 ft (2.5 m) high. The tabernacle model follows the precise biblical instructions specified in Exodus 25–28, with the exception of replacing genuine precious metals with synthetic materials.

The tabernacle was approached through the **OUTER COURT** where a large, **Brazen Sacrificial Altar** and **Bronze Laver** were located. The fire on the altar burned continually for the sacrifices or "burnt offerings" that were presented twice a day, morning and evening. The sacrifices were required to be male animals without blemish. The bronze laver was the washbowl in which the priests would scrub their hands and feet prior to entering and leaving the holy place.

Behind the outer court was the **HOLY PLACE**. Upon entering the Holy Place, to the right, was the **Table of Showbread** displaying twelve loaves of bread representing the twelve

tribes of Israel. To the left was the **Golden Lampstand** or "candelabra" that provided light for the priests. The **Altar of Incense** was positioned in the back, in front of the veil of the "Holy of Holies" (Exodus 40:26). At this location, the priests gave incense offerings morning and evening, which served as a shield to protect them from the glory of God (Leviticus 16:13). *Incense represents the prayers of God's people—a sweet aroma to the Lord.*

The **HOLY OF HOLIES** contained only the sacred **Ark of the Covenant** (right). The top of the Ark, with two cherubim, was known as the **mercy seat** or *Kaporet* in Hebrew, meaning "covering" or "atonement." Inside the mercy seat was a golden **pot of manna,** the budded **rod of Aaron,** and two **stone tablets** with the Ten Commandments. Only the high priest was allowed to enter the Holy of Holies—and only once a year on Yom Kippur, the Day of Atonement. The priest would sprinkle the blood of a goat seven times on the mercy seat as an offering for himself and the sins of the people of Israel that had been committed in ignorance (Hebrews 9:7). The priest then placed his hands upon the head of the goat, representing the transfer of the sins of God's people, foreshadowing the atoning blood of Yeshua, the Lamb of God.

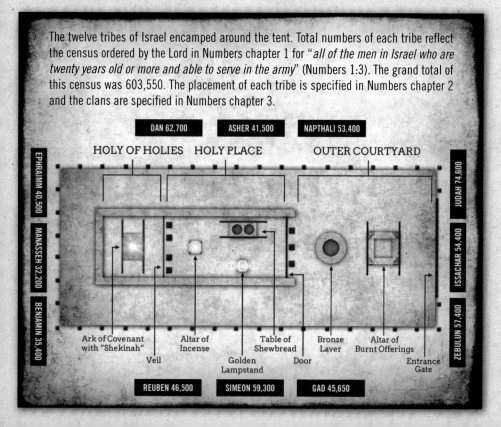

The twelve tribes of Israel encamped around the tent. Total numbers of each tribe reflect the census ordered by the Lord in Numbers chapter 1 for "*all of the men in Israel who are twenty years old or more and able to serve in the army*" (Numbers 1:3). The grand total of this census was 603,550. The placement of each tribe is specified in Numbers chapter 2 and the clans are specified in Numbers chapter 3.

DAN 62,700 ASHER 41,500 NAPTHALI 53,400

HOLY OF HOLIES HOLY PLACE OUTER COURTYARD

EPHRAIMM 40,500
MANASSEH 32,200
BENJAMIN 35,400

JUDAH 74,600
ISSACHAR 54,400
ZEBULUN 57,400

Ark of Covenant with "Shekinah"
Altar of Incense
Table of Shewbread
Bronze Laver
Altar of Burnt Offerings
Veil
Golden Lampstand
Door
Entrance Gate

REUBEN 46,500 SIMEON 59,300 GAD 45,650

THE SOUTHERNMOST, RESORT CITY of Eilat, with its array of exclusive hotels situated on the coast of the Red Sea, is a popular vacation spot. Eilat has been an important city for 3,000 years because of its direct access to the Red Sea and its prime location amid several major trade routes. Today, it is one of Israel's principal international seaports with imports from the Far East coming to Eilat's port.

Eilat is mentioned several times in the Bible. The city fell outside of the delineated boundaries of the Promised Land for the children of Israel. However, it was one of the stops on the Exodus journey from Egypt (Deuteronomy 2:8). King Solomon made Eilat's nearby port the base of his fleet for trading (1 Kings 9:26-28, 10:22, 22:48). Edomites moved into Eilat (2 Kings 16:6)

and King Uzziah rebuilt Eilat and restored it to Judah (2 Chronicles 26:2).

In the center of Eilat is the **Marina,** a large docking center for private and public boats and yachts. The surrounding Red Sea is home to over 270 species of coral and 2,500 species of underwater life. A spectacular display of these species can be viewed up close in **Coral World.**

Also, Eilat's coastal **Coral Beach Nature Reserve** is renowned as one of the most beautiful coastal reserves in the world, due its stunning coral reef. Another popular destination is **Dolfin Reef** which offers visitors the unique opportunity to observe and interact with bottlenose dolphins in their natural habitat. Contact with people is based entirely on the free will and choice of the dolphins!

EILAT STONE JEWELRY FACTORY

The Eilat stone is Israel's national stone. It is a stunning combination of malachite and azurite, mined in the nearby Solomon's copper mines of Timna Park. Stones are set in silver and gold, and many with diamonds right on the premises. Visitors can view the entire process of cutting, shaping, and polishing the Eilat stone, while learning all about its history. This exquisite showroom is a highlight for many! Phone: 972-8-637-8551; www.eilatstone.com

BLESS ISRAEL

The LORD had said to Abram, "Go from your country, your people and your father's household to the land I will show you. I will make you into a great nation, and I will bless you; I will make your name great, and you will be a blessing. I will bless those who bless you, and whoever curses you I will curse; and all peoples on earth will be blessed through you."

GENESIS 12:1–3

UNDERSTAND

Seek to understand Jewish history and the present-day mindset of most Jews toward the church. Read about forced baptisms, forced conversions, the Crusades, the Inquisition, Pogroms, and especially the Holocaust and events that led up to it. History repeats itself!

Read and avail yourself of beneficial resources to help your understanding. *Our Hands are Stained with Blood* by Dr. Michael Brown is a "Must-Read."

Blessing Israel also includes blessing the Arabs in Israel. Do your part to facilitate peace. The Lord created both Arabs and Jews, and Yeshua died for both.

"The foreigner residing among you must be treated as your native-born. Love them as yourself, for you were foreigners in Egypt. I am the LORD your God."
LEVITICUS 19:34

PRAY

Pray on your own or form a prayer group to regularly pray for Israel. See "Pray for the Peace of Jerusalem," p. 262.

Every Yom Kippur, while the Jewish people are repenting and fasting, either individually or as a group—you can pray and fast for Israel and the Jewish people.

GIVE

TAKE THE 1% CHALLENGE! FIRM (Foundation of Israel-Related Ministries) encourages believers to commit to tithing 1% of their income to Israel. Hudson Taylor believed what the apostle Paul had grasped thousands of years before: that the Word of God links the awakening of the Jews to the success in the church's vision to spread the Good News of the Messiah to the whole world. The Lord blesses those who bless Israel!

On January 1 each year, Hudson Taylor wrote a check to a group dedicated to blessing the Jews of Europe. On that check, he always wrote four simple words: "To the Jew first!" [Romans 1:16]

"Adopt" an Israeli church, ministry, IDF "lone soldier," or Holocaust Survivor. Pray regularly for them, provide financial support as you are able, communicate with them, and even visit them in Israel!

SUPPORT

SUPPORT ISRAEL'S ECONOMY: Patronize Israeli establishments. Counter the global boycott on Israel and buy Israeli-made products.

GO

Visit Israel! Take a tour that incorporates the biblical sites along with interacting with and serving the Israeli people.

SERVE

Volunteer individually or with a tour group. See options on pp. 270–271.

SHARE

As the tagline for "One for Israel" reads, *"The best way to bless Israel is through Jesus."* Share your faith with Jewish people *with sensitivity* when the opportunity arises. For helpful tips, type "How to share your faith—One for Israel" into your internet browser. Also, watch the dynamic YouTube video, "Isaiah 53–The Forbidden Chapter."

Send English speakers to www.imetmessiah.com and Hebrew speakers to igod.co.il for amazing testimonies!

(Excerpts from Our Hands are Stained with Blood, Dr. Michael Brown)

WIDESPREAD JEWISH VIEW OF CHRISTIANS:

"Instead of bringing redemption to the Jews, the false Christian messiah has brought down on us base libels and expulsions, oppressive restrictions and burning of our holy books, devastations and destructions, Christianity, which professes to infuse the sick world with love and compassion, has fixed a course directly opposed to this lofty rhetoric. The voice of the blood of millions of our brothers cries out to us from the ground: 'No! **Christianity is not a religion of love, but a religion of unfathomable hate!** All history, from ancient times to our own day, is the continuous proof of the total bankruptcy of this religion in all its segments.'" (anonymous Israeli writer, pp. 89–90)

"**We might be more inclined to give Christian claims some credence had we seen Christians through the ages behave as models of a redeemed humanity...** If anything, their social failings are especially discrediting of their doctrine for they claim to be uniquely free of human sinfulness and freshly inspired by their faith to bring the world to a realm of love and peace... Until sinfulness ceases and well-being prevails, Jews know that the Messiah has not come." (Professor Eugene Borowitz, pp. 90–91)

THE REMEDY:

"...The only way that these sins against the Jewish people will ever be blotted out, the only way that we will ever see a truly international revival, the only way that we will ever be ministers of God's grace to Israel, is if we fully acknowledge the guilt and shame of our 'Christian' ancestors, and with anguished heart, repent. Whether Catholic or Protestant — there is blood on our fathers' hands." (Catholic Edward Flannery, xiii)

"The Jewish nation remembers and will always remember. We seek reconciliation... there can be no reconciliation without remembrance. The experience of million-fold death is part of the every being of every Jew in the world, not only because people cannot forget such atrocities, but also because remembrance is part of the Jewish faith." (President of Germany, Richard Von Weizsaecker [1985], xi)

- All Christians should take it upon themselves to learn about and wrestle through the heartbreaking and shameful implications of Christian hatred and persecution to the Jewish people. If not, these sins that led to the Holocaust will lead to future sins and failures far worse.

- Even if we ourselves have not participated in these sins, we must all pray to avoid walking in the shameful manner of our forefathers (Nehemiah 1:5–11).

- Whether or not the Jewish people are guilty of sin, whether or not their sufferings are the result of divine judgments, God calls us to weep for and with them, ... "*Oh, that my head were a spring of water and my eyes a fountain of tears! I would weep day and night for the slain of my people.*" (Jeremiah 9:1)

- About one hundred years ago, a Christian minister to the Jews was asked what he thought wanting on the part of the friends of Israel. He replied, "more tears." **More tears is the urgent need on behalf of the Jewish people and the State of Israel today. "More tears" must flow from the Church's eyes—** *before* **tears of repentance, and then tears of joy, will flow from Israel's eyes. God grant us "More tears!" We must weep and lament because of the sins of our "Christian" forefathers against the Jewish people.** (p. 99)

PRAY FOR THE PEACE OF JERUSALEM

I have posted watchmen on your walls, Jerusalem; they will never be silent day or night. You who call on the LORD, give yourselves no rest, and give him no rest till he establishes Jerusalem and makes her the praise of the earth. ISAIAH 62:6-7

Jerusalem is called the house of the Lord. It is the world's center of His presence and His people, and will eventually be the place where the Messiah will return. Even though true and lasting peace will only come when the eternal New Jerusalem comes down (forever under the rule of the blessed Prince of Peace), the Word encourages us to actively seek Jerusalem's prosperity and pray for her peace and security.

An invaluable book to have in your prayer library is Penny Valentine's, *Praying for the Peace of Jerusalem.* The suggestions below are excerpted, with permission, from Penny's book.

PRAY THAT ISRAEL WILL MAKE GOD HER FIRST PRIORITY IN THE MIDST OF HER TROUBLES:

- She would not look to human solutions to solve her many problems, but both leaders and the people would see the futility of their own efforts and seek God's help, looking to His Word.

- She would not take His blessings for granted, nor take the credit for success, but give God the glory due His Name.

PRAY FOR ISRAEL'S PROTECTION:

- Protection from all her enemies and deliverance from every plan of the evil one to destroy her. Pray for encouragement for all those facing despair in the face of unrelenting hatred.

- The Lord's special provision and protection over Jerusalem, both physically and spiritually, and for the safety of all of her inhabitants and visitors.

- Uphold Israeli believers who are living in obedience to God's call. Pray for God to encourage them and provide for their health and safety, to grant them wisdom, discernment and boldness to do His will.

PRAY GOD'S NAME WILL BE LIFTED HIGH:

- That He will be glorified in all that happens in Israel and the Middle East, so that the nations may know that God is the LORD when they see His mighty acts.

- That the sufferings and evil experienced by the diverse peoples of Israel would lead many to faith in Yeshua — that God would remove the veil from their eyes and open their ears that they might hear the truth.

- That His people will be given much grace to forgive those who sin against them.

PRAY FOR ISRAEL'S LEADERS:

- God would raise up leaders of humility and integrity to be His servants and lead the nation according to His heart and the principles of His Word.

- God would guide the current leaders of Israel to place the welfare of the nation above that of their own personal or party interests.

- God would give Israel's leaders wisdom and strength in the immense, ongoing challenges they face, and use them to fulfill His perfect plan for Israel.

PRAY FOR ISRAEL'S BELIEVERS:

- They would "live a life worthy of the Lord and please him in every way: bearing fruit in every good work, growing in the knowledge of God." (Colossians 1:10)

- God would uphold those who are obedient to His call with wisdom and boldness, and with endurance and patience to live in the land and be a faithful witness to others.

- God would encourage the believers and provide for their health and safety.

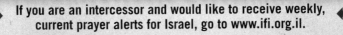

If you are an intercessor and would like to receive weekly, current prayer alerts for Israel, go to www.ifi.org.il.

HOTEL GILGAL, TEL AVIV

- Peaceful boutique hotel; only 2-minute walk to beach
- Original biblical art, biblical library, and photos
- Each room named after a place in Israel; corresponding photos
- Rich roof-top breakfast with a view of Tel Aviv and the Mediterranean
- Fully-equipped "Gates of Heaven" conference/meeting hall

Owned by Messianic believers, anointed atmosphere with beautiful decor
www.HotelGilgal.com ▪ 972-3-511-1000 ▪ reserve@HotelGilgal.com

CAESAREA VILLA, CAESAREA

- Luxurious three-story guesthouse in exclusive Caesarea neighborhood
- Five minutes from Caesarea National Park, sand dunes, and private beach
- Short and long-term rentals; Eight bedrooms, 20+ beds
- Fully-equipped kitchen, large outside pool—ideal for baptisms
- Hosts a weekly "Shalom House"—dinner for Holocaust Survivors

Ideal for family vacations, tour groups, individuals, celebrations/event hosting
volunteers.guesthouse@gmail.com ▪ Caesarea ▪ 972-54-747-1705

GALILEE GETAWAY, SOUTHERN GALILEE HILLS

- Serene get-away in quiet village with breathtaking views
- Exquisite one-bedroom apartment sleeps 6; atop home of Messianic believers
- Fully equipped kitchen, living/dining area, Jacuzzi, huge balcony
- Extraordinary views of Sea of Galilee, Jordan Valley, and the Golan Heights
- Hosts: tour guide, Rami Danieli and harpist/artist, Gabriela Danieli

Also available on property: stunning "Romantic Moroccan Escape," sleeps four
www.GalileeGetaway.com ▪ Poria Kfar-Avoda ▪ 972-52-802-1701

CNAAN VILLAGE BOUTIQUE HOTEL, NORTH GALILEE

- Voted #1 in Tripadvisor's "leading small hotels in the Middle East"
- Five luxurious suites with Jacuzzi, fireplace, wine, chocolate, and royal bed
- Private garden terraces overlooking a magnificent view of the Sea of Galilee
- Spa complex: heated pool with underwater music, dry sauna, massage
- Breakfast served by pool; homemade desserts, fruit, and coffee served all day

Romantic holiday for couples and couples' retreats!
www.cnaan-village.co.il ▪ 13, Had Nes, 12950 ▪ 972-4-682-2128

AUSTRIAN HOSPICE, OLD CITY JERUSALEM

- Great location: on Via Dolorosa near Western Wall and Old City sites
- Clean, spacious, and basic rooms with good, basic breakfast
- Rooftop terrace garden with panoramic views of the Old City
- Beautiful courtyard and garden adjoining their Viennese coffee-house
- Known for its apple strudel, schnitzel, and coffee

An oasis of tranquility in the hectic maze of the Old City
www.austrianhospice.com ▪ Via Dolorosa St 37 ▪ 972-2-626-5800

MT. ZION HOTEL, JERUSALEM

- Spectacular boutique hotel right outside the Old City
- Charming rooms, junior suites, extravagant suites and villas
- Breathtaking views of Mt. Zion, Hinnom Valley, Tower of David, & more
- Pool, jacuzzi, fitness center, Turkish steam bath, spa, massage
- Walking distance to Old City and Jerusalem's cultural and historical sites

Magnificent ambiance of old stone walls, columns, and arched windows
www.mountzion.co.il ▪ 17 Hebron Road ▪ 972-2-568-9555

ST. ANDREW'S GUESTHOUSE, JERUSALEM

- One of Jerusalem's best values for comfort, location, and setting
- Majestic, historic exterior and surrounding grounds; adjoining church
- Welcoming atmosphere of peace and tranquility
- Spectacular setting with unrivaled view of both Old and Modern Jerusalem
- Close proximity and walking distance to Old City

The Scottish Guesthouse is your home in the heart of Jerusalem!
www.scotsguesthouse.com ▪ 1 David Remez Street ▪ 972-2-673-2401

JERUSALEM HILLS INN, ABU GHOSH

- B & B operated by Messianic family and lovely staff of believers
- Beautiful, biblically-themed rooms with all the amenities of home
- Ten minutes from downtown Jerusalem; 30 minutes from the airport
- In Arab village of peaceful coexistence between Jews, Arabs, and Christians
- Road to Emmaus site; twenty-year resting place of the Ark of the Covenant

The best hidden secret of charming, affordable lodging in the Jerusalem area!
www.jerusalemhillsinn.com ▪ 9 Rehov HaTut ▪ 972-77-557-0948

YAD HASHMONA COUNTRY HOTEL, JUDEAN HILLS

- The only Messianic kibbutz (shared community) in Israel
- In the lush Judean Hills; 20 minutes to Jerusalem; 30 minutes to the airport
- Charming Finnish-Scandinavian log cabins and stone cottages
- Beautiful dining hall with an enormous variety of delicious food
- Unique "Biblical Garden" with artifacts and biblical plants

Groups can experience a biblical meal with a guided tour of the "Biblical Garden."
www.yadha8.co.il ▪ info@yadha8.co.il ▪ 972-2-594-2000

KRIVINE GUESTHOUSE, SDE BOKER

- Two fully equipped self-catering apartments available
- Peaceful and lovely surroundings with gardens and a fishpond
- Private terraces and garden access in each apartment
- Full English and Israeli breakfast included in stay
- Home-cooked three-course English dinners available

An authentic British B&B experience close to the beautiful Zin Valley overlook
www.krivine-guesthouse.com ▪ Neve Tzin 15, Sde Boker ▪ 972-52-271-2304

ABRAGE RESTAURANT, JAFFA

- High-class dining with a personal touch!
- A hidden jewel in Old Jaffa's central Kedumim Square
- Specializing in contemporary Mediterranean cuisine
- Wonderful range of fresh fish, seafood, bistro, meat, and gourmet dishes
- LOADS of food and amazing kabobs!

Relax at the Abrage with its arabesque arches and refreshing sea breeze!
www.abrage.rest-e.co.il ▪ 6 Kedumim Square, Jaffa ▪ 972-53-934-5526

AVI'S RESTAURANT, TIBERIAS

- Family atmosphere where you are welcomed by friendly, good-humored Avi!
- Five-minute walk to the Tiberias Promenade on the Sea of Galilee
- Middle Eastern cuisine—renowned juicy entrecote steak and tasty sea bass
- Fresh fish straight from the Galilee to the pan!
- Attractive prices for visitors on a budget

Popular, kosher restaurant with stone walls and arched, stained-glass windows
www.avi.rest.co.il ▪ 4 HaKishon Street, Tiberias ▪ 972-4-679-1797

DECKS RESTAURANT, TIBERIAS

- Beautiful setting and breathtaking views; directly on the Sea of Galilee
- Unprocessed lamb, cattle, and geese raised by farmers special for Decks
- Locally caught fish and fresh produce
- Ancient roasting methods used for preparing the finest kosher meats
- Meats grilled on charcoals made from olive, citrus and nut trees

All dishes are presented beautifully with high-quality artistic flair!
www.lido.co.il/home/decks ▪ Gdud Barak Rd. ▪ 972-4-671-0800

DAG AL HADAN, GOLAN HEIGHTS

- Serenely situated among trees, waterfalls, and the tranquil Dan River
- Rich selection of fresh fish grown in Dag al Hadan's adjoining fish farms
- Tour of fish farms available
- Renowned for their delicious grilled smoked trout
- Salads, appetizers, and freshly baked bread to accompany your main course

Magical setting amidst a breathtaking landscape with swans, ducks, and peacocks
Qiryat Shemona, near Tel Dan ▪ 972-4-695-0225

MAMILLA ROOFTOP, JERUSALEM

- Unsurpassed, spectacular view of the Old City
- Delectable food, pleasant music, and casual al fresco dining
- Large and varied menu with natural ingredients
- Great service and pleasant staff with attention to detail and presentation
- Very reasonable lunch prices—not to be missed!

High above the Old City, dine while viewing 5,000 years of Jerusalem's history!
www.mamillahotel.com/rooftop ▪ 11 King Solomon St. ▪ 972-2-548-2230

NAFOURA RESTAURANT, OLD CITY JERUSALEM

- Mediterranean, Middle Eastern and Armenian cuisine
- Located just inside the Jaffa Gate, adjacent to the Old City wall
- Over a quarter acre of dining areas and courtyards
- Set amidst archaeological columns, beautiful gardens, and fountains
- Known for its classy and romantic ambiance and warm, caring staff

A tranquil haven away from the noise and hustle of the Old City
18 Latin Patriarch Rd., Jerusalem ■ 972-2-626-0034

JACOB'S PIZZA, OLD CITY JERUSALEM

- Dubbed the "best pizza in Jerusalem," recipe passed down thru generations
- Friendly, welcoming staff and reasonable prices; open on Shabbat; WiFi
- Pizzas and plentiful toppings prepared daily using fresh, local ingredients
- Enjoy Jacob's salads, desserts, and various flavors of soft ice cream
- Options for eat-in, take out, or delivery

Located just inside Jaffa Gate—Old City charm; New City taste!
17 Latin Patriarchate St., Jaffa Gate ■ 972-2-627-5540

QUARTER CAFÉ, OLD CITY JERUSALEM

- Spectacular views of the Jewish Quarter and the Western Wall
- Israeli-European fare with healthy menu options
- Homemade recipes passed down through the family; superb salmon!
- Main dishes enhanced with delicious herbs and fresh local salads
- Recent, elegant renovation with handicap access

Second-generation restaurant with excellent, friendly service
11 Tiferet Israel St., Jewish Quarter ■ 972-2-628-7770

GAVNA RESTAURANT, GUSH ETZION

- Rustic wooden house nestled on a lush hillside, surrounded by history
- Family-owned restaurant with a varied menu (includes kids' menu)
- Popular venue for lunch, dinner, drinks, and special events
- Healthy, delicious selections served in a relaxing, cheerful atmosphere
- Southwest of Jerusalem—not far from the Elah Valley and Bethlehem

Relax and enjoy the delectable cuisine and breathtaking views of the Judean Hills!
Grove of Masuot Yitzhak, Gush Etzion ■ 972-2-533-6036

MUZA, ARAD

- A refreshing stop on the way to (or returning from) the Dead Sea and Eilat
- Quick service, great food, and friendly staff
- Extensive, varied menus for breakfast, lunch, and dinner (kids' menu)
- Generous portions, fresh salads, and great hamburgers!
- Sports bar renowned for its beer and popular entertainment venue

Unique atmosphere—tourist attraction for international sports fans and collectors
Road 31, Alon Gas Station Complex, Arad ■ 972-8-997-5555

CHOSEN PEOPLE MINISTRIES (CPM)

- Jerusalem center dedicated to evangelism and humanitarian aid
- Ministry to Russian-speaking Holocaust survivors
- Ramat Gan-Tel Aviv center runs a Gospel café and ministers to families
- Teaching: English, biblical counseling, parenting, and financial management
- Short-term outreach teams, Bible studies, and children's camps offered

CPM exists to pray for, evangelize, disciple, and serve Israeli Jews
info@chosenpeople.com ▪ Jerusalem and Ramat Gan ▪ 212-223-2252

FELLOWSHIP OF ISRAEL RELATED MINISTRIES

- Mobilizes Christians to support trusted ministries in Israel
- Helps Israeli ministries grow their potential for greater impact
- Connects ministries and ministry leaders to promote unity and cooperation
- 100% of donations given to FIRM Foundation directly fund member ministries
- Members are biblically sound, financially transparent, and accountable

"...to the Jew first and also to the Gentile." Romans 1:16
www.firm.org.il ▪ hello@firm.org.il ▪ 1-800-532-0706 ▪ Jerusalem

HAGEFEN PUBLISHING

- Publishing house with a mission to support congregations in Israel
- Translates Christian books from English to Hebrew
- Publishes books in both print and electronic form
- Primary focus on evangelism, discipleship, theology, and family life
- Currently translating the New Testament into modern Hebrew for teenagers

Assists Israeli Body of Messiah to grow in numbers and spiritual maturity
www.ha-gefen.org.il ▪ office@ha-gefen.org.il ▪ 972-3-966-1898

INTERNATIONAL CHRISTIAN EMBASSY JERUSALEM

- Global Christian ministry with branches in over 90 countries
- Hosts annual Feast of Tabernacles Celebration in Jerusalem
- Provides humanitarian aid to the needy in every sector of Israeli society
- Assists Jews around the world in making Aliyah (immigrating to Israel)
- Equips the global church to support Israel and the Jewish people

ICEJ exists to show concern for the Jewish people and the reborn state of Israel
icej@icejusa.org ▪ www.icejusa.org ▪ 1-615-895-9830

JEWS FOR JESUS

- Engages, equips, and inspires Jewish people to follow Yeshua
- Hosts weekly kids, youth, and soldiers meetings in Tel Aviv
- Ministers to homeless people, prostitutes, and drug addicts
- Trains and sends teams to reach young Israelis in India and South America
- Leads Hebrew courses, Bible studies, and day tours for Russian-speaking immigrants

Jews for Jesus exists to relentlessly pursue salvation of the Jewish people.
israel@jewsforjesus.org ▪ Tel Aviv ▪ 972-3-609-0925

NETIVAH YOUTH MINISTRY

- Evangelism and discipleship of Israeli youth
- National youth conferences and seminars
- Regional youth events including hiking and camping trips
- Teaching and discipleship for believing soldiers in the IDF
- Volunteers needed for kitchen staff and logistics teams

To equip, strengthen and support young Israeli believers
www.netivah.com

ONE FOR ISRAEL

- English and Hebrew online testimonies of Jewish believers in Yeshua
- Online apologetics and answers to objections regarding Jesus
- Only accredited Hebrew-speaking Bible college in the world
- One new man: Jews and Arabs work and study together
- Supports Holocaust survivors and women who choose not to abort

"The best way to bless Israel is through Jesus!"
www.OneForIsrael.org ■ www.imetmessiah.com ■ igod.co.il (Hebrew)

SCHINDLER'S ARK

- Founder—Rosemary Schindler Garlow, relative of Oskar Schindler
- Advocates for Holocaust Survivors worldwide
- Promotes believers to stand against anti-Semitism, racism, and injustice
- Coordinates Nights to Honor Israel and hosts pro-Israel conferences
- Advocates for government leaders to move their embassies to Jerusalem

Schindler's Ark continues carrying his torch to protect the Jewish people.
1-800-208-0219 ■ Rosemary@SchindlersArk.com

TREE OF LIFE MINISTRIES

- Ministry of Ariel and Shayla Hyde of the Kehilat HaCarmel congregation
- Evangelism through videos, websites, and special outreach events
- Street evangelism team prays for the sick and shares the gospel
- Evangelistic media (includes "The Forbidden Chapter—Isaiah 53" with 5M views)
- Distributes impactful outreach booklet, "Supernatural or Just Remarkable"

Equips believers through children's ministry, evangelism training, and discipleship
www.treeoflife.org ■ promises.israel@gmail.com ■ Haifa, Israel

UNCHARTED MINISTRIES

- Reaches out to Jews and Arabs in Israel; special focus on Holocaust Survivors
- Leads Bible tours and outreach trips to Israel and the West Bank
- Brings women's teams from abroad to uplift and reach out to Israeli women
- Provides inspirational books and resources by best-selling author Tom Doyle
- Launches believers into ministry in Israel and the Middle East

Be Amazed at How God Wants to Use You!
www.unchartedministries.com ■ 1-214-440-1118 ■ info@unchartedministries.com

ABUNDANT HOPE INTERNATIONAL

- Meets needs of Holocaust Survivors in 25 cities in Israel
- Dependent on international partners and volunteers
- Volunteers serve with compassion and unconditional love
- Adopt a Survivor with letters, prayers, small gifts, and $18 a month donation
- 100% of donations allotted for Survivors, goes to Survivors.

Help relieve the suffering of loneliness among the last of the Survivors now!
www.ahi-il.org ▪ adopt@ahi-il.org ▪ 717-592-0859 ▪ Akko, Israel

ALIYAH RETURN CENTER

- Assists the Jewish people to return to their Promised Land
- Assists Christians to understand their biblical Hebraic roots
- Shagririm.org.il trains believers to be ambassadors and advocates for Israel
- Allows believers globally to participate in the fulfillment of prophecy
- Needs volunteers in Galilee to assist new immigrants, the IDF, and much more

Volunteer, intern, or become an ambassador to Israel.
www.aliyahreturncenter.com ▪ 972-50-326-8850 ▪ watchaliyah@gmail.com

BE'AD CHAIM

- Pro-life organization with pregnancy centers across Israel
- "Operation Moses": provides needy mothers with basic baby needs
- Provides speakers for tour groups at their hotel or the Jerusalem office
- "Gardens of Life": plant a tree in honor and memory of your unborn baby
- Welcomes volunteers to help with clothing distribution and gardening

In 2018, the Israeli government paid for 19,000 abortions ($14 million+)
www.beadchaim.com ▪ 972-2-624-2516 ▪ info@beadchaim.org.il

BEAUTIFUL LAND INITIATIVE

- International tour groups clean up litter around the Sea of Galilee
- The Land is the inheritance of God's people; we are His stewards
- Volunteers help restore beauty and foster respect toward the Land
- In three years: 4,000 volunteers; 36 countries; 12,000 bags of litter
- Come and volunteer a couple of hours!

"To your descendants, I will give this Land." (Genesis 12:7)
www.BeautifulLand.org ▪ info@BeautifulLand.org

BIBLICAL TAMAR PARK

- Archaeological and biblical tel in the desert
- Restoration and maintenance of 55-acre historical site
- Educational center for Israeli students and tourists
- Interactive displays of history of Biblical Tamar
- Volunteers needed for archaeology, tractor repair, and maintenance

"...The wilderness will rejoice and blossom like the rose." Isaiah 35:1
www.blossomingrose.org ▪ 1-616-696-3425 ▪ info@blossomingrose.org

HAYOVEL

- International Christian volunteers come and fulfill prophecy
- Facilitates uniting Jews and Christians in Israel's restoration of the Land
- Coordinates volunteers to serve Jewish farmers in Judea and Samaria
- Encourages volunteers to harvest and prune vineyards and olive groves
- Equips volunteers to be effective ambassadors of the biblical heartland

"You shall yet plant vines on the mountains of Samaria…" (Jeremiah 31:5)
www.ServeIsrael.com ▪ 1-573-222-0460

HELPING HAND COALITION

- Humanitarian & social support to impoverished Holocaust victims
- Supports the most needy and destitute of Israel's populations
- Lobbies in the Knesset and provides a voice to victims of war and terror
- Strengthens ties with international friends of Israel
- Volunteers needed for Survivors, the elderly, children, and the handicapped

HHCoalition; the last line of defense for impoverished Israelis"
www.hhcoalition.com ▪ 972-2-689-7030 ▪ contact@hhcoalition.com

JOSEPH PROJECT

- Israel charity supported by the MJAA (Messianic Jewish Alliance of America)
- Largest importer of humanitarian aid in Israel
- Provides food, clothing, furniture, household goods, and medical supplies
- Has distributed $100 million in aid to Jews, Arab Christians, and Muslims
- Invites volunteers to help with food packing, distribution, and other needs

1.7 million Israelis live at or below the poverty line
www.mjaa.org/josephproject ▪ 1-800-225-6522 ▪ info@mjaa.org

LIGHT OF ZION

- Directs the national Israeli Prayer Network
- Passion and pursuit for Israeli revival
- Mobilizes God-loving, watchman-style intercessors for Israel
- Facilitates justice and humanitarian outreach
- Monthly prayer meeting and online Daily Prayer Guide for Israel

Dedicated to carrying Yeshua, who is the Light of Zion, to Israel and the nations
www. lightofzion.org ▪ info@lightofzion.org ▪ 1-949-533-8287 ▪ Jerusalem

VISION FOR ISRAEL

- Humanitarian aid, disaster relief, and community support for over 25 years
- New Millennium Center provides life-saving aid for the poor and needy
- School supplies for needy children through annual "Pack to School" project
- Physical, financial, emotional support to Holocaust Survivor, terror victims
- Medical supplies and ambulances for the elderly, first responders, and hospitals

Vision for Israel is devoted to helping build and restore Israel.
info@visionforisrael.com ▪ www.visionforisrael.com ▪ 972-8-978-6400

THE L'CHAIM EXPERIENCE

Bless Holocaust Survivors and Be Blessed!

Sponsored by the Israel Now Project USA non-profit foundation, in cooperation with Israeli Helping Hands Coalition and the Radiant Group.

The remaining 120,000+ Holocaust Survivors living in Israel today will only be with us for a few more years; their average age is 88 years old. These resilient souls have survived unspeakable suffering and loss, which they will carry with them to their grave. *L'Chaim* in Hebrew is a toast meaning "to life." You can help bring life, joy, and hope to some of these precious people.

COMING SOON:
An opportunity for tour groups to interact with local Israeli Holocaust Survivors.

TENTATIVELY, THIS WILL ENCOMPASS:

- A dinner and fellowship shared between a tour group and local Holocaust Survivors
- A brief introduction to the Holocaust and Israeli Holocaust Survivors today

- A Survivor testimony
- Israeli music and folk dancing
- An opportunity to interact with and "adopt" a Survivor as part of your extended family

Email Joan@IsraelNowProject.com for updates and reservations.
Visit www.IsraelNowProject.com

DEPOSIT PHOTOS

lzf: 76a
hurricane hank: 76b

DREAMSTIME

Sean Pavone: book cover, 24b, 150a, 182b, 189a
Rostislav Ageev: title page
Olkay: 12a
Eldadcarin: 12b, 95
Andrea Skjold: 17b
Lisa F. Young: 17c
Paul Cowan: 17e
Pavel Raigorodski: 17k
Claudio Monni: 17l
Zvonimir Atletic: 24a
Paul Prescott: 26C, 234a
Kristoffer Niclasen: 29a
Dgaertner: 32c, 33c
Mikhail: 32d, 37, 158a
Naetoo: 33a, 50
Kushnirov Avraham: 33e, 176b, 249b
Konstantnin: 34a
Mazor: 34c, 258a
Sergey Aleksandrov: 38b
Giordano Aita: 41
Mark Barry: 43
Leonid Spektor: 48, 210
Steve Allen: 51
Rafael Ben Ari: 61, 103b, 119, 124, 137a, 144b, 213a, 230c, 288a
Artem Derkachec: 67a
Ricky Goshen: 69
Iuliia Kryzhevska: 85
Viculia: 88a
Vladimir Blinov: 88c70c, 109
Rostislav Glinsky: 89a
Guter: 89b
Rainledy: 90a
Snake81: 90b, 110
Asaf Eliason: 91a
K45025: 93a
Hugoht: 94, 227
Aleksandar Todorovic: 96a, 196c, 203
Sergeiaviv: 98
minart: 101b
Kobby Dagan: 102a, 102b, 288e
Leonid Andronov: 102c
Aleksandr Penin: 104b
Alexirina27000: 105a, 128b, 166

Gkuna: 107, 194b
Slidezero: 113a
Mihai-bogdan Lazar: 113b
Yirmi Oppenhime: 122b, 134a
Ddkg: 125a
Zoya Yuzvak: 125b
mtsyri: 127b
Emkaplin: 128a
Oleg Lopatkin: 139a
Iryna Sosnytska: 139b
Dejan Gileski: 141, 232b
Thinkart: 143
Rrodrickbeiler: 144a, 180
Mariadubova: 149a
Itay.G: 152
Aron Brand: 153
Sapateka: 157
Suronin: 163, 175b, 178, 195b
ChameleonsEye: 168b
Lucidwaters: 150d, 172
Alex Gulevich: 174c
Alefbet26: 179
Ionut David: 182a, 194a
ImagoGestalter: 186a
Farek: 186b
Yosef Erpert: 196b
Rawpixelimages: 201
Geothea: 205b
Pavel Bernshtam: 212, 247
Noam Armonn: 217
Michal Ninger: 229
Vicspacewalker: 230b
Meoita: 231b
Maryna Kriuchenko: 235
Laser143: 244a
Gorshkov13: 245, 250, 252a, 252b, 254a, 254b, 254c, 254d, 254e
Serge Novitsky: 255a
Rkckwwjd: 256a
Paulus Rusyanto 259
Boris Diakovsky 288c
Moshemc 288f

SHUTTERSTOCK

Ryan Rodrick Beiler: 1, 288b
Rostislav Glinsky: 15, 150b, 200
Rus S: 17a
Mike Donenfeld: 22a
Hermitis: 22b
Mikhail: 29b, 288d

George Muresan: 30a
Aron Brand: 30b
Howard Sandler: 33d
Anneka: 32a, 34b
ChameleonsEye: 39a, 134b, 138a, 138b, 249a
Andrey Burmakin: 84
Flik47: 93b
pokku: 99
Tal Naveh: 103c
Alexandre Grigoriev: 103d
irisphoto1: 106b
Yosefer: 106c
k45025 Rita K: 114a
Khirman Vladimir: 126b, 130
Roman Sigaev: 131
makarenko7: 137b
Yan Vugenfirer: 155
Sean Pavone: 168a, 176a
VojtechVlk: 176c
Protasov AN: 114, 184-185
InsatiableWanderlust: 204b
WDG Photo: 205a
Aleksandar Todorovic: 205c
Sergei25: 255b
Vlad61: 258b, 258c

WIKIMEDIA COMMONS

27, 28, 38a, 55, 67b, 96b, 106a, 145a, 145b, 151, 158b, 159a, 159c, 165a, 165b, 170b, 171a, 177, 181, 183, 197c, 207a, 213b, 214a, 214b, 216, 221, 224, 226, 230a, 231a, 233b, 238a, 240, 248, 251

INDIVIDUALS/SITES

Cheri Walker: 17f, 17g,17h,17j, 23b, 26b, 32b, 35, 86b, 86c, 101a, 104a, 122a, 138c, 149b, 150c, 160a, 160b, 160c, 160d, 161a, 161b, 161c, 161d, 169a, 174a, 174b, 175a, 185b, 186c, 190b, 191a, 191b, 194c,

195a, 196a, 197a, 197b, 198a, 198b, 244b
Bruce Gregg: 23c, 23d, 23e, 26a, 111a, 111b, 126a, 127a, 167a, 167b, 167c, 170a, 189b, 190a, 192, 232a, 256b, 257
Andrea Grinberg: 33b
Jim Bouck: 39b, 159b, 199a, 199b, 204a, 206b
Answers in Genesis: 60
Deerland: 64
Helping Hand Coalition: 66
One for Israel: 49
Palmach Museum: 97a
Ayalon Institute: 97b
Joan Peace: 103a, 112a, 112b, 113c, 114b, 135a, 136, 146a, 146b, 146c, 169b, 171b, 206a
Carolyn Hyde: 115a
Tamar Bakfar: 115b, 115c
Gabriela Danieli: 117a, 117b, 117c
Golan Magic Center: 123
Avinoam Mich: 135b, 200, 236, 237, 239a, 239b
Genesis Land: 140
Friends of Zion Museum: 148
Chamber of the Holocaust Museum: 187a, 187b, 187c
First Fruits of Zion: 188
City of David: 193
Gush Etzion Winery: 207b
Caliber 3: 208a, 208b
Courtesy of Eating with Ziggy: 215
maxresdefault: 220a
Hayovel: 220b, 225
Shelley Neese: 233a, 233c
www.biblewalks.com/sites /kerioth.html 238b
Fountain of Tears: 238c, 242a, 242-243, 243a, 243b
Kfar Hanokdim: 238d, 241a, 241b, 241c, 241d
Yotvata: 253
Eilat Stone Factory: 258d

SHALOM!